R. Finlay Heron

The Law and Practice of Municipal Elections in Ireland

With an appendix and a copious index

R. Finlay Heron

The Law and Practice of Municipal Elections in Ireland
With an appendix and a copious index

ISBN/EAN: 9783337323561

Printed in Europe, USA, Canada, Australia, Japan

Cover: Foto ©Suzi / pixelio.de

More available books at **www.hansebooks.com**

THE LAW AND PRACTICE

OF

MUNICIPAL ELECTIONS IN IRELAND,

WITH

AN APPENDIX OF STATUTES AND A COPIOUS INDEX.

BY

R. FINLAY HERON, M.A.

Senior Moderator, T.C.D.

Secretary to the Blackrock Township Commissioners.

DUBLIN:
ALEX. THOM & Co. (LIMITED), 87, 88, & 89, ABBEY STREET,
THE QUEEN'S PRINTING OFFICE.
WILLIAM M'GEE, 18, NASSAU-STREET.

LONDON:
STEVENS & HAYNES, BELL YARD, TEMPLE BAR.

1891.

PREFACE.

At the present time Municipal Elections in Ireland cause a considerable amount of interest and are keenly contested; it is therefore important—with a view of avoiding litigation—that they should be conducted in strict accordance with the statutes which govern them, as interpreted by the most recent legal decisions.

It is a well recognised fact, that the Law relating to Municipal Elections in Ireland is exceedingly complicated and confusing, and in regard to some points positively obscure.

This is caused to a great extent by so many provisions of statutes relating to Municipal Elections being inconsistent and irreconcilable with one another, and the language used in them ambiguous. It occasionally happens, too, that a portion of an Act passed with a view to Parliamentary Elections—to which it is perfectly adapted—is brought into force in regard to Municipal Elections to which it is difficult to apply it.

There are some fifty Acts of Parliament, the whole or portions of which affect Municipal Elections in different places in Ireland. (See List given, pp. 210-213).

It can be readily understood that this bewildering array of legislative enactments, and the judicial decisions (many of which are of a conflicting character), recorded in interpretation of them, render it necessary for any one who requires information on the subject to unearth it—from a very voluminous and scattered mass of legal literature.

It is admitted that a repeal and codification of the various Acts bearing on Municipal Elections in Ireland is urgently required, and it is to be hoped that at no distant date a reform of this character will be undertaken by the Legislature.

Such a reform has been carried out in England and Wales by the passing of the Municipal Corporation Act of 1882 (45 & 46 Vic., c. 50), which consolidates about seventy previous statutes.

The law and practice in regard to Parliamentary Elections has been treated in the most complete and exhaustive manner by several writers, but no work has appeared dealing—in anything like a comprehensive manner—with the subject of Municipal Elections in Ireland.

An attempt has been made in the following pages to supply this want to some extent, and to deal with the difficulties which present themselves in practice, in carrying out the provisions of the Acts referred to; and it is hoped that it will be found to be of use in this respect to Returning Officers and Town Clerks in Ireland, upon whom this duty necessarily devolves. I have to acknowledge, with many thanks, the assistance I obtained from Mr. Constantine Molloy, Q.C., and Mr. Robert Keating Clay, Solicitor, in the preparation of this work, and for the information so freely placed at my disposal by the Town Clerks throughout the country.

Valuable aid has also been obtained from the following and other sources, to which reference is made :—

    Haig :—The Municipal Corporation Acts of Ireland, 2nd Ed., 1845.

    Meara's Law and Practice of Elections, 1847.

    Leigh and Le Marchant's Election Law, by Leigh and Anderson, 1880.

    Bushby on the Practice of Parliamentary Elections, by Hardcastle, 1880, &c.

    Parker :—The Powers, Duties, and Liabilities of an Election Agent, and of Returning Officer at a Parliamentary Election in England and Wales, 1885.

Cunningham:—Law of Parliamentary and Municipal Elections, by G. Tyrrell Giles, 1885.

O'Mally and Hardcastle:—Reports of the Decisions of the Judges for the trial of Election Petitions.

A compendium of the principal statutes (and parts of statutes) which bear on Municipal Elections (Ireland) has been added in the form of an Appendix, which will be found convenient for reference.

This work has been produced under some difficulty owing to the pressure of official business, and the author trusts that his attention may be drawn to any errors or omissions which may be discovered in it, with a view to their correction.

R. FINLAY HERON.

Town Hall, Blackrock, Co. Dublin,
    7th September, 1891.

	Page
Abbreviations,	13
Table of Cases cited,	15
Table of Statutes,	21

Chapter
- I.—The Register of Voters, ... 23–41
- II.—Qualifications of Voters under 9 Geo. IV., c. 82, 42–44
- III.—Qualifications of Voters under the Municipal Reform Act, 1840, . . . 44–48
- IV.—Qualifications of Voters under the Towns Improvement (Ireland) Act, 1854, ... 49–55
- V.—Qualifications of Voters in Townships formed under Local Acts, ... 55–71
- VI.—Qualifications of Town Councillors and Commissioners, ... 72–74
- VII.—Persons disqualified from being elected or acting as Town Councillors, ... 74–80
- VIII.—Agents, ... 81–86
- IX.—Returning and Presiding Officers, . 87–94
- X.—Nominations, ... 94–116
- XI.—Preparations for taking the Poll, . . 117–132
- XII.—The Poll, ... 132–157

Chapter	Page
XIII.—Counting the Votes,	158–186
XIV.—Election of Mayor, Aldermen, &c.,	186–189
XV.—Occasional Vacancies,	190–191
XVI.—Corrupt Practices,	191–203
XVII.—Controverted Elections,	203–208
Table of Boroughs, Towns, and Townships in Ireland,	209
Table of Acts of Parliament bearing on Municipal Elections in Ireland,	210–213
Appendix,	i to lxxxiv
Index,	lxxxv to xcviii

ABBREVIATIONS.

A. & E.,	Adolphus and Ellis' (Queen's Bench) Reports.
Ap.,	Appendix of Statutes.
B.A.,	The Ballot Act, 1872 (35 & 36 Vic., c. 33).
B. & A.,	Barron and Austin's Election Cases, 1842.
B. & C.,	Barnwall and Cresswell's (Queen's Bench) Reports, 1823-30.
Black. Com.,	Blackstone's Commentaries on the Laws of England.
Bushby,	Bushby's Practice of Parliamentary Elections, by Hardcastle, 1880. 5th Ed.
C.B.,	Common Bench Reports, or Manning, Grainger, and Scott's Reports.
Cunningham,	Cunningham's Law of Parliamentary and Municipal Elections, by G. Tyrrell Giles, 1885. 3rd Ed.
C. & R.,	Cockburn and Rowe's Election Cases, 1833.
E. & B.,	Ellis and Blackburne's (Queen's Bench) Reports, 1852-8.
F. & F.,	Falconer and Fitzherbert's Election Cases, 1835-38.
Haig,	Haig's Municipal Corporation Acts of Ireland, 1847.
Ir.R.C.L.,	Irish Reports, Common Law.
K. & O.,	Knapp and Ombler's Election Cases, 1834-5.
L.R.C.P.,	Law Reports, Common Pleas, 1865-75.

L.R.C.P.D.,	Law Reports, Common Pleas Division, 1875–80.
L.R.Q.B.,	Law Reports, Queen's Bench, 1865–75.
L.R.Q.B.D.,	Law Reports, Queen's Bench Division, 1875–90.
L.J.N.S.,	Law Journal, Reports. New Series.
L.T.N.S.,	Law Times, Reports. New Series.
T.L.R.,	Times Law Reports.
Leigh,	Guide to Election Law, 3rd Ed., 1880, by Leigh and Le Marchant.
Meara,	Law of Practice of Elections, 1847, by Wm. Meara.
O. & H.,	O'Malley and Hardcastle's Reports of Election Petitions, 1869–1704.
Owen,	The Ballot Act, 1872, by Hugh Owen, jun.
Parker,	The Powers, Duties, and Liabilities of an Election Agent, and of a Returning Officer at a Parliamentary Election in England and Wales, 1885, by Frank R. Parker.
P. & K.,	Perry and Knapp's Election Cases.
Salk.,	Salkeld's (King's Bench) Reports, 1695–1704.
Taunt.,	Taunton's (Common Pleas) Reports, 1807–19.
W. & B.,	Wolferstan and Bristowe's Election Reports, 1859–64.

TABLE OF CASES CITED.

A.
                                                                          Page

Ackers v. Howard (L.R., 16, Q.B.D., 739), .   180, 181, 183
Athlone (3 O. & H., 57), ... 140
Aylesbury (4 O. & H., 63), ... 83

B.

Baker v. Marsh (4 E. & B., 144), ... 49
Belfast (B. & A., 561), ... 118
—— (Ir. R., 7, C.L., 30), ... 131
Bedford (P. & K., 147), ... 70
Berwick-on-Tweed (44 L.T.N.S., 290)(3 O. & H. 178), 140, 177, 178
Bodmin (1 O. & H., 122), ... 199
Bolton (2 O. & H., 141), ... 144, 145, 196
Bowden v. Besley (4 T.L.R.Q.B., 590), ... 106
Bradford (1 O. & H., 37), ... 199
Budge v. Andrews (L.R., 3, C.P., 511), ... 100
Buckrose (4 O. & H., 115), . . . 142, 172, 175, 178
Burgoyne v. Collins (L.R. 8, Q.B.D., 450), . . 99, 100
Barnstable (32 L.T.N.S. Q.B. 602), ... 179
Birkbeck v. Bullard (54 L.T.N.S., 626), . . 195, 199, 204

C.

Canterbury (K. & O., 131), ... 141
Carrickfergus (1 O. & H., 265), ... 199
Cashel (1 O. & H., 288), ... 84, 85
Clementson v. Mason (L.R., 10, C.P., 209), . 84, 82, 126, 146
Coventry (P. & K., 345 ; C. & R., 289), . . . 103

D.

	Page
Davies v. Lord Kensington (L.R., 9, C.P., 729),	107
Down (3 O. & H., 122),	202
Drinkwater v. Deakin (L.R. 9, C.P., 626),	79, 80
Drogheda (2 O. & H., 206),	121, 125, 131
Dublin (1 O. & H., 273),	196
Dudley (2 O. & H., 121),	147
Dungannon (3 O. & H., 101),	83
Drewe v. Collins (2 Luder's Election Reports, 245),	90

F.

Fanagan v. Kernan (8 Ir. L.R., 44),	87, 89

G.

Galway (Town) (1 O. & H., 306),	200
Gledhill v. Crowther (60 L.T.N.S., C.P., 866),	106
Gloucester (2 O. & H., 60),	201
Gothard v. Clarke (L.R., 5, C.P.D., 253),	101, 107
Gravesend (3 O. & H., 84),	197
Greenock (1 O. & H., 249),	119
Gribbin v. Kirker (Ir. R., 7, C.L., 30),	131
Guildford (1 O. & H., 15),	197

H.

Hackney (2 O. & H., 88),	128, 131
Harwick (3 O. & H., 69),	194
Harmon v. Park (L.R., 7, Q.B.D., 369),	102
Harmon v. Park (L.R., 6, Q.B.D., 323),	104
Hastings (1 O. & H., 218),	195, 197
Henry v. Armitage (L.R., 12, Q.B., 257),	101, 106
Howes v. Turner (45 L.J.N.S., C.P., 550; L.R.I.C.P.D., 670, 671),	31, 96, 98, 100, 101, 102

I.

Ipswich (4 O. & H., 74),	194

K.

	Page
Kidderminster (2 O. & H., 173),	200
Kingstown (18 Ir., L.R. (Q.B.), 179)	113

L.

Lewis v. Carr (L.R., Ex.I.D., 484),	75
Lichfield (3 O. & H., 137),	198, 203
Liffin v. Pitcher (Dowling's Reports, N.S., Q.B., 769),	31
Lisburn (W. & B., 225),	197
Londonderry (4 O. & H., 103),	138
Longford (2 O. & H., 7),	130, 200
Lowering v. Dawson & others (L.R., 10, C.P., 723),	204
Launceston (2 O. & H., 129),	198

M.

Mallow (2 O. & H., 21),	196
Mather v. Brown (L.R., 1, C.P.D., 683),	105
Mayo (2 O. & H., 194),	101, 107
M'Laren v. Home (L.R., 7, Q.B.D., 477; 3 O. & H., 178; 44 L.T.N.S., Q.B, 289),	171, 179
Monks v. Jackson (35 L.T.N.S., C.P., 95),	100
—— (L.R., 1, C.P.D., 683),	99
Monmouth (K. & O., 415),	57

N.

New Windsor (K. & O., 160),	56
Norfolk (1 O. & H., 243),	199
Northallerton (1 O. & H., 169),	198, 201
Northcote v. Pulsford (L.R., 10, C.P., 484),	94, 102, 103, 182
Norwich (2 O. & H., 41),	195

O.

Oldham (1 O. & H., 153),	141, 180, 194

P.

	Page
Packard v. Collings (54 L.T.N.S., 619),	196
Pickering v. James (L.R., 8, C.P., 489),	180
Pickering v. Startin (28 L.T.N.S., C.P., 112),	181
Phibbs v. Kearns (Ir. R., 11, C.L., 294),	45
Pryce v. Belcher (4, C.B., 866),	64, 137

R.

Reading (F. & F., 553),	70
Reg. v. The Mayor of Tewkesbury (L.R., 3, Q.B., 629),	80, 90
Reg. v. Bradley (30, L.J., Q.B., 180),	106
Reg. v. Parkinson (L.R , 3, Q.B., 11),	113
Reg. v. Oldham (L.R., 4, Q.B., 290),	75
Reg. v. Crosthwaite (Ir. R., 17, C.L., 174),	51
Reg. v. Cunningham (L.R., 20 Q.B., 490),	78
Reg. v. The Justices of Armagh (6 Ir. Jurist., N.S., 212),	33
Reg. v. Harrald (L.R., 8, Q.B., 418),	140
Reg. v. Tugwell (L.R., 3, Q.B., 704),	140
Reg. v. Byrne (22 Ir. L.R., 330),	191
Reg. v. Hazley (11 Ir. L.R., 360),	191
Reg. (Parker) v. Power (26 Ir. L.R., 380),	48
Reg. (Byrne and others) v. Lord Mayor of Dublin (28 Ir. L.R., 296),	48
Reg. (Collins and others) v. Lord Mayor of Dublin (28 Ir. L.R., 313),	48
Reg. v. Mayor of Belfast (Ir. R., 15, C.L., 162),	46
Reg. v. Uncles (Ir. R., 8, C.L., 50),	146
Reg. v. St. Mary Kalendar (9 A. & E., 630),	47
Renfrew (2 O. & H., 213),	186
Reg. v. Mayor of Bangor (L.R., 18, Q.B.D., 349),	186
Reg. v. Mayor of Exeter (L.R., 4 Q.B., 110),	43

S.

Sligo (Powell, Rodwell, and Davis Reports, 208),	111
—— (1 O. & H., 302),	198
Soper v. Basingstoke (L.R., 2 C.P., 444),	107

	Page
Spilsbury v. Micklewaite (1 Taunt., 146), . . .	103
Stafford borough (1 O. & H., 230), ...	83
Staleybridge (1 O. & H., 66 ; 20 L.T.N.S., C.P., 75), .	197
Stannanought v. Hazeldine (L.R., 4 C.P.D., 191), . .	145
Stowe v. Jolliffe (L.R., 9, C.P., 446), . . 138, 148, 207
Stepney (4 O & H., 43), . . 143, 171, 178, 197, 201

T.

Tamworth (1 O. & H., 86), ...	200
Tipperary (3 O & H., 21), ...	100
Tralee (28 Ir. L.R., 10), ...	89, 130
Tewkesbury (L.R., 3 Q.B., 629), . . .	. 80, 90

W.

| Wakefield (B. & A., 270), ... | 90 |
| Westminster (1 O. & H., 95), . . . 83, 85, 197, 199 |
Wigan (1 O & H., 191), ...	83
Wigtown (2 O. & H., 216), ...	181
Windsor (New) (K. & O., 139), ...	56
Woodward v. Sarsons (L.R., 10 C.P., 746-7-8), 164, 179, 180
Worcester (3 O. & H., 189), . . . 132, 146, 134, 138

Y.

| Yates v. Leach (L.R., 9, C.P., 608), . . . | 80 |

TABLE OF STATUTES AND PORTIONS OF STATUTES IN THE APPENDIX.

	Page
The Commissioners Clauses Act, 1847 (10 Vict., c. 16),	i–ix
The Towns Improvement Clauses Act, 1847 (10 & 11 Vict., c. 34),	ix–x
An Act to amend the Laws which regulate the Qualifications and Registration of Parliamentary Voters in Ireland, and to alter the Law for rating Immediate Lessors of Premises to the Poor Rate in certain Boroughs, 1850. (13 & 14 Vict., c. 69),	x–xiv
The Corrupt Practices Prevention Act, 1854 (17 & 18 Vict., c. 102),	xv–xx
The Towns Improvement (Ireland) Act, 1854 (17 & 18 Vict., c. 103),	xx–xxv
The Municipal Election Act, 1859 (22 Vict., c. 35),	xxv–xxviii
The Local Government (Ireland) Act, 1871 (34 & 35 Vict., c. 109),	xxviii–xxxi
The Ballot Act, 1872 (35 & 36 Vict., c. 33),	xxxii–lvii
The Corrupt Practices (Municipal Elections) Act, 1872. (35 & 36 Vict., c. 60),	lix–lxxi
The Municipal Elections Act, 1875 (38 & 39 Vict., c. 40),	lxxi–lxxviii

	Page
The Municipal Elections (Ireland) Act, 1879 (42 & 43 Vict., c. 53),	lxxviii–lxxix
The Town Councils and Local Boards Act, 1880 (43 Vict., c. 17),	lxxix–lxxx
The Elections (Hours of Poll) Act (48 Vict., c. 10),	lxxx–lxxxi
The Municipal Voters Relief Act, 1885 (48 Vict., c. 9),	lxxxi–lxxxii
The Medical Relief Disqualification Removal Act, 1885 (48 & 49 Vict., c. 46),	lxxxii
The Public Bodies Corrupt Practices Act, 1889 (52 & 53 Vict., c. 69),	lxxxii–lxxxiv

CHAPTER I.

The Register of Voters.

The first matter to be considered in relation to an election is the preparation of the Register of Voters.

Rule 66 of the Ballot Act, 1872 (35 & 36 Vic., c. 33), (in applying the provisions of Part II., Schedule I., to Municipal Elections in Ireland) enacts:—

"The expression 'register of voters,' in addition to the meaning specified in such part,* means, in relation to any municipal borough subject to the provisions of a Local Act requiring an annual revision of the lists of voters at municipal elections, the register of voters made in conformity with the said provisions of such Local Act, and in relation to municipal boroughs to which Part II. of the Local Government (Ireland) Act, 1871, applies, the list to be made under the provisions of section twenty-seven of the said Act, and in relation to other municipal boroughs, a list which the town clerk of every municipal borough is hereby authorized and directed to make in like manner in every respect as if the provisions of the said section were applicable to and in force within such municipal borough."*   (Ap. l.)

---

* Viz.:—"The burgess roll of the burgesses of the borough, or, in the case of an Election for the Ward of a Borough, the Ward list." (B.A., r. 64 (a) Ap. xlix.

† A Municipal Borough is defined by the Ballot Act, 1872, as follows:—

"The expression 'Municipal Borough' means any place for the time being subject to the Municipal Corporation Acts, or any of them:

"The expression 'Municipal Corporation Acts' means—

"(c.) As regards Ireland, the Act of the session of the third and fourth years of the reign of Her present Majesty, chapter one hundred and eight, intituled 'An Act for the Regulation of Municipal Corporations in Ireland,' the Act of the ninth year of George the Fourth, chapter eighty-two, The Towns Improvement (Ireland) Act, 1854, and every local and personal Act providing for the election of Commissioners in any towns or places for purposes similar to the purposes of the said Acts." (B.A., s. 29).   Ap. xl.

Four Classes of Boroughs.]

There are four classes of Municipal Boroughs† referred to in this section—

I. Those in which a " Burgess Roll " is kept—viz., those under the Municipal Reform Act, 1840 (3 & 4 Vic., c. 108), Schedule A.

II. Those having a Local Act requiring an annual revision of the list of voters by a revising barrister.

III. Those to which Part II. of the Local Government (Ireland) Act, 1871, refers—viz., those under the Towns Improvement (Ireland) Act, 1854 (17 & 18 Vic., c. 103), or any town or borough having a special Act incorporating the whole or any portion of the said Towns Improvement Act.

IV. Every other borough not included in the three former classes.

How the Burgess Roll is to be prepared.]

I. In Boroughs under Schedule A of the Municipal Reform Act, 1840 (3 & 4 Vic., c. 108), the Burgess Roll is to be made out in accordance with the provisions of that Act, as amended by 6 & 7 Vic., c. 93;* as follows :—

On or before the 8th September, in every year, the Town Clerk is to enter in a book the names of all persons who appear to be entitled to be Burgesses, in respect of inhabitancy, occupation, and rating† ; the names of such persons are to be arranged alphabetically and numbered consecutively in this book, which is to be according to the annexed form.

---

* Unless where the provisions of these Acts are amended in regard to any of these boroughs by subsequent legislation.

† He is to take the "rating" from the valuation given in the Poor Law Rate Books.

Register of Voters.

LIST of Persons appearing entitled to be enrolled as Burgesses of the Borough of ———— (in the Ward of ————) in the Burgess Roll next to be made, in right of Inhabitancy, and Occupation and Rating.

Dated this 8th September, 1843.

JOHN THOMPSON, Town Clerk.

Number.	Name.	Residence.	Situation of Qualifying Property.	Description of Property.	Poor Rate.	Paving Rate.	And so for any other rates or cesses as the case may be.
1	Adams, John,	3, John-street,	3, John-street,	House,			
2	Albin, William,	9, Park-street,	6, High-street,	Shop,			
3	Burn, Edward,	Booterstown,	10, Essex-street,	Warehouse,			
4	Casey, Patrick,	Chapelizod,	12, Mount-street,	Shop,			

Where a borough is divided into wards, there are to be separate books for each ward.

The town clerk is two days at least before the 8th of September to summon, or cause to be summoned, the collectors of all rates* for the relief of the poor, and of Grand Jury and Municipal Cesses, and of all rates and taxes payable in respect of premises within the borough, and also the treasurer of the borough, and if there be no treasurer the mayor of the borough, to attend at his office at such time or times within the seven days next succeeding the 8th September as he shall think necessary, with all necessary books, vouchers, and accounts; and they shall themselves, or by sufficient deputies, attend accordingly at the office of the town clerk, and shall, in such order as the town clerk shall direct, for the more convenient dispatch of business, enter in the columns of the said book appropriated to the taxes, rates, or cesses, within their collection, respectively, the amount of the last tax, rate, or cess, paid by each person named in such book, or paid on account of the premises in respect whereof such person may be entitled to be enrolled, and the date of each payment, and the amount of the tax, rate, or cess (if any) then due and unpaid by each such person or in respect of such premises as aforesaid, and the date when the same became due and payable, and shall sign the said columns; and on the completion of the entries so to be made in the said book, the town clerk shall cause a notice thereof to be fixed on or near the outer door of the town hall, or in some public and conspicuous place within the borough, and shall keep the said book in his office and permit it to be perused by any person without payment of any fee at all reasonable times during the last ten days of

---

* Public notice to be given in regard to the payment of rates (3 & 4 Vic., c. 108, s. 30). The office for receiving taxes is to be kept open each day (Sunday excepted) from 10 till 4 o'clock for one month before the 31st day of August (3 & 4 Vic., c. 108, s. 38). If the office be not open, the occupier may pay or tender the rates to the treasurer of the borough, and if there be no treasurer, to the mayor.

September (Sunday excepted), and shall deliver a copy thereof, or any extract therefrom, to any person requiring the same on payment of a reasonable price, not exceeding one halfpenny for every name, and with the entries attached thereto, which may be included in such copy or extract so required; such copy or extract to be delivered by the town clerk within four days from the date of the application.—(6 & 7 Vic., c. 93, s. 2).

* Any mayor, treasurer, or collector, who neglects to perform the duties herein-before specified, shall forfeit a sum of £20.—(*id.*, s. 3.)

The town clerk shall, on or before the 20th day of September, make out an alphabetical list of all persons entitled to be enrolled in the burgess roll of that year within such ward of such borough, excluding therefrom the name of every person who shall not appear (by the entries made in the book referred to by the several collectors, &c.) to have paid all rates and cesses required to be paid in order to qualify such person; and shall sign such lists, and shall, on the said day (20th September), deliver a true copy of such lists, signed by himself, to the mayor of the borough; and he shall himself keep such original list to be perused by any person, without payment of any fee, at all reasonable times between the 20th and 30th of September, and shall cause a copy of the said lists to be fixed on or near the outer door of the town hall, or in some public and conspicuous place within the borough, on every day during the eight days next preceding the 1st day of October.— (3 & 4 Vic., c. 108, ss. 41, 42; and 6 & 7 Vic., c. 93, s. 4.)

Persons who find that their names have been improperly omitted from the lists, may give notice in the form given in Schedule D, No. 2 (3 & 4 Vic., c. 108) to the town clerk

---

* Haig (p. 17) says:—" 6 & 7 Vic., c. 93, s. 1, has repealed the clauses directing the preparation of the lists, and made new provisions without imposing a penalty on the town clerk for breach of the new enactments. See sects. 25 and 54 of 3 & 4 Vic., c. 108. The effect appears to be that there is no penal clause now affecting a town clerk neglecting to discharge this duty."

on or before the 1st of October. Notices as to persons whose names are objected to as having been improperly inserted on the lists, must be given to the town clerk and also to the person objected to, (or left at the premises in respect of which his name shall have been inserted in such list,) in the form given in Schedule D, No. 3 (3 & 4 Vic., c. 108) on or before the 1st of October.—(6 & 7 Vic., c. 93, s. 4.)

Names of claimants and persons objected to, to be published.]

The town clerk shall cause a list of all claimants and all persons objected to, to be fixed on or near the outer door of the town hall, or in some public conspicuous place within the borough, during eight days (Sunday excepted) next preceding the 20th October.

He is to keep a copy of the names of the claimants and persons objected to, to be perused by any person, during all reasonable hours, without any charge, during the eight days next preceding the 20th October (3 & 4 Vic., c. 108, s. 43; and 6 & 7 Vic., c. 93, s. 4).

Revision Court.]

A Revision Court is to be held in each borough between the 20th October and the 10th November, under the mayor and two assessors. Three clear days'* notice is to be given of the holding of this court.†

The court may adjourn from time to time, but cannot sit after the 10th of November.

The lists to go before the Revision Court are:—

1. The qualification list as prepared from the poor law rate books by the town clerk.
2. The list of claimants.
3. The list of persons objected to.

* See foot note, post p. 31.

† Notices to be affixed on or near the door of the town hall, or in some public and conspicuous place in the borough.

The mayor is empowered to take evidence on oath and to require the collectors, &c., to attend with their books. The proceedings are to be carried on in open court. All claims or objections duly made are to be heard, and names to be inserted or expunged on the proof of such claims or objections. The mayor is to expunge from the lists the name of any person found to be dead, and to correct any mistake, or supply any omission, which shall be proved to have been made in any of the said lists in respect of the name or place of abode, or local description of the property of any person who shall be on any such list.

Names not objected to are to be retained on the list. The fact of the name of any person being on the burgess roll of the preceding year is *primâ facie* evidence of his title to be enrolled on that for the current year.

No name is to be expunged from the lists, unless notice has been served as provided by 3 & 4 Vic., c. 108, s. 43. The mayor is, in open court, to write his initials against the names respectively struck out, or inserted, and against all amended errors in the said lists, and sign his name to every page of the several lists so settled (3 & 4 Vic., c. 108, s. 46; 6 & 7 Vic., c. 93, s. 4).

The lists, when revised and signed, are to be delivered to the town clerk, who is to take charge of same and cause them to be copied into a book provided for the purpose. The names are to be arranged alphabetically in each ward, and numbered consecutively from the first name in the first ward to the last name in the last ward. This book—which is to be called the Burgess Roll—is to be completed before the 20th November, and constitutes the register of voters entitled to vote at any election which may be held.*—(3 & 4 Vic., c. 108, ss. 45, 46; and 6 & 7 Vic., c. 93, s. 4).

The mayor shall provide true copies of the burgess roll or ward list for each polling station.—(B. A., r. 64 (a)). Ap. xlix.

* He is not required to have copies of the Burgess Roll printed. The old Burgess Roll is to remain in force till the new is made out (3 & 4 Vic. c., 108, s. 47.)

Application may be made to the Court of Queen's Bench for a mandamus to the mayor to put a burgess on the roll.—(3 & 4 Vic., c. 108, s. 49).

The right of anyone who shall have been admitted and enrolled upon the burgess roll may be questioned by appeal to the Court of Queen's Bench.—(3 & 4 Vic., c 108, s. 50).

The Freeman's Roll.]

The Freeman's roll is to be prepared by the town clerk. The mayor, in boroughs under 3 & 4 Vic., c. 108, schedule A, and a person appointed by the Lord Lieutenant in boroughs under 9 Geo. IV., c 82, is afterwards to hold a court for revising it. The town clerk is to attend at the revision and to permit inspection of corporation books and other documents by claimants or persons acting for them, or by any registered Parliamentary elector of the borough.

A true copy of the Freeman's roll, when revised, is to be kept by the town clerk, and he is to allow a free perusal of it at all reasonable times, and supply copies of it, or extracts from it, on receiving payment of certain fees.—(3 & 4 Vic., c. 108, ss. 7, 8.)

The admission or rejection by the mayor of a claimant may be the subject of an appeal to the Court of Queen's Bench.—(3 & 4 Vic., c. 108, s. 9).

Annual Revision by Revising Barrister.]

II.— In towns or boroughs having Local Acts requiring an annual revision of voters by a revising barrister, the register of voters is prepared in substantially the same way as the burgess roll is prepared in boroughs under Schedule A of the Municipal Reform Act, 1840 (3 & 4 Vic., c. 108).

Some of these Acts have provisions requiring the town clerk, before the preparation of the lists is commenced, to publish a notice stating that no person will be entitled to have his name inserted on the list of voters unless certain rates are paid before a specified date, and providing for the sale of printed copies of the register when finally revised. If the town clerk fails to publish the names of persons objected to, a mandamus may be obtained to compel him to do so.—See *Kingstown* case 1885 (18 Ir. L.R., 179).

Voters' List made out by the Town Clerk.]

III.—The register of voters is made out by the town clerk in boroughs to which Part II. of the Local Government (Ireland) Act, 1871 (34 & 35 Vic., c. 109), refers, viz. :— Those under the Towns Improvement (Ireland) Act, 1854 (17 & 18 Vic., c. 103), or under a special Act incorporating the said (Towns Improvement) Act in whole or part. This class comprises by far the greater number of towns and boroughs in Ireland. (See table *post* p. 209.)

The 27th section of the Local Government (Ireland) Act, 1871 (34 & 35 Vic., c. 109), enacts :—

"The clerk to the commissioners, at least fifteen days* before the day appointed for the annual election of commissioners in each year, shall make out an alphabetical list of the names of all persons, with their respective residences, entitled to vote at such election in respect of premises within the town, as they appear in the rates made for the purposes of the principal Act, and also of all persons entitled to vote at such election in respect of property within the town."

"Such list shall be evidence that the persons therein named are entitled to vote at the next annual election for commissioners, and also at any other election for one or more commissioners which may be held before the next annual list is made out.

"The clerk to the commissioners shall forthwith cause to be printed copies of the list to be made out by him in every year as aforesaid, and shall deliver a copy of such list to all persons requiring the same, on the payment of the sum of one shilling for each copy, and shall cause a copy of such list to be fixed on or near the outer door of the office of the commissioners, and in some other public and conspicuous situation within the town, on every day† during the ten days next preceding the day appointed for the election of the commissioners in each year."—(Ap. xxx.)

In making out the list, the Town Clerk should be careful to give the names and residences of occupiers *exactly* as

---

* Means fifteen *clear* days, without counting Sundays.—*Howes* v. *Turner*, (1876), 45 L.J.N.S.C.P., 550, and *clear* days are reckoned exclusively of the first and last days, see case of *Liffin* v. *Pitcher*, 1842, 1 Dowling's practice reports, new series, Q.B., 769. The list need not be published, it will be observed, till 10 days before the election.

† Should the day fixed for the election fall on a Sunday, the election is to take place on the following day (Monday).

they appear in the Poor Law Rate Book, and of Immediate Lessors as they appear in the Township Rate Book.

Publication of Notice.]

When any public notice is authorized or required by the Ballot Act, 1872, it is to be given by advertisements, placards, handbills, or by such other means as the returning officer thinks best calculated to afford information to the electors. (B.A., r. 46.) Ap. xlvii.

The Registration Act, 1868 (13 & 14 Vict., c. 69, s. 40), enacts, in regard to the publication of notices and lists in connection with Parliamentary elections—

"That in all cases in which any notice, list, copy of register, or other document shall, pursuant to the provisions aforesaid, be affixed on any such place as aforesaid, the same shall continue so fixed for a period including two consecutive Sundays, at the least, next after the day on or before which the same is hereinbefore required to be published; and in case the same shall be destroyed, mutilated, effaced, or removed before the expiration of such period, the party hereinbefore required to publish the same as aforesaid shall, as soon as conveniently may be, publish in like manner in its place another notice, list, copy of register, paper, or other document so destroyed, mutilated, effaced, or removed."

And section 42 (*id.*) provides that the list shall not be invalidated by imperfect publication, but makes the party responsible for the publication of it liable to penalties.

These provisions however, have not been brought into force in regard to Irish municipal elections.

In England the name of the printer must be affixed to any notices or placards which are issued in connection with an election (46 & 47 Vic., c. 51, s. 18).

Machinery for preparing List unsatisfactory.]

The Legislature has cast the important and responsible duty of preparing the list "of persons entitled to vote" upon the town clerk, but has failed to provide him with the necessary machinery for satisfactorily performing it; yet the voters' list as prepared by him is as conclusive, as regards the qualification of a person to vote, as the one which (as we have seen,) has been revised and settled in open court, upon sworn evidence, by the mayor and assessors or by the revising barrister, after a preliminary list has been published, and time allowed for the service of notice of claims and objections to it, and for the publication of such claims and objections. The town clerk without these aids and safeguards prepares his list not in public but privately in his office. He decides there—on the best evidence he can get—whether a person is, or is not, qualified to vote; and his decision is absolute, and without appeal. It is not necessary for him to assign any reason for having put the name of one person on, or omitted the name of another from, the list. He may endeavour to discharge this duty in the most painstaking, impartial, and strictly legal manner, yet he is liable to error; and, besides, it is unsatisfactory for those ratepayers whose names are omitted from the list not to know the grounds upon which they are disqualified to vote.

It may perhaps be open to anyone who considers that he has been unfairly, or with malicious intent, disfranchised, to take an action, or institute a criminal prosecution against the town clerk.

The town clerk would not, however—his duties being of a judicial character in regard to the preparation of the list—be liable for any mistake he might make through an error of judgment.—See *The Queen* v. *the Justices of Armagh*, 1861 (6 *Irish Jurist*, N.S., p. 212), where it was held that the preparation of the lists of jurors is a judicial act.

An elector would not have time to obtain a mandamus to compel the town clerk to place his name on the list of voters, because he could not ascertain that his name had been omitted from the list until the date on which the list is published—viz., ten days before the election.*

* In towns under the Towns Improvement (Ireland) Act, 1854, elections are held on the 15th October (17 & 18 Vic., c. 103, s. 23), so that the list need not be published till the 4th of October, at which time the Court of Queen's Bench would not be sitting.

The list is conclusive and final even upon an election tribunal, except in regard to persons inherently disqualified.—See *post*, p. 138–9.

Suggested Course with regard to the preparation of the List.]

The Act says:—"The town clerk shall make out an alphabetical list *of all persons entitled to vote.*" To do this he must know *who* are entitled to vote: consequently the Legislature imposes upon him the duty of ascertaining this; and it is submitted that he ought to take all such steps as he legally can, for properly discharging this important duty.* And it is suggested, for the consideration of those town clerks who are required to make out an annual list of voters, whether it might not be advisable in preparing these lists to follow to some extent the course which the law requires to be followed in those boroughs where the lists are revised by a revising barrister, and to publish,† say on the 1st September, a notice as follows:—

Notice to the electors of the township (town or borough) of ⸺⸺.

I, being town clerk, of the said township (town or borough) am now (in accordance with the provisions of the Local Government (Ireland) Act, 1871) about to prepare a list (which will be published on the 4th day of October next) of all persons qualified to vote for the forthcoming election of commissioners for this township (or borough), to be held on the 15th day of October next, 18   .

---

* The Legislature has left him to a great extent in the dark as to how he is to proceed to ascertain who are entitled to vote.

It merely directs him "to make out an alphabetical list of the names of all persons, with their respective residences, entitled to vote at such election in respect of premises within the town as they appear in the rates made for the purpose of the principal Act (*i.e.*, The Towns Improvement (Ireland) Act, 1854); and also of all persons entitled to vote at such election in respect of property within the town," but does not afford him any assistance as to how he is to obtain information or evidence as to the qualifications of persons to vote, other than that obtainable from the rate books; *e.g.*, it affords him no means of ascertaining whether a person has been "in occupation during the qualifying period" or whether he is of "full age," or whether he is "an alien," &c.

† By placards extensively posted through the locality.

Register of Voters.

A preparatory list of persons (who appear from the evidence at my disposal) qualified to vote is now ready and can be seen at this office on any week-day after this date, between the hours of 10 a.m. and 1 p.m. up to, and including the 14th September (instant). Any person having an objection to make to the name of any person being retained on this list, or any person whose name is not on this list, claiming to have his name inserted thereon, is hereby required to send me a notice of same, stating the grounds of such objection or claim, as the case may be, on or before the 15th day of September (instant).

A list of persons 'claiming to vote,' and of those 'objected to' will be published by me on the door of the town hall* on the 16th September (instant).

Those persons objected to can ascertain the grounds upon which they are objected to, by calling at this office between the 16th and 20th inst., and may submit a statement in writing or a sworn declaration† (to be delivered to me on or before the 21st inst.) of any facts which they consider calculated to refute such objections.

And I further give notice that I will attend here between the hours of 10 o'clock, a.m., and 1 o'clock, p.m., on the 26th day of September inst.,‡ for the purpose of finally revising said list of voters, and during said final revision persons claiming to have their names inserted on the voters' list, or persons objecting to the names of any other persons being retained thereon, who have given notice of such objection or claim as aforesaid; and the persons objected to may attend and ascertain the grounds upon which such claims or objections have been admitted or rejected, and may inspect the township rate book, the rate collector's certificates of 'persons not in occupation during the qualifying period,' and of 'persons whose rates have not been paid on or before ———,' and a certified copy of the Poor Law rate book.

  Town Clerk's Office,
   Town Hall,
    September 1st, 18 .
     Signed,———,
        Town Clerk.

Note.—Forms of notice of claim or objection may be obtained at this office.

---

* Need not be printed.
† Under the Statutory Declaration Act, 1835 (5 & 6 Wm. IV., c. 62). The Town Clerk has no power, like the revising barrister, to take evidence on oath.
‡ This being 15 clear days (Sundays excluded) before the 15th October; date on which elections under the Towns Improvement (Ireland) Act, 1854, are held.

NOTICE OF CLAIM.

To the Town Clerk of the Township (or Borough of ——).

I hereby give you notice that I claim to have my name placed on the voters' list of the township (or borough or ward) of ———— as a rated occupier (*or immediate lessor*),* and I append herewith particulars of my qualifications as such.

PARTICULARS OF QUALIFICATIONS.

(1.)	(2.)	(3.)	(4.)	(5.)	(6.)	(7.)	(8.)	(9.)
Name in full.	Residence.	Qualifying property.	Rateable value of qualifying property.	Period in occupation of qualifying property.	Date on which borough or township rates assessed (within ———) have been paid.	Of full age.	If a natural born subject, or if not whether letters of naturalisation have been taken out.	Rated for relief of the poor in respect of such qualifying property.

Dated this ———— day of ———— 18 .

(Signed)

* For claims of immediate lessors, columns 5, 6, & 9 need not be filled in.

NOTICE OF OBJECTION.

To the Town Clerk of the Borough of

I hereby give you notice that I object to the name of   of   being retained on the voters' list of the town (borough, or township) of   on the ground that (*here insert reason for alleged disqualification*).

Dated this   day of   18 .

(Signed)

Points in favour of course suggested.]

It is submitted that (in the absence of any prohibitory enactment) there is nothing illegal in the course here suggested.

The point to be considered is whether, in the present deficient and unsatisfactory state of the law, it would not be advisable to adopt any expedient, which can legally and inexpensively be adopted, for securing greater accuracy in the lists of voters, and carrying out the revision or preparation of them in as public a manner as possible, and giving every ratepayer an opportunity of making his claim, and of knowing, if disqualified, the grounds on which he is disqualified.

Objections against it.]

Objections may possibly be advanced against it, viz. :—

(1). That the payment of the expenses incurred for printing and posting the notices referred to (the publication of such notices not being specifically authorised by statute) would be an illegal payment, and might be surcharged by the Local Government Board auditor.

(2). That even although legal, the town council might refuse to sanction such an expenditure.

(3). That by admitting the public at the final revision of the lists the proceedings might be interrupted or disturbed by disorderly persons attending it, and that the town clerk would have no means of preserving order by causing the arrest or removal of the persons so disturbing.

Objections considered.]

(1). The expenditure is not, it is true, in terms authorised by the Act, but the course suggested for adoption is a means of carrying out the requirements of the Act, and it is extremely doubtful whether such an expenditure could legally be surcharged.

(2). The expenditure would not exceed £1, and the members of a town council who refused to sanction this trifling expenditure—thereby preventing the town clerk from adopting the course which he considered necessary for satisfactorily discharging a public duty imposed upon him by statute—and affecting so sacred a constitutional right as the municipal franchise—would place themselves in an unenviable position in regard to the public and to their constituents.

(3.) The town clerk would have no such power as the returning officer has, when sitting to determine the validity of nomination papers (in boroughs under 3 & 4 Vic., c 108) to order the arrest or removal of any person disturbing the proceedings during the revision of the lists in public; but in the unlikely event of a disturbance occurring, the town clerk could at once adjourn the proceedings; or bring them to a close and complete the revision in private, as carrying it out in public is voluntary, and not obligatory, on his part.*

Form in which the lists of voters are to be published in towns or boroughs which have adopted the provisions of the Towns Improvement (Ireland) Act, 1854 (17 & 18 Vic., c. 103) in regard to the qualifications of voters :—

---

* If the procedure suggested here is considered too cumbersome, or if any practical difficulties arise in carrying it out, the town clerks might at least give the agents or representatives of each political party a copy of the preliminary list, and invite them to be present, and submit claims or objections when the list is being finally revised

Price One Shilling.

A LIST of the NAMES of ALL PERSONS, with their respective Residences, entitled to Vote at the Election of Town Commissioners under the Towns Improvement (Ireland) Act, 1854, for (the   Ward, in) the Borough of   , at the annual election of such Commissioners to be held on the 15th day of October, 18   , and at any other election which may be held before the next Annual List is made out.

Registered No.	Christian and Surname.	*Numbers on Rate Book.	Residence.	*Qualification.	*Premises within the Town from which the Property or Rating Qualification is derived.
1	Adams, John J.,	450,	8, Main-street, Ardee,	Tenant and occupier,	House and yard, Main-street.
2	Allan, James,	1,150, 2,	3, Henry-street, do.,	Rated as immediate lessor,	Two houses, Newtown-avenue.
3	Atkinson, Charles C.,	25, 80, 97,	1, Mary's-lane, Dublin,	Immediate lessor,	Three houses, Ovoca-avenue.
4	Ball, Richard,	10,	2, Prince Edward-terrace, Ardee.	Rated joint occupier,	House and garden, Conduit-street, jointly rated and occupied with John Meadows.
5	Barton, Henry,	550,	22, Main-street, Ardee,	Rated joint occupier,	House and yard, Main-street, jointly rated and occupied with Mary Jones.
6	Boyd, Joseph J.,	—	4, Church-street,	Tenant and occupier,	House and land, Church-street.

Dated this 29th day of September, 18   .

(Signed),
Town Clerk of the Borough of   .

* It is to be observed that the particulars given in the third and last two columns are not required by the 27th section of the Local Government (Ireland) Act, 1871 (34 & 35 Vic., c. 109).

Every other Borough not included in the preceding classes.]

IV.—The rule (66. B.A.) provides that the list of voters is to be made out in accordance with the 27th section of the Local Government (Ireland) Act, 1871—in every other borough not dealt with, in the preceding portion of the clause.

The only boroughs not included in the preceding portion of the clause are those under 9 Geo. IV., c. 82. But elections in these boroughs are only held every three years; and the 27th section of the Local Government (Ireland) Act, 1871, refers to an annual election, and an annual preparation of the list of voters; having regard, however, to the language used in the Act—viz., that the list is to be made out "in like manner in every respect as if the provisions of the said section were *applicable to* and in force in such municipal borough " (B.A. r. 66), it is submitted that the intention of the Legislature will be best fulfilled by the adopting (in boroughs under 9 Geo. IV., c. 82), the provisions of the 27th section, Local Government (Ireland) Act, 1871, in regard to the preparation of the voters' lists, reading the word "annual" "triennial" in the said section.

It is generally (but it is submitted erroneously) held, that the 27th section of the Local Government (Ireland) Act, 1871, does not apply to elections in these towns, and that the voters' list should be prepared under the provisions laid down in 9 Geo. IV., c. 82.

Under sec. 21 (9 Geo. IV., c. 82), the Commissioners are "to cause to be kept, and from time to time, with all diligence and care, and upon all reasonable requests at all times, to revise and amend a register of all the householders resident within such city, town, ... and occupying houses of the annual value of £5 or upwards; and such registry shall distinguish such of the said householders as shall occupy houses of the annual value of £20 or upwards; their description or abode."

As by the operation of the Town Councils and Local Boards Act, 1880 (43 Vic., c. 17)—any person qualified to vote is qualified to be elected a commissioner,* and therefore it is not now necessary in making out the list to distinguish the householders valued at £20 and upwards.

The register shall be conclusive evidence of qualification. (9 Geo. IV., c. 82, s. 16).

The election is held triennially on the first Monday in July. The notice of it must specify the places for polling, and must be affixed (1) on the principal outer door of every parish church (if any) within the borough; (2) on the principal market house, or place where markets are usually holden there; (3) on the guild hall or town hall; (4) on the door of the quarter session house for the borough or for the division of the county in which the town or any part of it is situate; (5) it ought to be advertised three times in one of the newspapers of the town, or the one published nearest thereto.—(ss. 4, 16, id.)

Notice must be given at least ten days and not more than twenty-one days, before the day of election.—(id.).

The Municipal Reform Act of 1840 preserved the vested rights of freemen to vote in boroughs under 9 Geo. IV., c. 82, named in schedules B. & I.

Sec. 7 (3 & 4 Vic., c. 108) enacts: "That in every borough named in either of the said schedules (B. & I.) to which no charter of incorporation shall have been granted by virtue of this Act, the Lord Lieutenant of Ireland shall appoint from time to time a fit person to make out a list, to be called the 'freeman's roll,' of such borough, and to act in respect thereto, as hereinafter mentioned."—(See also secs. 8 & 9).

* The converse of this does not always hold good, as for example, in the Bray Township, Co. Dublin, a person may be qualified to be a Commissioner, but yet not qualified to vote.

CHAPTER II.

The Qualifications of Voters.

The qualifications necessary to entitle persons to vote at municipal elections* in Ireland depend upon the provisions of the particular Acts in force in the different towns or townships or boroughs, and vary considerably. They may be considered under four heads, viz. :—

I. In towns or boroughs under 9 Geo. IV., c. 82, and 6 & 7 Vic., c. 93.

II. In boroughs under the Municipal Reform Act, 1840 (3 & 4 Vict., c. 108), Schedule A., and 6 & 7 Vic., c. 93 (where the provisions of these Acts in regard to the qualifications of voters have not been subsequently altered by special Local Acts), or in boroughs having municipal commissioners.†

III. In towns under the Towns Improvement (Ireland) Act, 1854 (17 & 18 Vic., c. 103).

IV. In townships formed under special Local Acts.

Qualification of voters in towns or boroughs under 9 Geo. IV., c. 82.]

The qualification of voters in towns or boroughs under 9 Geo. IV., c. 82, is settled by sections 16 & 21 of that Act, and by the 15th section of 6 & 7 Vic., c. 93.

Sec. 21 makes residence within the town or borough a necessary qualification—hence the word "occupy" in sec.

---

* The Ballot Act, 1872 (35 & 36 Vic., c. 33), s. 29 (c)—defines municipal election as regards Ireland to mean "An election of any person to serve the office of alderman, councillor, commissioner, municipal commissioner, township commissioner, or assessor of any municipal borough." Ap. xl.

† There is only one borough under municipal commissioners, viz., *Carrickfergus*, in which the qualification of voters is the same as that in the boroughs under Schedule A, 3 & 4 Vic., c. 108.

16 must be taken to mean inhabitancy occupation*—the qualifications of voters being as follows :—

(1) The person (male) must have inhabited a dwelling-house (2) for twelve months previous to date of the election at which he votes; (3) such dwelling-house to be situated within the borough or its suburbs or liberties, as defined by the commissioners; (4) such dwelling-house must be of the net annual value of £5 at least, according to the poor law valuation.

The payment of poor rate † only applied to the first election.

Persons must reside in a dwelling-house of the value of £5 at least according to the poor law valuation. Separate houses or premises occupied by the same person, each under the required valuation (say one at £1, another at £2, another at £4), would not give the necessary qualification for voting, as, of course, a person could not inhabit more than one house at the same time.

Nine towns under 9 Geo. IV., c. 82.]

The Act of 9 Geo. IV., c. 82, cannot now be adopted.—(17 & 18 Vic., c. 103, s. 19), Ap. xxii. There are only nine towns in which this Act is now in force—viz., *Armagh, Bandon, Downpatrick, Dungannon, Fethard, Monaghan, Omagh, Wicklow, Youghal.*

Jointly rated Householders.]

Jointly rated householders do not seem qualified to vote —the Act is silent on the point. In boroughs under the Municipal Reform Act, 1840 (3 & 4 Vict., c. 108), and in towns under the Towns Improvement (Ireland) Act, 1854 (17 & 18 Vict., c. 103), "jointly rated occupiers" are qualified to vote, but express provision is made giving them

---

* Continual unbroken residence not necessary to make a person an "inhabitant."
—*Haig*, p. 27. See also *Reg.* v. *Mayor of Exeter*, 1860, L. R., 4 Q. B. 110.
† 6 & 7 Vic., c. 93, s. 12, abolishes vestry rate.

the right of voting.—(See 3 & 4 Vic., c. 108, s. 34; 17 & 18 Vic., c. 103, s. 22, and *post*, p. 71).

Haig (p. 29) however says: "The joint owners of a house occupied by them as partners in trade, are each a 'householder' in respect of the premises so occupied: *Reg.* v. *Hall*, 1 B. & C., 123; *Reg.* v. *Poynder*, 1 B. & C., 178."

Minors; unpardoned felons; and aliens, who have not become naturalized, are inherently disqualified.

Women are not qualified to vote, no matter how highly rated they may be.

Any previously existing rights of freemen to vote in boroughs under 9 Geo. IV., c. 82, are preserved. (See *ante*, p. 41).

CHAPTER III.

QUALIFICATIONS OF VOTERS IN BOROUGHS, UNDER 3 & 4 VIC., CAP. 108, AND 6 & 7 VIC., CAP. 93, WHERE NOT ALTERED BY MORE RECENT ENACTMENTS.

II.—In those boroughs named in schedule A* of the Municipal Reform Act, (3 & 4 Vic., cap. 108), and in Carrickfergus, the voter's qualification (where not altered by subsequent legislation)† is determined by 3 & 4 Vic., cap. 108, and 6 & 7 Vic., cap. 93 (which Acts are to be construed together), and is as follows :—

Voter's qualification.]
Every male inhabitant householder of full age who has for six months previous to the 31st day of August resided

---

* Viz., Belfast Clonmel, Cork, Drogheda, Dublin, Kilkenny, Limerick, Londonderry, Sligo, Waterford.
† Voters' qualification has been altered in Dublin by the Dublin Improvement Act, 1849, 12 & 13 Vic., c. 85, and in Belfast by the Municipal Corporation of Belfast Act, 1887 (50 & 51 Vic., c. cxviii., local and personal), by sec. 10 of which latter Act the municipal franchise was extended to women.

within the borough or within seven statute miles of it,* and who has occupied either as owner or tenant any house, warehouse, counting-house, or shop within the borough which, either separately or jointly with any land within such borough, is of the clear yearly value of not less than £10, to be ascertained and determined in the manner following and not otherwise, that is to say, such value shall be a sum composed of the net annual value at which the premises so occupied by such man shall be rated (as they are hereby required to be) to the relief of the poor under the Act for the more effectual Relief of the Destitute Poor in Ireland,† and of the amount of the sums at which the landlord's repairs and the landlord's insurance shall be estimated and stated in any rate to be made in pursuance of the said Act. ‡

Provided that he has been in occupation of such premises or other premises of the like nature, within the borough,

---

* This is modified by the Municipal Voters' Relief Act, 1885 (48 Vic., c. 9), which enacts, in sec. 2, that "a man shall not be disqualified from being enrolled or voting as a burgess at any municipal election in a borough in respect of the occupation of any house, by reason only that during a part of the qualifying period, not exceeding four months in the whole, he has, by letting or otherwise, permitted such house to be occupied as a furnished dwelling-house by some other person, and during such occupation by another person has not resided in or within seven miles of the borough."

† This referred to secs. 64 and 65 of 1 & 2 Vic., c. 56 (An Act for the more effectual Relief of the Destitute Poor in Ireland, 1838), subsequently repealed.

‡ The valuations are now prepared under the direction of the Commissioner of Valuation, in pursuance of the Valuation Acts, 15 & 16 Vic., c. 63, &c.; but 6 & 7 Vic., c. 92 (An Act for the further Amendment of an Act for the more effectual Relief of the Destitute Poor in Ireland, 1843), s. 10, enacts that the Poor Law Rate books shall in regard to rateable hereditaments in boroughs under 3 & 4 Vic., c. 108, contain, in addition to the estimated net annual value of such hereditaments, an estimate of the probable annual average cost of the landlord's repairs and landlord's insurance.

15 & 16 Vic., c. 63 (An Act to amend the Laws relating to the Valuation of Rateable Property in Ireland, 1852), repealed the Act 9 & 10 Vic., c. 110, which in section 12 contained a similar provision, but left the section in 6 & 7 Vic., c. 92, undisturbed.

It was held in the case of *Phibbs* v. *Kearns* (1860), Ir. R. 11, C.L. 294, that:— A person claiming to be enrolled as a burgess cannot add to the net annual value at which the premises occupied by him are rated a sum for landlord's repairs and insurance, so as to make up the amount of qualification required by 3 & 4 Vic., cap. 108, sec. 30, unless such sum be stated in the rate; and, therefore, a custom in a borough of allowing a fixed sum for landlord's repairs and insurance, the same not being stated in the rate, is bad.

for the space of twelve months next preceding the 31st day of August,* and has been rated for the relief of poor in respect of such premises, and has paid, on or before that day, all poor rates, grand jury and municipal cesses, and all rates and taxes which shall have become payable by him in respect of such premises during his occupation thereof, except such as shall have become payable within three calendar months next before 31st day of August;† the premises in respect of the occupation of which any person shall be qualified to vote in any year need not be the same premises, but may be different premises, occupied in immediate succession by said person in the same parish or union, or in different parishes or unions.—(3 & 4 Vic., c. 108, s. 30, and 6 & 7 Vic., c. 93, s. 27).

Freemen.]

The existing right of freemen to vote is preserved by the Municipal Corporations Act, 1840, to the fullest extent, but sec. 5 (3 & 4 Vic., c. 108), enacts that after the passing of this Act no person shall be elected, made, or admitted a burgess or freeman of any borough by gift or purchase.

Bonâ fide occupier not named or misnamed in the "rates."]

The fact of any *bonâ fide* occupier not being named or being misnamed, or insufficiently described, in the "rates," will not disqualify him from being enrolled as a burgess, provided that he is the person liable for the rates, and has been called upon to pay, and has actually paid them, within

---

* Under this section the party must show, not merely that he was in occupation of premises within the borough, for a period of twelve months prior to the last day of August, but also that the premises (whether the same premises throughout, or different premises occupied in succession), were during the whole period of his respective occupation, rated to the relief of the poor, and that to an amount not less than £10, as evidenced by the rate book for the time being in force.—(Judge Hayes' Judgment, *Queen v. Mayor of Belfast*, 1862, Ir. R. 15, C. L. 162).

† Public notice regarding the payment of taxes to be given; see 3 & 4 Vic., c. 108, s. 31.

the specified time as provided (3 & 4 Vic., c. 108, s. 30, and 6 & 7 Vic., c. 93, s. 27).—See *post*, p. 140.

Seven miles—how to be computed.]

The distance of seven miles is to be computed by the nearest public road, or way by land or water (3 & 4 Vic., c. 108, s. 35).

Carrickfergus.]

The qualifications of voters in Carrickfergus are the same as in those boroughs under Schedule A., 3 & 4 Vic., c. 108; see 6 & 7 Vic., c. 93, s. 26.

What constitutes a householder.]

As to what constitutes a householder, Haig (pp. 28, 29), says:—

"It is considered to be now settled, that where a house is let out in separate portions to different tenants, and the owner or landlord does not reside on the premises, though there is but one outer door common to all the tenants, each distinct portion so let is the house of the occupier. Rawlinson's Municipal Acts, 18, see *Reg. v. Trapshaw*, 1 Leach, 427; *Reg. v. Carroll, id.*, 237; *Reg. v. Bailey*, Moody, C.C., 23; and Littledale, J., in *Reg. v. Mayor of Eye*, 9 A. & E., 680."

"So chambers in the Inns of Court are each the dwelling-house of the occupant . . . . in such cases there is a common stair-case, and one common passage open to the air; but it seems that such chambers would not cease to be several dwelling-houses, though the common entrance was closed by an outer entrance door common to all the chambers.". . . .

"A salaried clerk occupying a house belonging to his employer, and liable to be dispossessed at pleasure, is not a householder; *Gorman's Case*, 1 Ir. Law Rep., 282. And no lodger, though having the exclusive possession of a principal part of a house, and however long the term for which he has taken it, is a householder for the purpose of qualification. See 1 Nolan, P.L., 178; *Reg. v. North Collingham*, 1 B. & C., 578; *Lee v. Gansell*, 1 Cowp., 1." . . . .

Occupation.]

"Occupation may take place without personal residence, for a man may occupy by bales of goods; per Denman, *C. J. Reg. v. St. Mary Kalendar*, 9 A. & E., 630" (*id.*)

No person who occupies *land* only, within the borough, is entitled to be enrolled as a burgess.

Aliens and Paupers disqualified.]

No person who has within twelve months next before the 31st August, received any relief from poor law guardians or any allowance from certain charitable trustees (other than medical or surgical assistance),* is qualified, but the fact of a person having his child at a public or endowed school is not a disqualification. (3 & 4 Vic., c. 108, s. 32).

Aliens are disqualified (see *post*, p. 67).

Felons.]

Felons disqualified (see *post*, p. 70).

Joint occupiers.]

Joint occupiers are entitled to be enrolled in respect of premises which they jointly occupy, provided that the value of such premises (to be ascertained and determined as aforesaid, *i.e.*, as in sec. 30, 3 & 4 Vic., c. 108) shall be of an amount, which, when divided by the number of such occupiers, shall give for each occupier a sum not less than the sum which would entitle such person to be enrolled or to vote as aforesaid if he occupied separately but not otherwise. (3 & 4 Vic., c. 108, s. 34).

Weekly tenants.]

Weekly tenants occupying premises in the Municipal Borough of Dublin are entitled to be placed on the Burgess Roll if they claim to be rated, and pay or tender the full amount of the last made rate then payable in respect of the premises. *The Queen (Parker)* v. *Power*, 1890 (26 Ir. L.R., 380). See also *The Queen (Byrne and others)* v. *The Lord Mayor of Dublin*, 1891 (28 Ir. L.R., 296); and *The Queen (Collins and others)* v. *The Lord Mayor of Dublin* (*id.* 313).

* See also Medical Relief Disqualification Removal Act, 1885 (48 & 49 Vic., c. 16), Ap. lxxxii.

CHAPTER IV.

Qualifications of Voters in Towns under the Towns Improvement (Ireland) Act, 1854.

III. The *qualifications of voters at elections for commissioners in towns under the Towns Improvement (Ireland) Act*, 1854 (17 & 18 Vic., c. 103) are fixed by 22nd section of that Act. (Ap. xxii.)

(1.) Every person of full age, who is the immediate lessor of lands, tenements, and hereditaments, within the town, of the value of £50 and upwards according to the last poor law valuation, and who resides within five miles of the boundary of such town; and

(2.) Every person of full age who shall have occupied as tenant or owner or joint occupier, or shall have been the immediate lessor* rated for such premises to the relief of the poor, to the net annual value† of four pounds or upwards (and in the case of joint occupiers, rated in respect of premises of the net annual value of four pounds or upwards for each of such joint occupiers of any lands, tenements, or hereditaments, within such town—and shall have been rated for the relief of the poor in respect of such premises‡ for the period of twelve months preceding the first day of January in the year in which any such election is held, and shall have paid all rates under any Local Act in force in such town, payable by him in respect of such premises within six months next preceding the day of election.

---

* *i.e.*, An owner who occupies.

† The words "annual value" refer to the actual rateable value. *Baker v. Marsh*, 1854, 4 E. & B., 144.

‡ The valuation of the premises must be over £4 (at least £4 5s. 0d.), otherwise the occupier of the premises cannot be rated to the relief of the poor (6 & 7 Vic., c. 92, s. 1): but if the property occupied by the same person in any Union amount, in the aggregate, to more than £4 net annual value, the occupier is to be rated.—*See* Mooney's Compendium of Poor Law Acts, p. 63.

Payment of Poor Rates and Grand Jury Rates now abolished.]

The provision in this section making the payment of poor rates and grand jury rates necessary to qualify a person to vote is repealed by the Local Government (Ireland) Act, 1871 (34 & 35 Vic., c. 109), s. 26 (Ap. xxx.)

Means of ascertaining payment of rates provided in this section cannot now be adopted.]

The section further provides:—

> "And of the payment or non-payment of such rate, a receipt, certificate, or certified list, under the hand of . . . . . the collector under any Local Act in force in the city or town, shall for such purpose be deemed sufficient evidence, and which certificate or certified list such collectors . . . . . are hereby required to furnish to the person or persons presiding at such election ; and if any controversy shall arise at such meeting as to the qualification or right to vote of any person claiming to vote or to be qualified, such controversy shall be determined by the person or persons presiding at such meeting upon reference to the rate book, which the clerk of the union is hereby required to produce at such meeting."

The portion of this section—which provides for evidence being produced or gone into, or requires the collectors to furnish certified lists to the presiding officers at the election of persons whose rates have or have not been paid, with a view of determining their qualification to vote in this respect—is virtually repealed by the Ballot Act; being incompatible with the provisions of it.—(B.A., s. 32, Ap. xli.)

The question then arises as to the date on which the rates must be paid in order to qualify a person to vote — whether a person is qualified to vote who pays his rates on the day of election immediately before presenting himself to vote, or whether his rates must be paid at the time the voters' list is being made out. (For a full consideration of this matter see *post*, pp. 63-7).

Women disqualified.]

Females are disqualified from voting at elections under the Towns Improvement (Ireland) Act, 1854.

In the case of the *Queen* v. *Crosthwaite*, 1864, the Court of Common Pleas held that women of full age, and possessing the required qualification, were admissible to vote under the twenty-second section (17 & 18 Vict., c. 103), Judge Fitzgerald adding: " I am not to be taken as concurring in any expression indicating an opinion that ladies are not entitled to sit as town commissioners if the electors choose to elect them."—(Ir. R. 17, C.L., 174).

An appeal was brought to the Court of Exchequer Chamber, which reversed the decision of the Court of Queen's Bench. (The appeal was heard before Monahan, *C.J.*, Pigot, *C.B.*, Ball, Keogh, and Christian, *JJ.*, and Fitzgerald and Deasy, *BB.*; Monahan, *C.J.*, Pigot, *C.B.*, and Ball, *J.*, dissented from the decision, being of opinion that the judgment of the Court of Queen's Bench should be affirmed).

Baron Deasy said :—

" If it were not for the glossary clause in the first section of this Act, there would be no doubt that the twenty-second section of this Act gave the right of voting to men only ; and the question we have to decide is, whether that clause controls and qualifies the plain words of the twenty-second section, which, if taken by themselves, would leave the franchise in towns, situated as the town of Kingstown is, in precisely the same condition, so far as sex, as the franchise in towns under 9 George IV., or the Municipal Reform Act. Now the glossary clause, so far as relates to the present question, is that words importing the masculine gender, except only the word male, shall include females. But that is contradicted by the general saving at the commencement of the clause, unless there is something in the subject or context repugnant to such construction. Is there anything then in the context repugnant to such construction ? I think there is. The seventh section, which defines the qualifications of persons who are to vote at the meeting which is to decide whether the Act is to be adopted or not, uses terms quite as general as the twenty-second section, and differs from it only in the amount of the qualifications required. But it is plain from schedule A. that by the general words then used the Legislature did not intend to include females ; for, by the form of notice of meeting given in that schedule, males only were to attend to vote. Again, in section 25, where the qualification of commissioners is defined, words equally general are used; and yet, it is plain, I think, both from the language of that section, particularly the exception as to ecclesiastics, and from the nature of the duties imposed upon and the powers given to the commissioners, that it never was intended that a female should be elected to the office. . . . I think, therefore, that looking to the provisions of this Act and its object, and the provisions of analogous Acts dealing with the same subject-matter, that we ought not to control the plain words of the twenty-second section by the general declaration in the glossary clause, but that we ought to give it such a construction as will give effect to every part of it, and at the same time make it, or rather keep it, consistent with the previous enactments of the Legislature, and the policy there expressed. But I am unwilling to rest my judgment exclusively upon the provisions of the statutes regulating the local government of towns in Ireland. I think that there is a far more exclusive principle involved in the case; and that is, the right of women to intervene personally by their votes in contested elections for public officers entrusted with powers of government, either local or general. I think the general policy of the law is to exclude from them any such intervention; and that the policy is founded, partly on the supposition that such subjects are beyond their cognizance, as requiring a judgment superior to that which they possess,* and partly upon the ground that it is inconsistent with the delicacy and modesty of their sex that they should be mixed up in the strife and turmoil of a contested election."—(Ir. R. 17, C.L., 471).

Qualifying Premises.]

The (male) person must occupy and be rated for lands or tenements of the value of £4† or upwards, according to the last poor law valuation; but separate houses (or lands) occupied by the same person, within the borough, each under the required valuation (say one for £3, another for £1), the aggregate value of which amounts to £4, will not give him the necessary rating qualification for voting, as no occupier is rated for township rates for premises, unless

* Pigot, C.B., who took the opposite view, said—"I cannot hold that in this realm in which a female not only may reign, but does reign, in her own right, there is in women a common law inability arising out of mental incapacity," and referred to Queen Elizabeth, of whom Lord Plunkett said—"No monarch ever better knew the royal art of reigning."—(Id., 483.)

† A person cannot be rated for the relief of the poor unless the aggregate valuation of the lands or premises he occupies is at least £4 5s. 0d. See footnote p. 49.

the valuation of the same is at least £4.—(17 & 18 Vic., c. 103, s. 64).

Occupation.]

It is to be observed that occupation does not mean residence, and that a person can "occupy" premises with his furniture or with a bale of goods. In the glossary of the Towns Improvement (Ireland) Act, 1854, the word "occupier" is made "to extend to and include an immediate lessor made liable under this Act to assessments," &c., ... but not to include "a lodger or a party in occupation as tenant of a furnished house for a less period than one year, but shall include the party by whom such furnished house is so let." (17 & 18 Vic., c. 103, s. 1)—Ap. xx.

The Voters Relief Act, 1885 (48 Vic., c. 9), has no practical effect in towns unless residence forms part of the qualifications of the voter.

Lodgers are not "occupiers," nor can they be rated for the relief of the poor (6 & 7 Vic., c. 92, s. 4), and therefore are not qualified to vote.

Weekly or Monthly Tenants.]

Weekly or monthly tenants, or persons occupying separate apartments in a house, are not qualified to vote.

All occupiers are rated for the relief of the poor (1 & 2 Vic., c. 56, s. 61), unless the valuation of the premises they occupy is not more then £4—in which case the immediate lessor is rated (6 & 7 Vic., c. 92, s. 1), or unless they are let in separate apartments, or to lodgers (6 & 7 Vic., c. 92, s. 4). Hence, weekly or monthly tenants of premises over the valuation of £4, must be rated for the relief of the poor.

The Towns Improvement (Ireland) Act, 1854 (17 & 18 Vic., c. 103), sec. 60, provides that the commissioners shall assess all occupiers of premises, rated in respect of such premises for the relief of the destitute poor—and sec. 61 that the clerk of the union shall, on the requisition of the commissioners, produce the rate book of the union, &c.—Ap. xxiv.

The Towns Improvement (Ireland) Act, 1854, s. 65 (Ap. xxv.), however, expressly incorporates so much of the Towns Improvement Clauses Act, 1847 (10 & 11 Vic., c. 34), as relates to the manner of making rates, and sec. 181 of this latter Act enacts that the *owners* of rateable property which is let to weekly or monthly tenants, or in separate apartments, or to lodgers, shall be rated instead of the occupiers thereof.—(Ap. x.)

It is submitted therefore that weekly or monthly tenants are not liable to be rated, and could not, therefore, comply with the provision as to the payment of township rates, and are consequently not qualified to vote.*

Police.] Not disqualified (see *post*, p. 71).

Joint Occupiers.]

Joint occupiers are entitled to vote, provided that the valuation of the premises which they jointly occupy is of an amount which, when divided by the number of such occupiers, gives for each occupier a sum of not less than £4. If the amount of the valuation of the premises is not sufficient to give each male occupier a valuation of £4—then no one is qualified to vote in respect of such premises.

If, for example, the valuation of the premises is £20, and there are six occupiers jointly rated for it, none of them are entitled to vote; nor would the case be altered if five of the jointly rated occupiers were male, and one a female.

---

* The 184th section (10 and 11 Vic., c. 34) only gives yearly tenants the right of demanding to be rated, and to pay the rates, and thus—"exceptio probat regulam"—in effect provides against such a right being exercised by weekly tenants.

Weekly tenants belonging, as they almost always do, to the working classes, are frequently obliged to change from place to place as their term of service or work is finished, and the Legislature recognised that it would be useless to hold them liable for the payment of rates, because owing to the nature of their tenancy, they could readily evade payment by vacating the premises when the rates became due.

The intention of the Legislature was that no person should have the right of voting in respect of the occupation of premises, unless the person who is actually liable for the payment of the rates, hence the franchise was not extended to weekly tenants.

The fact that weekly tenants have the right to vote in Dublin (see *ante*, p. 48) does not affect the general principles of legislation here referred to.

Joint Immediate Lessors.]
Joint immediate lessors do not seem to be entitled to vote, unless, of course, they are rated occupiers. (See *post*, p. 71).

Aliens]
Aliens (who have not taken out letters of naturalisation) are not qualified to vote (see *post*, p. 67).

Felons.] Disqualified (see *post*, p. 70).

CHAPTER V.

QUALIFICATIONS OF VOTERS IN TOWNSHIPS FORMED UNDER LOCAL ACTS.

The qualifications of electors in townships formed under Local Acts vary of course according to the special provisions which these Acts contain in regard thereto. We will take as an example of these:—The Blackrock township (Co. Dublin), which was formed under the Blackrock Township Act, 1863 (26 & 27 Vic., c. cxxi.), Local and Personal, as the clause which specifies the qualifications of voters in this Act, is substantially the same as that in several of the Local Acts in force in other townships.*

Sect. 21 of the Blackrock Township Act, 1863 (26 & 27 Vic., c. cxxi., Local and Personal), specifies the qualifications of persons entitled to vote at an election for commissioners in that township.

"The Commissioners to be elected under this Act for every ward shall be elected by all male persons of full age, who are immediate lessors of lands, tenements, or hereditaments within the ward, of the yearly value of fifty pounds or upwards, according to the then last Poor Law valuation, and whose names have been on the Township Rate Book as immediate lessors for three months at least before the day for the election, and by all male persons of full age respectively rated to the relief of the poor within the respective wards for any lands, tenements, or hereditaments, of the yearly value of eight pounds or upwards, who, on or before the fifteenth day of July next before the day

* Viz.—Pembroke, Clontarf, etc.

for the election, have occupied the lands, tenements, or hereditaments, in respect whereof they respectively claim to vote for not less than three months; provided that no person shall be qualified to vote unless he, before voting, have paid all rates for the relief of the poor, and under this Act payable by him within the township, except those which are assessed within three months next before the day for the election."

There are two classes of voters (1)—" Immediate Lessors," and (2) " Rated Occupiers."

Immediate Lessors.]

This term " Immediate Lessor" is frequently used in the statutes in regard to municipal affairs—but no definition is given of it—but from the sense in which it is applied, it evidently means the person who receives the " rack rent,"* and who stands in the relation of immediate landlord to the tenant who pays the rack rent.

What constitutes Full Age.]

(a.) An immediate lessor must be of full age—it is to be borne in mind that a person comes to full legal age on the day before his 21st birthday.

Meara in his " Law and Practice relating to Parliamentary Elections," p. 60, says :—" Full age is accomplished on the day preceding the anniversary of a person's birth. (1 Bl. Com., 463 1 ; † Salk. 44, 2 ; Salk. 625.) So that if A. be born on 1st January he is of age on the morning of the last day of December, though he may not have lived twenty-one years, by nearly 48 hours; the reason assigned is, that the law does not notice the fraction of a day."

" In England the Common Law in this respect is enforced and declared by Statute 7, 8 Will. 3, c. 25, s. 8."

" In the *New Windsor* Case, K. & O., 160, the committee determined that the vote of a minor, against whom

---

* Rack rent is defined by the Towns Improvement (Ireland) Act, 1854, to mean a rent which is not less than two-thirds of the full net annual value of the property out of which the rent arises (17 & 18 Vic., c. 103, s. 1). A similar definition is given in sec. 2 of the Public Health (Ireland) Act, 1878 (41 & 42 Vic., c. 52).

† Salkeld's (King's Bench) Reports, 1695—1704.

no objection had been made before the Revising Barrister, was a good vote." (*Monmouth, ib.* 415.")

Property Qualification.]

(*b*) He must be an immediate lessor of lands, tenements, or hereditaments, within the ward (for which he shall be entitled to vote for the election of a commissioner) of the yearly value of £50 or upwards, according to the then last Poor Law valuation.

Joint Immediate Lessors.]

Joint immediate lessors do not appear entitled to vote under this section. (See *post*, p. 71).

Payment of Rates.]

An immediate lessor is only liable to be assessed when the rateable value of premises is £4 and under* (17 & 18 Vic., c. 103, s. 64,—Ap. xxv.), so that there are no rates payable by an immediate lessor of £50 and upwards, and he is entitled to vote, whether the rates on the property which qualifies him have been paid or not.

The next condition with regard to the qualification of an immediate lessor is that his name shall have been on the township rate book for at least three months before the day of election.

Name to be on Township Rate Book.]

Property is constantly changing hands; an immediate lessor may die or dispose of his qualifying property, and the commissioners have no means of knowing of his death or in what way his property has been disposed of. An immediate lessor, when he acquires qualifying property, should make application to the commissioners, giving evidence of his claim to have his name placed on the township rate-book in respect of same—the commissioners having power to amend the said rate book (see Towns Improvement (Ireland)

---

* Unless in some cases for water or sewer rate, or where the premises are let to weekly or monthly tenants. See *ante*, p. 54.

Act, 1854 (17 & 18 Vic., c. 103,) s. 61, Ap. xxiv.; Towns Improvement Clauses Act, 1847, 10 & 11 Vic. c. 34), s. 174 (Ap. ix.), incorporated* by the Towns Improvement (Ireland) Act, 1854, s. 65, (Ap. xxv.) which last mentioned Act is incorporated* by the Blackrock Township Act, 1863 (26 & 27 Vic., c. cxxi. (Local and Personal), s. 4).

As immediate lessors are generally ignorant of the course which it is necessary for them to take in order to secure their franchise, it is suggested that a notice as follows might be published, say about four months, before the day of election :—

TOWNSHIP OF ———

NOTICE TO IMMEDIATE LESSORS.

Notice is hereby given that a printed list of all persons whose names appear on the Township Rate Books as immediate lessors of property valued at £50 and upwards, and who are consequently qualified to vote at next annual election of Commissioners, in respect of such qualification, is now ready, and may be seen at the office of the Commissioners any week day between the hours of 10 a.m. and 1 p.m.

Persons whose names do not appear on this list, and who claim to be immediate lessors of property valued at £50 and upwards, should apply in writing to the Commissioners on or before Tuesday, 2nd July, giving full particulars and evidence in support of their claims, with a view to having their names placed on the Township Rate Books, otherwise they will not be eligible to vote, under sects. 21, 26 & 27 Victoria, cap. 121.

——— Town Clerk.

Town Hall,
 Dated this 15th June, 18 .

The Commissioners, of course, must have satisfactory evidence that the claim of any person applying to have his name enrolled as an immediate lessor on the Township Rate Book is well founded.

The right of owners of property in fee to vote is not recognised by the Legislature.

---

* Except where expressly varied or excepted.

Second Class—Rated Occupiers.]

Rated occupiers must—

- (*a.*) Be 21 years of age.
- (*b.*) Of the masculine gender.
- (*c.*) Be rated for hereditaments valued at £8, or upwards, for the relief of the poor.
- (*d.*) Have been in occupation for a period of three months from the 15th April to 15th July.
- (*e.*) Have paid before voting all township rates payable by him assessed within three months next before the day of election.

Full age.]

He must be twenty-one years of age. A person comes to full legal age the day before his twenty-first birthday. (See *ante*, p. 56).

Women disqualified.]

Women are not qualified to vote for the election of Commissioners in the Township of Blackrock—the section expressly provides that the voters shall be *male* persons.

Rated for the Relief of the Poor.]

The poor law Union rate book is the source from which the town clerk must obtain evidence as to a man's being rated for the relief of the poor.

The poor rate books are open to inspection for fourteen days before the rate is struck, of which notice is given,* so that if a duly qualified person finds that his name has been omitted from the rate book he can, during this period, call upon the guardians to have it inserted therein.

* 12 & 13 Vic, c. 104.—(An Act to Amend the Act for the more effectual Relief of the Destitute Poor in Ireland), sec. 21 enacts "that the Guardians of the Poor of the several Unions shall, before the making of every rate, leave the rate books open for the inspection of any ratepayer between the hours of ten in the forenoon and four in the afternoon, during 14 days at the least, before the making of every such rate; and that such Guardians shall give the same public notice of the deposit of such rate books for inspection as they are now required to give in relation to the making of such rates, and that in all cases the names of occupiers for whom the immediate lessor is primarily liable for the payment of rate shall be inserted in the rate book."

After the rates are made an occupier rated for £8 or upwards, can claim to be rated, but he must make a written application to the guardians and sign it, tendering the amount of poor rate due (if any) on the premises in respect of which he claims to be rated.*

FORM OF APPLICATION.

To the Board of Guardians of the   Union.

I,
occupier of
situate at
in the   Union,
hereby claim to be rated in respect of said premises, and to have my name *inserted in the last made rate*, pursuant to the Statutes in that case made and provided.

Dated this   day of   18 .

} *Name.*
} *Residence.*

Occupation.]

They must have been in occupation for three months from the 15th April to 15th July. Occupation does not imply residence, and a man may occupy a house, or premises, or land, with some of his property (see *ante*, p. 47), nor will

---

* 13 & 14 Vic,. c. 69, s. 110, enacts "that it shall be lawful for any person who shall occupy any lands, tenements, or hereditaments rated under the Acts for the more effectual relief of the destitute poor in Ireland at a net annual value . . . . of eight pounds or upwards in any city, town, or borough in *Ireland*, in which there shall be a rate for the relief of the destitute poor, and whose name shall have been omitted from such rate, to present to the guardians of the union a claim to be rated in respect of such premises, and such claim shall be in writing, and signed with his name; and upon such occupier so claiming and actually paying or tendering the full amount of the rate or rates (if any) then due in respect of such premises, the guardians of the union shall insert the name of such occupier in such rate in respect of such premises aforesaid; and in case such guardians shall neglect or refuse so to do, such occupier shall for the purpose of this Act be deemed to have been rated in respect of such premises in the rate in respect of which he shall have claimed to be rated as aforesaid."

letting his house furnished disqualify him,* hence the Voters Relief Act, 1885 (48 Vict., c. 9), has no practical effect in the Blackrock Township.

The rate collector ought to be the best informed person, and is, in fact, the recognised authority with regard to the occupation of lands or premises in the township, and he should furnish to the town clerk, say on or before 25th of August, a certified list of all persons who were not in occupation of the qualifying lands or premises during the required period.

A person must occupy and be rated for premises or lands, of the value of £8 or upwards, according to the last poor law valuation; but separate houses, or premises, or lands within the township, occupied by the same person, each under the required valuation (but being of the valuation of £4 or upwards, say one at £5, another at £4, the aggregate valuation of which amounts to £8 or upwards) will give him the necessary rating qualification. (See footnote *ante*, p. 49).

Weekly or Monthly Tenants.]

A weekly or monthly tenant occupying a house valued at £8, or upwards, is not qualified to vote in respect of same. (See *ante*, p. 53).

Receipt of Parochial Relief.]

Being the recipient of parochial relief does not disqualify a person from voting.

Bankruptcy.]

Bankruptcy does not disqualify a voter.

If voter qualified for two wards.]

If a person is qualified to vote in two wards, his name is to be placed on the list of voters for both wards; but he

---

* A person who lets his furnished house for more than a year ceases to be an "occupier," and a person in occupation of a furnished house for more than a year becomes the "occupier."—Towns Improvement (Ireland) Act, 1854 (17 & 18 Vic., c. 103), s 1, Ap. xx

can only vote in one ward, and the ward in which he first votes will be held to be the ward in which he has elected to vote in. (See *post*, p. 140).

Payment of Rates.]

He must have paid all rates under this Act, payable by him within the township, except those which are assessed within three months before the day for the election.

Of Poor Rates.]

There is some doubt as to the payment of poor rates being a necessary qualification.

The 26th sec. of the Local Government (Ireland) Act, 1871 (34 & 35 Vict., c. 109), is brought into force in the Blackrock Township by the Public Health (Ireland) Act, 1878 (41 & 42 Vict., c. 52, s. 294, Schedule A).* This section repeals so much of the 22nd section of the Towns Improvement (Ireland) Act, 1854, as made the payment of poor rates and grand jury rates by any person necessary for qualifying such person to vote at the election of commissioners.

However the portion of the 22nd section of the Towns Improvement (Ireland) Act, as to the qualifications of electors for the election of commissioners, was not incorporated by the Blackrock Township Act, 1863 (see sect. 4 of that Act).

There being some doubt on the point, the payment of poor rates should not be insisted upon as an indispensable condition—as where reasonable doubt exists on a matter of this kind—the benefit of the doubt should be given for, not against, the right of exercising the franchise.

Township Rates.]

There would seem, however, to be no doubt as to the payment of township rates being a necessary qualification

---

* The repeal, by the Public Health (Ireland) Act, 1878 (41 & 42 Vic., c. 52), Schedule A of section 3 of the Local Government (Ireland) Act, 1871 (34 & 35 Vic., c. 109), which contains the definition of " Principal Act," has no practical effect.

—but considerable difficulty arises as to *when* these rates must be paid—the section here does not fix any date but enacts " before voting," but these words must of course be interpreted having regard to, and so as to be consistent with the provisions of the Local Government (Ireland) Act, 1871, sect. 27, as to the preparation of the lists and the provisions of the Ballot Act, 1872, relative to the taking of the poll.

It has been suggested that in the case of a man otherwise qualified who has not paid the township rate—made and assessed more than three months before the election—there should be put after his name on the voters' list something to show that he is not entitled to vote, unless before voting he has complied with the proviso, which might be somewhat in this form, viz. :—an asterisk placed after his name with a note as follows :—

A.B.*

* " Provided that before voting he shall have paid the portion of the Blackrock Township rate made and assessed on the ——— day of ————, 18—, under the Blackrock Township Act, 1863, payable by him, which was due and unpaid at the time of making out this list."

And it is contended that if such an elector pays, before he presents himself to vote, the rate due, he should be allowed to vote,—and that the collector should make out a list for each ward (certified by him) of the persons who have so paid, up to the morning of the day of election, and that such certified list ought to be taken as sufficient evidence (under section 22 of the Towns Improvement (Ireland) Act, 1854) * of a person's having complied with the proviso ; and that as others may, during the voting, and since the collector made out the list, have paid the rate, they should on the production of the collector's receipt be allowed to vote, or if necessary the presiding officer might send for the collector and ascertain the fact.

* Ap. xxii.

It is submitted, however, that this mode of solving the difficulty might involve the presiding officers in serious trouble.

A presiding officer, if required by the agent acting on behalf of any candidate, is to put to the elector at the time he tenders his vote, before handing him the ballot paper, but not afterwards, either or both of the following questions, that is to say :—*

(1). Are you the same person whose name appears as A.B. on the register of voters now in force for the city (or town or borough, *as the case may be*) of———?

(2). Have you already voted either here or elsewhere at this election for the city (or town or borough, *as the case may be*) of———?

He is not to put, or permit to be put, to any elector any other question whatsoever. (See *post*, p. 135).

Hence, if A.B.'s name were on the list, with the proviso suggested as to his rates being paid before voting, he might demand his ballot paper, and the presiding officer would have no right to put any question to him as to whether he had, since the preparation of the list, paid his rates, or to require him to produce a receipt for the payment of same; and if he answered the two required questions and took the required oath an action would lie against the presiding officer if he refused to give him a ballot paper.

In an English election case it was held that the returning officer in refusing to admit the vote of a person whose name was on the register, and who had answered the questions, had mistaken his duty, and might have subjected himself to a criminal prosecution for the breach of a public duty. (*Pryce v. Belcher*, 1847, 4 C.B., 866.)

---

* The provisions of the Ballot Act in regard to all that relates to taking the poll apply to Municipal as well as Parliamentary elections (B.A., s. 20). Ap. xxxvii.–vlii.

The Ballot Act, by Schedule VI., incorporates amongst other sections (in relation to the mode of taking the poll) section 89 of 13 & 14 Vic., c. 69.

This section enacts that it shall not be lawful to require any voter at any election for members of Parliament "to take note or affirmation either in proof of his freehold, occupation, or of his residence, age, or other qualification or right to vote, or of his qualification continuing, or of *his not owing* any cesses, rates, or taxes whatsoever, any law or statute, local or general, to the contrary notwithstanding," &c.—(Ap. xi.)

And the Ballot Act (Schedule VI.) repeals the 27th section of the Commissioners Clauses Act, 1847 (10 Vic., c. 16), which gave the presiding officer power to summon and interrogate rate collectors, and to enquire into the qualification of voters on the day of the election, and although it does not expressly repeal sect. 22 of the Towns Improvement (Ireland) Act, 1854—which gave a similar power to the presiding officers —yet sect. 32 (B.A.) enacts that "all other enactments inconsistent with this [the Ballot] Act are hereby repealed." —Ap. xli.

That this section is inconsistent with the Ballot Act is obvious, as it is clearly the intention of the Ballot Act that no evidence is to be gone into at the taking of the poll (going into evidence would cause controversy* and seriously delay the poll), and that any question as to the qualifications of voters must be settled at the time the list is made out, the list being conclusive according to L.G. (I.) Act, 1871 (34 & 35 Vic., c. 109), s. 27, Ap. xxx.-i., and to C.P. (M.E.) Act, 1872 (35 & 36 Vic., c. 60), s. 10.—Ap. lxii.

It is submitted, therefore, that as the provisions of the previous Acts can only be put in force as far as they are

---

* By 1 Geo. IV., c. 11, s. 16, and 4 Geo. IV., c. 55, s. 58, it was enacted that no person shall speak, or barrister plead, during the time of polling.

Meara says (p. 68):—"The objection on the ground of alienage, is difficult to sustain; it would appear, from later authorities to be incumbent upon the objector to prove not merely that the persons was born 'hors' the allegiance, but that the incapacity has not been removed.'

Bedford, P. & K. 147. C. & R. 98. Godfrey Levi's Case—"The evidence produced to prove the alienage was that of a brother of the voter and of another witness who had known him as an infant in *Germany* and afterwards in *England*. It was contended in favour of the vote, that there was no proof that one of the parents of the voter was not an English subject (*b*). Vote good.

"*Reading*, F. & F. 553, Pierre Chaville De Barthes was objected to, being an alien. Pierre Barthes, brother of the voter, proved that he was a native of *Bourdeaux*, and ten years older than the voter. That the voter was born at *Bourdeaux* whilst he was living in his father's family. That the voter came to *England* in 1826, and had not to the knowledge of the witness been naturalised or received letters of denization. Vote good."

Vide *Levi's* Case, *ib.* 437.

In regard to this (the *Reading* Case), which was heard before a Parliamentary Committee, Cunningham (p. 390) says:—"It was held that the onus lies on the person impugning the vote of such person of proving as a fact that he was not naturalised or become a denizen. But this decision seems contrary to the first principles of evidence."

Felons.]

A person convicted of treason or felony is disqualified to vote at municipal elections until he shall have suffered the punishment to which he had been sentenced, or shall have been pardoned.—(33 & 34 Vic., c. 23, s. 2).

Joint Occupiers not entitled to vote.]

Joint occupiers are not entitled to vote, no matter what may be the valuation of the land, &c., jointly occupied by them.

The 22nd section of the Towns Improvement (Ireland) Act, 1854 (17 & 18 Vic., c. 103), contains provisions for joint occupiers voting, and consequently in boroughs and towns under this Act (where the qualifications of electors have not been altered by subsequent legislation) joint occupiers are entitled to vote.

But the 22nd section (17 & 18 Vic., c. 103), as regards the qualification of electors, is not incorporated by the Blackrock Township Act, 1863, and different qualifications, as we have seen, are laid down in the 21st section of this (latter) Act for voters in Blackrock.

This section makes no provision for joint occupiers voting, and hence they are not entitled to vote.

This is shown by an analogous case in regard to the Parliamentary franchise of joint occupiers in counties and boroughs. Under sections 1 and 5, which (like the 21st section of the Blackrock Act) do not contain any provision for joint occupiers in counties voting, joint occupiers in counties were not entitled to vote. Under section 6, which contained a provision for joint occupiers voting in boroughs (like sect. 22 of Towns Improvement (Ireland) Act, 1854), joint occupiers in boroughs were entitled to vote.

Joint occupiers in counties continued disqualified till the passing of 31 & 32 Vic., c. 49, which by sect. 6 gives joint occupiers the right to vote.

Police.]

Members of the Dublin Metropolitan Police force, or the Royal Irish Constabulary, are not debarred by statute from voting at municipal elections.

A natural born subject is a person born within the dominions of the crown of England.

"An alien, is a person born out of the dominions of the crown of England; out of the allegiance of the king."—Blackstone's Commentaries on the Laws of England, 366.

"An alien, as being ignorant of the laws and customs of the realm, and unable or unlikely to promote the interest of the State to which he is not naturally allied, has always been ineligible."—Simeon on Elections (1789), 24.

"The children of aliens born within the dominions of the crown of England are natural-born subjects."—Blackstone, 374.

A "denizen" is an alien born who has obtained "ex donatione legis," letters patent to make him an English subject. He is in a kind of middle state between an alien and a natural born subject."*

"By several Irish statutes, naturalization is conferred on foreigners under particular circumstances."

"By stat. 14, 15 Car. II., c. 13—amended and perpetuated, as far as relates to the encouraging Protestant strangers—by Stat. 4 Geo. I., c. 9, *all aliens* of the *Protestant* religion, and all *merchants*, &c., or *seamen*, inhabiting in, or arriving in this kingdom with intent to reside, upon taking the oaths prescribed by 3 W. & M., c. 2 E. & I., are declared to be natural subjects. By 19 & 20 Geo. III., c. 29, 23 & 24 Geo. III., c. 38, and 36 Geo. III., c. 48, *all foreigners* settling in Ireland, upon taking the necessary oath (or affirmation, if a quaker), and obtaining licences from the chief governor in council, shall be deemed natural subjects; except as to being a member of the privy council, or sitting in Parliament, or holding any office or place of trust under the crown."—Meara, p. 68.

* Parker, pp. 48, 49.

The Naturalization Act, 1870 (33 & 34 Vic., c. 14), s. 7, provides that :—

"An alien, to whom a certificate of naturalization is granted shall, in the United Kingdom, be entitled to all political and other rights, powers, and privileges, and be subject to all obligations to which a natural born British subject is entitled or subject in the United Kingdom, &c.

Aliens therefore are not entitled to vote; and if the town clerk receives an objection from anyone in regard to a person's name being placed on the list of voters on the ground that that person is an alien and has not become naturalized, and if he (the town clerk) is satisfied from the evidence laid before him that the objection is well founded, it is submitted that he would not be justified in putting the name of that person on the list of persons qualified to vote unless the alleged alien is in a position to show that he is not an alien, or that he has taken out letters of naturalization, and the town clerk might send him a notice to the following effect :—

SIR,
 I have to inform you, that I am now preparing a list of persons qualified to vote at the forthcoming election of commissioners for this township, and that an objection has been made in regard to your name being placed as a voter on the said list on the ground that you are an alien and have not become naturalized; be good enough, therefore, to furnish me with satisfactory evidence, on or before the 26th September instant, of your having been born within the British Dominions, or if you are an alien, that you have taken out letters of naturalization, as in the absence of such evidence I will not be able to place your name on the list of persons qualified to vote.

       I am, Sir,
        Yours etc.,
         ———-Town Clerk.

The town clerk should be guided by the same evidence as would be likely to determine the decision of a revising barrister in a similar case.

consistent and compatible with those of the Ballot Act, that no question of payment of rates or any other element of qualification can be considered after 26th day of September, the date upon which the list is to be made out, and that the list required to be made out by the 27th section of Local Government (Ireland) Act, 1871, must be interpreted to mean a list of all persons entitled *at the time the list is being made out* to vote at such elections;—(it is difficult to conceive how it could mean anything else, or to understand how the town clerk could make out a list of persons who were not at the time he was making out the list qualified to vote, but who might become qualified before the date of the election; nor how he could possibly tell what persons might become disqualified by death or other causes before the date of the election;)—and that consequently no person otherwise qualified to vote is entitled to have his name placed on the voters' list unless his township rates are paid on the 26th September.*

There seems no other alternative, unless it be held that the effect of the Ballot Act is to abolish the payment of rates as a necessary qualification of voting in townships.

If the view taken in regard to this matter, viz.: that the payment of township rates at the time the list is being made out is necessary in order to entitle a person to have his name placed thereon, is correct, every possible means should be adopted to make this fact known to the electors, and a notice as follows should be given on the 1st September:—†

---

* That is fifteen clear days, Sundays excluded, before the 15th day of October, the 26th of September being the last day. See *post* footnote, p. 31.

† By placard extensively posted throughout the town, and advertisements in the newspapers.

Township of——— \} NOTICE TO THE ELECTORS.
to wit.

I hereby give notice that no person will be entitled to have his name inserted as a rated occupier on the list of persons qualified to vote at the ensuing election of commissioners for this township (or borough) to be held on the 15th day of October, 18 , in respect of any lands, tenements, or hereditaments, unless he shall have paid, on or before 26th day of September (instant), all township or borough rates payable on same, except those assessed within three months before date of said election.

The township rate collector will attend in his office at the town hall from 9.30 till 1 o'clock on every week day for ten days preceding the said 26th day of September (instant) for the purpose of receiving payment of rates.

Dated the 1st day of September, 18 .

Town Hall   (Signed), ———,
                                Town Clerk.

In addition to this notice it would also be desirable that the rate collector should issue notices on 1st September to those rate-payers whose rates were not paid, informing them that they would not be entitled to vote unless their township rates were paid on or before the 26th of September.

Aliens.]

Aliens, who have not become naturalized or made denizens by letters patent, are not entitled to vote.

Under the 5th section of 7 & 8 Vic., cap. 66, aliens were only debarred from voting for the election of members of Parliament, and could, therefore, vote at township elections; but the Naturalization Act, 1870 (33 & 34 Vic., c 14), Sched. Part I. repealed this Act, and by its second section this Act greatly improved the position of aliens with regard to holding property, yet it, at the same time, enacted that nothing in this (2nd) section shall qualify an alien for any office or for any parliamentary, municipal, or other franchise.

CHAPTER VI.

QUALIFICATIONS OF TOWN COUNCILLORS AND COMMISSIONERS.

The Town Councils and Local Boards Act, 1880 (43 Vic., c. 17), entitled, "An Act to abolish the property qualification for members of Municipal Corporations and Local Governing Bodies,"* sec. 1 enacts that :—

"Every person shall be qualified to be elected and to be a member of a local authority who is at the time of election qualified to elect to 'any membership of that authority.'"† (Ap. lxxix.)

Local Authority.]

And section 2 (*b*) defines the term "Local Authority" to mean the Town Council of any Town Corporate, Commissioners appointed by virtue of 9 Geo. IV. c. 82, and any Municipal Town or Township under any general or local Act; and thus this Act is applicable to the whole of Ireland. (Ap. lxxix).

Other Qualifications not repealed.]

The qualifications mentioned in this section are to be alternatives, and are not to repeal or take away any other qualifications (sec. 3). Ap. lxxx.

Existing Disqualifications not removed.]

Section 4 enacts that :—

"Nothing in this section shall qualify any person for any office who is disqualified for the office by the existing law by reason of office, contract, bankruptcy, or any other matter of disqualification or disability." Ap. lxxx.

---

* It will be seen that the title and the 3rd section of this Act are directly at variance. The title states that it is "an Act to abolish property qualification," and the section provides that other qualifications (*i.e.* property qualifications), are not to be taken away. The operation of this Act produces some curious effects, *e.g.*, in the Township of Bray, County Dublin, a person may (in respect of property) be qualified to be elected a Commissioner, but (from not being a resident) not entitled to vote.

† Some local Acts, which are in force in towns and boroughs which are divided into wards, contain a provision which requires a person to possess a higher property qualification for election as a commissioner if he does not reside within the ward for which he seeks to be elected; but such provisions are abolished by the operation of this Act, and now if a person is qualified to vote in one ward, he is qualified to be elected to "any membership," that is, as a commissioner for any of the other wards.

Residence.]

And section 5 enacts that:—

"If a person qualified under this section ceases for six months to reside within the borough or 'district' in which he has been elected to an office, he shall cease to be qualified under this section, and his office shall become vacant, unless he was at the time of his election, and continues to be, qualified in some other manner."—Ap. lxxx.

Hence any person who does not reside, for at least six months in each year, within the "borough" must (in order to be qualified to be elected a member of the "Local Authority" of that borough) possess the property or occupation qualification which is required in the case of non-residents by the local or general Act in force in regard to that "borough"; but if persons reside for at least six months within a "borough" their qualifications for election in that borough are identical with their qualifications to vote.— (For *Qualifications of Voters* see preceding chapters).

Qualifications of non-residents.]

We now proceed to consider the qualifications of non-residents (*i.e.* of persons who cease to reside for six months in the year within the borough) for election.

The qualification of persons *non-resident*, in boroughs under 3 & 4 Vic., c. 108, Schedule A, is (where not modified by more recent local or personal Acts) "to be on the *Burgess Roll, and to be seized or possessed of real or personal estate, or of both, of the clear value of £1,000 above what will satisfy his debts for twelve months preceding the day of election, or to be in occupation† of a house within the borough rated for relief of the poor of the net annual value of £25 or upwards." (3 & 4 Vic., c. 108, s. 58).

In towns under the Towns Improvement (Ireland) Act, 1854 :—to have been for twelve months preceding the first

---

* Being on the Burgess Roll does not necessarily imply residence within the borough (see 3 & 4 Vic., c. 108, s. 30).

† Occupation here does not mean "residence."

Clauses Act, 1847, and therefore the provisions in these sections above quoted are in force in such townships.

Felons.]

Persons convicted of treason or felony are disqualified.—(33 & 34 Vic., c. 23, s. 2).

Bankrupts.*]

The Bankruptcy Act, 1883 (46 & 47 Vic., c. 52), s. 32 enacts—(1) " Where a debtor is adjudged bankrupt he shall, subject to the provisions of this Act, be disqualified for:—

"(a.) Being elected to, or holding or exercising the office of mayor, alderman, or councillor.

"(b.) Being elected to, or holding or exercising the office of . . . . member of a sanitary authority . . . . .

" 2. The disqualifications to which a bankrupt is subject to under this section shall be removed and cease if and when—

"(a.) The adjudication of bankruptcy against him is annulled; or

" (b.) He obtains from the court his discharge, with a certificate to the effect that his bankruptcy was caused by misfortune without any misconduct on his part.

"The court may grant or withhold such certificate as it thinks fit, but any refusal of such certificate shall be subject to appeal.

" 3. The disqualifications imposed by this section shall extend to all parts of the United Kingdom."

Notice must be given of the disqualification of a Candidate.]

If a candidate is disqualified, at the time of election, and due notice of his disqualification is given to the electors, all votes polled for him after such notice will be held on petition to have been as if not given or thrown away; and if,

---

* Compounding with creditors does not disqualify Commissioners under the Towns Improvement (Ireland) Act, 1854, or under the Commissioners Clauses Act, 1847.—*Reg. (Cochrane)* v. *Cunningham*, 1887, L. R. 20 Q. B., 490.

when these votes (given after notice of the disqualification), have been deducted from the votes obtained by that candidate, the candidate on whose behalf the seat is claimed, has a majority of valid votes, he will be declared elected, without a new election being held. Cunningham (p. 402), says :—

"This would be a very different result from that of a respondent being unseated on the ground that he was disqualified (where no sufficient notice was given), as in this latter case, though the respondent would be unseated, yet the petitioner would not in consequence thereof be entitled to the seat merely as being the next qualified candidate on the poll ; he must show that he has an actual majority of legal and valid votes in order to obtain the seat."

If an agent has conclusive proof that an opposing candidate is disqualified, he should at once notify the fact to the voters.

Form of notice.]

The notice may be in the following form : --

NOTICE OF DISQUALIFICATION OF A CANDIDATE.

To the electors of the borough (or township, &c.) of

Municipal election to be held on   18 .

Whereas, *A.B.*   of   a candidate for the election now about to be held for the (ward or borough or township) of   has been convicted of a corrupt practice, viz. : (*or state the facts or whatever the ground of disqualification is*), and is in consequence disqualified and incapacitated under (*state statute or statutes,*) from being elected a commissioner.

I hereby give you and each of you notice that all votes given for the said *A.B.* will be thrown away and wholly null and void.

Dated this

Signed,
Agent for

See form of notice adopted by the agent of Drinkwater— *Drinkwater* v. *Deakin*, 1874, L. R., 9 C. P. 626.

Unless the disqualification is notorious " the votes will

"No person shall, however, be disqualified by reason of his being a proprietor or shareholder of or in any company which shall contract with the council or commissioners of such borough for lighting or supplying with water any part of the said borough, or insuring against fire any property therein" (*id.* s. 59).

5 & 6 Vic., c. 104, s. 1, enacts that the word "contract" shall not be construed to extend to any lease, sale, or purchase of any lands, tenements, or hereditaments, or to any agreement for any such lease, sale, or purchase, or for the loan of money, or to any security for the payment of money only.

Sec. 2 (*id.*) provides that members of council are not to take part in discussions if pecuniarily interested.

Sec. 7 (*id.*) that councillors, &c., are not to be disqualified on account of having any interest in any lease of lands, &c.

In towns under Towns Improvement (Ireland) Act, 1854 (17 & 18 Vic., c. 103).]

The Commissioners Clauses Act, 1847 (10 Vic., c. 16), sec. 7* enacts that:

"The same property is not to qualify one person as an '*owner*' and another as an '*occupier*.'"

Sec. 8 (*id.*) that:

"No bankrupt or insolvent, or person not qualified as required by the special Act shall be capable of being or continuing a commissioner."—(See *post*, p. 78).

Sec. 9 (*id.*) that:

"Any person who at any time after his appointment or election as a commissioner shall accept or continue to hold any office or place of profit, under the special Act, or be concerned or participate in any manner in any contract, or in the profit thereof, or of any work to be done under the authority of such Act, shall thenceforth cease to be a commissioner, and his office shall thereupon become vacant."

Sec. 10 (*id.*), however, enacts:

"Provided always, that no person being a shareholder or member of any joint stock company established by Act of Parliament, shall be prevented from acting as a commissioner by reason of

---

* Sections 7, 8, and 9 of the Commissioners Clauses Act, 1847, are incorporated by the Towns Improvement (Ireland) Act, 1854, sec. 24.

any contract entered into between such company and the commissioners; but no such commissioner being a member of such company, shall vote on any question relating to the execution of this or the special Act in which such company is interested."

Ecclesiastics of any religious denomination are disqualified.—(17 & 18 Vic., c. 103, s. 25), Ap. xxiii.-iv.

Every Commissioner who, for the space of six months after his appointment, neglects to make and subscribe the statutory declaration, or who for six months in succession is absent from all meetings of the commissioners, shall cease to be a commissioner.—(10 Vic., c. 16, s. 16), Ap. v.

Women, minors, aliens (who have not become naturalized), felons, and persons proved guilty of corrupt practices, are disqualified for election in all municipalities in Ireland.

Any person convicted of being personally guilty of any corrupt practice at an election shall be disqualified for holding or exercising any municipal office or franchise for seven years (35 & 36 Vic., c. 60, s. 4); or if found guilty of any corrupt practice by an agent he shall be disqualified for being elected to, and for holding any municipal office in the borough for which the election was held, and if he was elected his election shall be void (*id.* s. 5.—see also 55 & 53 Vic., c. 69, s. 2).

A Candidate, if Returning Officer, is disqualified.]

Any person acting as a returning officer at an election for which he is a candidate is disqualified. (See *post*, p. 89).

Interest in a Newspaper not a disqualification.]

Town councillors are not disqualified by having an interest in a newspaper in which the advertisements of the council are published.—(15 & 16 Vic., c. 5., ss. 2 & 5).

In many of the townships having special local Acts, the local Acts incorporate, amongst other sections, the 24th section of the Towns Improvement (Ireland) Act (1854), which incorporates secs. 7, 8, 9, & 10 of the Commissioners

day of January in the year in which the election is held, the immediate lessor of lands, tenements, and hereditaments within the town of the value of £50 or upwards, according to the last Poor Law valuation, and to reside within five miles of the boundary of such town; or to be a householder or occupier (of full age) of a dwelling-house in the town of £12 and upwards, according to the last Poor Law valuation, and to be rated for the relief of the poor. (17 & 18 Vic., c. 103, s. 25)—Ap. xxiii.

In towns or boroughs under 9 Geo. IV., c. 82, a person to be qualified either as a voter or as a commissioner must be an "inhabitant occupier;" so that a non-resident would not be qualified, no matter what property he possessed. Hence in these towns or boroughs the qualifications for a commissioner are identical with those of a voter.

In townships under local Acts the qualification varies considerably; in some townships persons must be immediate lessors of property, within the township, of the rateable value of £200, in others of £100, and in others of £50.

CHAPTER VII.

Persons Disqualified from being Elected or Acting as Town Councillors or Commissioners.

Under 9 Geo. IV., c. 82, & 6 & 7 Vic., c. 93.]

A commissioner neglecting to attend some one of the three meetings of commissioners which shall be held immediately subsequent to his election, and thereat to take the required oath or make the required affirmation, shall cease to be a commissioner, unless he can show to the satisfaction of the other commissioners that his absence was caused by illness or other sufficient cause. Or he will be disqualified if absent—after having received notice—from the meetings of commissioners for more than six months in succession (9 Geo. IV., c. 82, s. 20).

Any commissioner interested directly or indirectly in any contract with the board or council of which he is a member, becomes disqualified and subject to a penalty of £100 (*id.*, s. 69).

But if such contract devolved upon him by demise, succession, or inheritance, he is forthwith to discover the same; and in such case he will not be subject to any penalty, but he will cease to be qualified as a member of the board (*id.*, s. 70).

An uncertified bankrupt is disqualified (see *post*, p. 78). Clergy do not appear to be disqualified from being elected commissioners under 9 Geo. IV., c. 82.

Under 3 & 4 Vic. c. 108.]

In boroughs in which the Municipal Reform Act, 1840 (3 & 4 Vic., c. 108), is in force the following persons are disqualified from being elected:—

Any person (1) in Holy Orders, or the regular minister of any dissenting congregation.*

(2) † Holding any office or place of profit under the council.

(3). Being an uncertified bankrupt, or compounding with creditors.‡

(4). Or having an interest directly or indirectly by himself or his partner in any contract§ or employment with, by, or on behalf of the council of which he seeks to become a member. (3 & 4 Vic., c. 108, s. 58).

---

* Does not apply to the case of a person who preaches during a temporary vacancy.—*Reg.* v. *Oldham*, 1869, L. R. 4 Q. B., 290.

† The office of mayor is expressly excepted.

‡ See Debtors (Ireland) Act, 1872 (35 & 36 Vic., c. 57, s. 20).

§ It has been held that the word "contract" in the corresponding English Municipal Act of 5 & 6 Will. IV., c. 76 (Municipal Corporation Act, 1835), refers to continuing contracts, not to mere sales of goods over the counter, or even sales for ready money.—*Lewis* v. *Carr*, Ex. 1 D , 484. Quoted by Leigh, p. 234.

be lost unless notice is given."— *Yates* v. *Leach*, 1874,*
L. R., 9 C. P. 608.

Notice should be given by placards and advertisements in the newspapers; and each voter as he goes to the poll should be verbally informed—or handed a notice warning him—that his vote will be lost if he votes for the disqualified candidate.

It is to be observed, that the fact upon which the disqualification is grounded must be established at the time. It is not enough merely to know that a candidate is guilty of a corrupt practice—he must have been convicted of it.

It was held in the case of *Drinkwater* v. *Deakin*, 1874, that bribing by a candidate at an election, though it renders his election void, if he be found guilty of it on petition, does not incapacitate him at that election in the sense that the votes given for him by voters with knowledge of it, will be thrown away, and that no disqualification arises in the sense of the term until after the candidate has been found guilty of bribery on petition.—(L. R., 9 C. P. 626).

It was held in the *Tewkesbury* case 1868 (L.R., 3 Q.B. 629) that the mere knowledge on the part of the voters of the fact that a candidate was returning officer did not amount to a knowledge that he was disqualified in point of law as a candidate; and therefore their votes were not thrown away, so as to make the election fall on the next candidate.

An agent should be quite sure of the disqualification of a candidate before he publishes a notice of it, as he might render himself liable to an action for libel, &c. Parker (p. 135) says:—

"Allegations of bribery and corruption, or that one is 'incapacitated and disqualified from being elected as a member of Parliament,' are libellous, and the candidate, agent, and printer responsible for the notices might be cast in heavy damages."

A candidate in respect of whom a notice of disqualification is published, may give a counter-notice rebutting the alleged disqualification.

* In all references to cases the year in which the decision was given is added.

CHAPTER VIII.
AGENTS.

Three classes of agents.]

In parliamentary elections there are three classes of agents—(1) 'expense" agents, (2) "personation" agents, and (3) "counting" agents, and the appointment of "expense" agents is obligatory on the candidates; but in municipal elections the appointment of all classes of agents is optional. No "expense" agents need be appointed, as all the necessary expenses in connection with a municipal election are not borne by the candidates,* but are defrayed out of the borough rates.

Appointment of agents authorized.]

The Ballot Act, 1872 (35 & 36 Vict., c. 33), sec. 20, sub-sec. 6 enacts:—

"Nothing in this Act shall be deemed to authorize the appointment of any agents of a candidate in a municipal election; but if in the case of a municipal election any agent of a candidate is appointed, and a notice in writing of such appointment is given to the returning officer, the provisions of this Act, with respect to agents of candidates, shall, so far as respects such agent, apply in the case of that election."—Ap. xxxviii.

The wording of this section caused some doubt to arise as to whether there was any actual authority for the appointment of agents at municipal elections; however, no doubt should now exist. Sec 24, part iii., of this same (Ballot) Act, which deals with personation at municipal as well as parliamentary elections, enacts that:—

"The provisions of the Registration Acts, specified in the third schedule to this Act, shall in England and Ireland respectively apply to personation under this Act, &c."—Ap. xxxix.

The provisions (specified in the third schedule) referred to, as regards Ireland, are sections 92-96 (both inclusive) of 13 & 14 Vic., c. 69—an Act to amend the laws which

---

* There seems, however, no limitation by statute of the expenditure which a candidate may make in promotion of his candidature at a municipal election, provided that it is legitimate expenditure.

F

regulate the qualification and registration of Parliamentary voters in Ireland.

Now, the 92nd sect. of this Act—(thus incorporated by Ballot Act)—authorizes in clear and unmistakable language the appointment of personation agents:—

"It shall be lawful for any candidate at any election of a member or members to serve in Parliament . . . . previous to the time fixed for taking the poll at such election, to nominate and appoint an agent or agents in his behalf, to attend at each or any of the booths appointed for taking the poll at such election, for the purpose of detecting personation; and such candidate shall give notice in writing to the Returning Officer or his respective deputy, of the name and address of the person or persons so appointed by him to act as agents for such purpose, and thereupon it shall be lawful for every such agent to attend during the time of polling at the booth or booths for which he shall have been so appointed." Ap. xii.

Rule 31 (B. A.), enacts that the candidates may appoint agents to attend at the counting of the votes, and rule 52 provides that the name and address of every agent of a candidate appointed to attend the counting of the votes shall be transmitted to the returning officer, one clear day at the least, before the opening of the poll, and rule 64 makes (with certain modifications) the provisions of Schedule 1 applicable to municipal elections. Ap. xliv.-viii.-ix.

In this way the Ballot Act authorizes the appointment of agents at municipal elections, and their appointment has been recognised and upheld by various legal decisions; see, for example, the decision of Mr. Justice Denman in the case of *Clementson* v. *Mason*, 1875 (L. R. 10 C. P. 209).*

Notice of appointment must be given.]

Unless notice is given to the returning officer of the appointment of agents, he need not admit anyone on the ground of his being an agent, to the poll or the counting of the votes; but if the candidates appoint agents, and give a

---

* He said—"Though the present is the case of a municipal election, I think that the agents appointed by the candidate are personation agents, having precisely the same duties as those appointed in the case of a Parliamentary election."

written notice of such appointment to the returning officer, then all the provisions of the Ballot Act with regard to the agents of candidates at a parliamentary election come into force in regard to such agents.

What constitutes an Agent.]

It is difficult to give a definition of an agent*; a person may become an agent to a candidate not only by express appointment, but by the recognition or acceptance of his services. A candidate is bound by his agent as a master is by his servant.

"It is, in point of fact, making relation between a candidate and his agent the relation of master and servant, and not ot principal and agent."—*Westminster* (1869), 1 O. & H. 95. See also *Aylesbury* (1886), 4 O. & H. 63.

"The relation of master and servant imposes upon the master a liability for an unlawful act done by the servant in the course of his employment, notwithstanding a prohibition which may have been given to him by his master; notwithstanding that the instant before an accident occurred he had impressed upon his servant or coachman the necessity for driving with the utmost possible care, if the next moment that man disobeys the order received from his master and inflicts an injury upon another, the master is responsible for it, and why? Because the relation of master and servant exists between them and creates this liability. —*Wigan Judgments*, 205; 1 O. & H. 191;" quoted by *Leigh*, p. 52.

Baron Fitzgerald, in the *Dungannon* case (1880), said:—'I think it must be made out that the party, before he is chargeable as an agent, must be a party found to be entrusted in some way or other by the candidate whose agent he is intended to be, with some material part of the business which is ordinarily performed by the candidate in his own person' (3 O. & H. 101)."

Treacherous Agents.]

It is to be observed however that a candidate would not be responsible for any acts corruptly done by an agent with a view to betray him. *Stafford Borough*, 1869, (1 O. & H. 230).

Rules with regard to Agents.]

Agents are required to make the declaration of secrecy. (B. A., r. 54,) Ap. xlviii.

* For a full treatment of the question of agency the reader is referred to Cunningham, pp. 245-273.

The returning officer or his partner or clerk is precluded from acting as an agent for a candidate.—(B. A., s. 11.)

A person proved guilty of corrupt practices is not to be employed as an agent during a period of seven years from the date of conviction (35 & 36 Vic., c. 60, s. 3), Ap. lx.

Although there is no limit to the number of agents to be appointed by each candidate laid down by statute, the returning officer would be justified in refusing to admit an unreasonable number to the polling stations or to the place where the votes are counted.

A candidate may himself undertake the duties which any agent of his, if appointed, might have undertaken.*—(B. A., r. 51), Ap. xlviii.

Notice of appointment of Counting Agents.]

The name and address of every agent appointed to attend the counting of the votes is to be sent one clear day at least before opening of the poll to the returning officer.—(B. A., r. 52,) Ap. xlviii.

Persons on Register not to be employed as paid Agents.]

No one whose name is on the register is to be employed as a paid canvasser; if so employed he and the candidate who employs him will be liable to a penalty of £10 (35 & 36 Vic., c. 60, s. 7).

A paid agent or canvasser who votes is liable to a penalty of £10, and his vote will be struck off on scrutiny. The vote of a paid agent will be bad, even if given for a candidate for whom he is not acting (*id.*)

Retainer to Voter not bribery.]

Giving a voter a retainer to act as an agent at an election, in order to incapacitate him from voting for either party is not necessarily bribery.—(*Cashel*, 1869, 1 O. & H. 289.)

---

* A candidate is not required to take the declaration of secrecy, but if he acts as his own agent and infringes the secrecy required by the 4th section of the Ballot Act, he renders himself liable to punishment. See *Clemenston* v. *Mason*, L. R. 10, C. P. 209.

Refreshments to paid Agents.]
Refreshments given to paid agents will not, of course, avoid the election or render the candidate liable for any penalty.

—— to voluntary Agents.]
Giving refreshments—even on the day of election—to voluntary agents, who are *bonâ fide* engaged in work connected with it, is not illegal—Martin B. in the *Westminster* case, 1869, said :—" I cannot think that giving food to persons doing work on the day of election is a corrupt Act." (1 O. & H., 91.)

Ballot Box to be shewn empty.]
The ballot box is to be shewn empty, to the agents who may be present, before the commencement of the poll.—(B. A., r. 23), Ap. xliii.

Personation.]
For agents' duties in regard to "personation," see *post* p. 143.

Votes of illiterate voters, &c., to be taken in presence of agents, if present.—(B. A., r. 26,) Ap. xliii.

Bribery by wife of Agent.]
A candidate is liable for an act of bribery by the wife of his agent.* (*Cashel*, 1869, (1 O. & H., 288).

May be removed from Polling Station.]
An agent may be removed for misconduct from the balloting station by direction of the presiding officer.—(B. A., s. 9,) Ap. xxxv.

May affix Seals.]
Agents have the right of affixing their seals to the ballot boxes and packets made up by the presiding officer. —(B. A., r. 29,) Ap. xliv.

At the counting of the Votes.]
Agents are to get notice in writing of the time, and place at which, the votes will be counted.—(B. A., r. 32,) Ap. xlv.

Agents are to be allowed to be present at the counting of the votes.—(B. A., r. 33,) Ap. xlv.

---

* But he is not responsible for acts done by the son of his agent.—*Westminster* (1886), 1 O. & H. 96.

The returning officer is in the presence of such agents of the candidates as may be in attendance, to open the ballot box, and to count the number of ballot papers.—(B. A., r. r. 32, 34,) Ap. xliv.-v.

Unless the agents agree, the counting of votes cannot be proceeded with between 7 o'clock at night and 9 o'clock on the succeeding morning. During the precluded time agents may affix their seals to the ballot boxes, &c.—(B. A., r. 35,) Ap. xlv.

Agents are entitled to take a copy of the returning officer's report, as to the result of his verification of the ballot paper account to the town council.—(B. A., r. 37,) Ap. xlvi.

Conveyance of Voters]
The candidate or his agent is prohibited from paying for the conveyance of voters under a penalty of £5.—(35 & 36, Vic., c. 60, s. 8,) Ap. lxi.

At Nominations.]
The Municipal Elections Act, 1875 (38 & 39 Vic., c. 40), s. 3, authorises the attendance of an agent on behalf of each candidate at the nomination of candidates.—Ap. lxxii.

Absence of Agents.]
The non-attendance of agents will not invalidate any act or thing done (B. A., r. 55),—A. xlviii.

It has been observed that the agent's duty is to watch the interest of the candidate at the poll, not to afford him information.

If Agent dies.]
If a personation or counting agent dies, or becomes incapable of acting during the time of election, the candidate may appoint another agent in his place, but must forthwith give to the returning officer notice in writing of the name and address of the agent so appointed.—(B. A., r. 53), Ap xlviii.

CHAPTER IX.

Returning and Presiding Officers.

Definition of term "Returning Officer."]

The Ballot Act (1872), 35 & 36 Vic., c. 33, Part II., sec. 20, sub-sec. 1, enacts that :—

"The term 'returning officer' shall mean the mayor or other officer who, under the law relating to municipal elections, presides at such elections" (Ap. xxxviii.)

And by sec. 23. sub-sec. 1 (in the application of this part of the Act to Ireland). the term 'mayor' is made to include the 'chairman of commissioners,' 'chairman of municipal commissioners,' 'chairman of town commissioners,' and 'chairman of township commissioners.'*—App. xxxviii.

Provision made in event of Mayor being unable to act.]

In municipal boroughs in which the Municipal Reform Act, 1840 is in force, provision is made for the appointment of a returning officer in the event of the mayor being unable to act.

If the mayor be dead, absent, or otherwise incapable of acting† at an election, the council shall forthwith choose an alderman to execute the powers and duties of the mayor. (3 & 4 Vic., c. 108, s. 71).

---

* Towns having commissioners appointed by virtue of an Act made in the ninth year of the reign of George the Fourth, intituled " An Act to make provision for the Lighting, Cleansing, and Watching of Cities and Towns Corporate, and Market Towns in Ireland in certain cases," are styled " commissioners."

Towns having municipal commissioners under 3 & 4 Vic., c. 108--" the municipal commissioners."

Towns having town commissioners under the Towns Improvement (Ireland) Act, 1854 (17 & 18 Vic., c. 103), or under any Local Act, " the town commissioners."

Townships having commissioners under local Acts, "township commissioners." (34 & 35 Vic., c. 109, sched.)--Ap. xxxi.

† " Incapable of acting" does not refer merely to physical incapacity, but to legal disqualification.—*Fanagan* v. *Kernan*, 1831, 8 Ir. Law Rep. 44.

But in towns or boroughs not under the Municipal Reform Act, 1840, no provision is made in the event of the chairman being unable to act; however, no difficulty can arise in those municipalities in which provision is made for the appointment of a vice and deputy vice-chairman, as in the absence of the chairman the vice-chairman becomes *de facto* the chairman, and is invested with all his powers.

If, therefore, from absence, illness, death, or other causes, the chairman be unable to act, then the vice-chairman becomes the returning officer. And in the event of the vice-chairman being also unable to act, then the deputy vice-chairman becomes the returning officer.

If neither the chairman, vice-chairman, or deputy vice-chairman can act, then the municipal council or board of commissioners must elect a returning officer.

In the event of the chairman being unable to act in places where no provision exists for the appointment of a vice-chairman, the council must appoint a substitute. Indeed, as a matter of precaution, the council should, some time before the election, appoint one of its members to act in the event of the chairman becoming incapable of acting.

Cannot appoint a Deputy to act for him.]

The returning officer cannot appoint a deputy to act for him, because he cannot delegate his judicial functions to any one else—"*delegatus non potest delegare;*" but he can employ others to carry out his ministerial duties.

Want of Title.]

Any informality in the appointment of, or any want of title in the person acting as the returning officer, will not vitiate an election otherwise valid.—See 3 & 4 Vic. c. 108, s. 89; Commissioners Clauses Act, 1847 (10 Vic, c. 16,) s. 34.

If a Candidate, disqualified.]

If the mayor or chairman be a candidate for election, he is incapacitated from acting as returning officer; if he acts, his doing so will render void his own election, but will not otherwise affect the validity of the election.

At an election for an alderman for a ward in the city of Dublin the outgoing alderman, who was a candidate for re-election, presided and acted as returning officer. His election was held void on the ground that, being interested in the result of the election as a candidate, he was incapacitated from presiding.—*Fanagan* v. *Kernan* (1881), 8 Ir. L. R. 44.

In this case of *Fanagan* v. *Kernan* Judge Lawson remarked:—

"There is no more sacred maxim of our law than that no man shall be a judge in his own cause, and such force has that maxim that interest constitutes a legal incapacity to a person being a judge in every case. In a remarkable case in the House of Lords, *Dimes* v. *the Proprietors of the Grand Junction Canal* (3 H. L. C. A. 759) Lord Cottenham happened to be a trustee for a shareholder in a canal company, with respect to which he affirmed a certain decree pronounced by the Vice-Chancellor. It afterwards went to the House of Lords, and on the ground that the judge was a trustee of shares in the company his decree was set aside. That constitutional judge, Lord Campbell, makes observations which are well worthy of our consideration. He says (at p. 793): 'It is of the last importance that the maxim that no man is to be a judge in his own cause should be held sacred, And that is not to be confined to a cause in which he is a party, but applies to a cause in which he has an interest.'"

In the *Tralee* municipal election case 1890 (28 Ir. L. R. 10), a candidate, who was seeking re-election, presided and acted as returning officer, and gave his casting vote between two, who had an equal number of votes, for the last place. He was himself elected as third on the list of successful candidates, and declared himself duly elected.

Held,—(upon petition, by the candidate who had been voted against by the returning officer)—that the acting presiding officer was disqualified by his personal interest as a candidate,* and that his election was void,† but that the election of the remaining commissioners was valid, being unaffected by the want of title in the returning officer. The returning officer was made liable in this case for the costs. See also *Reg.* v. *Tewkesbury* 1868 (L. R. 3 Q. B. 629).

It should be borne in mind that under no circumstances can the returning officer return himself. It was even held in the *Wakefield* Parliamentary election case, 1842, that the return of a candidate who was returning officer, and then resigned, was invalid.

"The candidate who was returned was the returning officer, but had resigned, and another person was nominated in his stead. The committee, however, held that he continued to be the returning officer notwithstanding the resignation, and was, consequently, ineligible; and further, that the vote of a person to whom a notice of the disqualification had been given before his voting was thrown away.—*B. & A.*, 270."

To Prosecute Personators]

It is the duty of the returning officer to institute a prosecution against any person whom he believes has been guilty of personation.—(B. A., s. 24).

Liability of Returning Officer.]

Returning or presiding officers are liable for any breach of their ministerial duties (see *post*, p. 180), but (if not influenced by fraud or malice) are not liable for any mistake in regard to their judicial duties (see *post*, p. 104).

"If a Returning Officer be not influenced by fraud or malice, but act in the conscientious discharge of his duty, no action can be maintained against him."—*Drewe* v. *Collins* (2 Luder's Election Reports, 245)," quoted by Ward,‡ p. 9.

---

* The court ordered a new election to be held to fill his place.

† Ward's *Practice of Parliamentary Elections.*

‡ In a borough or township where there are more wards than one, the mayor or chairman may, of course, act as presiding officer in a ward for which he is not a candidate, if appointed by the returning officer.

Presiding Officers.*]

The section 22 of the Commissioners Clauses Act, 1847 (10 Vic. c. 16), (which is incorporated by section 24 of the Towns Improvement (Ireland) Act, 1854 16 & 17 Vic. c. 103) enacts:—

"Where the appointment of the returning officer to act at the election of commissioners is not provided for by the special Act, the chairman of the commissioners shall be the returning officer; and if the commissioners are to be elected for wards, the said chairman shall act as the presiding officer at the election for the ward for which he was elected a commissioner, and he shall appoint some other commissioner for each of the other wards to be presiding officer at the election for such ward; and in case of the death of any such presiding officer, or of his declining or becoming incapable to act, the commissioners shall appoint another of their body to be the presiding officer in the place of the person so dying or declining or becoming incapable to act, and the clerk to the commissioners shall, two clear days at least before each election, by advertisement, placard, or otherwise, give public notice of every such appointment." †—Ap. vi.

The duties (involving serious responsibilities) thrown on the returning officer by the Ballot Act 1872 are generally quite sufficient to fully occupy his time and attention, and render it extremely inadvisable that he should undertake, in addition to his own particular duties, those of a presiding officer.

Returning Officer may act as Presiding Officer for any Ward.]

The Ballot Act 1872, Schedule 1, Rule 47 enacts:—

"That he may, if he think fit, preside at any polling station"

Thus the obligation which was thrown upon him by the section quoted above of presiding at the ward for which he was elected a commissioner is removed.

---

* See Instructions to Presiding Officers, post, p. 151.

† It is to be observed that although Schedule VI. of Ballot Act repeals sections 23, 26, 27, and part of section 28 of the Commissioners Clauses Act of 1847, it does not repeal this section, which must, however, be interpreted so as to be consistent with the enactments in the Ballot Act.

"All other enactments inconsistent with the Act are hereby repealed."--(B.A., s. 32.)

Presiding Officers appointed by the Returning Officer.]

Rule 21* (B. A.), gives him authority to appoint a presiding officer to preside at *each* station, and would seem to leave these appointments entirely in his hands, so that in the event of the death of a presiding officer, or of his declining or becoming incapable to act, it would be the duty of the returning officer, not that of the commissioners, to make a fresh appointment.

Indeed, in many cases it would be quite impossible for the commissioners to make a fresh appointment, because a presiding officer appointed by the returning officer might die or decline or become incapable of acting, say, for instance, on the day before the election, and there would not be sufficient time to summon a meeting of the commissioners to elect one of their members to fill his place, nor in a case of this nature could the commissioners or the returning officer comply with the statute by giving the required two clear days notice, before the day of election, of such appointment.

Appointment of Presiding Officers must be made from amongst the Commissioners.

The returning officer would seem, however, under the 22nd section of the Commissioners Clauses Act, 1847, to be confined in making his selection of presiding officers to " other commissioners."

The statutes only contemplate the appointment of *one* presiding officer for each ward. "He shall appoint some other commissioner for each of the wards;" 10 Vic., c. 16, s. 22 ; B. A. r. 21 ; 3 & 4 Vict. c. 108, s. 64.

Several Presiding Officers for each Ward.]

As Presiding officers, being aldermen or commissioners, are not entitled to receive any remuneration for their services,† it would be unreasonable to require them to sit

---

* Ap. xlii. † The services of the returning officer are also gratuitous. See 4 Geo. IV., c. 55, s. 73.

continuously for twelve hours (from 8 a.m. to 8 p.m.), and there does not seem to be any reason why two or more presiding officers should not be appointed for each ward, who could relieve one another. In the case of parliamentary elections, as the payment of only one presiding officer is provided for, for each polling station, it is of course different. And although the presiding officers may do, by the clerks appointed to assist them, any act which they are required or authorised to do by the Ballot Act at their polling stations, except ordering the arrest, exclusion, or rejection from the polling station of any person (B. A., r. 50), yet they would not be justified in absenting themselves from the polling stations of which they have charge for any considerable time, and leaving the poll clerks to discharge their duties.

Declaration of Secrecy.]

The returning officer must make the declaration of secrecy —before the opening of the poll—before a justice of the peace ; the presiding officer before the returning officer or a justice of the peace (B.A., r. 54).

Penalties for neglect of Duty.]

Sec. 11 (B. A.) enacts that—

"Every returning officer, presiding officer, and clerk who is guilty of any misfeasance or any wilful act or omission in contravention of this Act shall, in addition to any other penalty or liability to which he may be subject, forfeit to any person aggrieved by such misfeasance, act, or omission a penal sum not exceeding one hundred pounds ;" (Ap. xxxv.)

and brings into force the 13* section of the Representation of the People (Ireland) Act, 1868 (31 & 32 Vict., c. 49), which is as follows :—

Shall not act as Agent for a Candidate.]

"No returning officer for any county, city, town, or borough, nor his deputy, nor any partner or clerk or either of them,

* See B. A., sec. 17. Ap. xxxvii.

shall act as agent for any candidate in the management or conduct of his election as a member to serve in Parliament* for such county, city, town or borough; and if any returning officer, his deputy, the partner or clerk, or either of them, shall so act, he shall be guilty of a misdemeanor."

CHAPTER X.
NOMINATIONS.

Uniformity of Nominations from 1872 to 1879.]

From the passing of the Ballot Act in 1872 to the passing of the Municipal Elections (Ireland) Act, 1879 (42 & 43 Vic., c. 53), nominations for municipal elections in Ireland were, or at least, ought† to have been carried out in a uniform manner in accordance with sec. 23 (sub-sec. 2) of the Ballot Act, 1872, which enacted that the provisions of the Municipal Elections Act of 1859 (22 Vic., c. 35), in relation thereto, shall apply to nominations in every "municipal borough" in Ireland.

Municipal Borough defined.]

And in sec. 29 (B. A.) "municipal borough" is defined to mean any place for the time being subject to the "Municipal Corporation Acts" or any of them, and the expression "Municipal Corporation Acts" means, as regards Ireland,

---

* This of course applies to municipal elections, being a provision in relation to a returning officer, consequently one which is "concerned with" the poll.

† But considerable confusion existed, as it was thought by some that the form of nomination papers which the Ballot Act enacts (sched. II., s. 1.) shall be used in parliamentary elections—was to be adopted in municipal elections (and not the form in 22 Vic., c. 35, as directed by sec. 22, B. A.), owing to a note in the Schedule II. (B. A.) as follows:—

"The form of nomination paper in a municipal election shall as nearly as circumstances admit be the same as in the case of a parliamentary election."

It would seem, however, that the note was intended merely as a direction with regard to the mode of printing the paper, and had no reference to the nomination paper being subscribed by eight assenting burgesses (see *Owen*, p. 86); and the case of *Northcote* v. *Pulsford*. L. R. 10 C. P. 484, where it was held that the rules regarding nominations in the Ballot Act do not apply to municipal elections. Further confusion arose on the passing of the Municipal Elections Act, 1875 (38 & 39 Vict., c. 40), which, owing to the words "United Kingdom" being used in it, was thought to be an Imperial one, and consequently to be in force in regard to Ireland. It was only on the passing of the Municipal Elections (Ireland) Act, 1879, that all doubt was removed.

3 & 4 Vic., c. 108; 9 Geo. IV., c 82; Towns Improvement (Ireland) Act of 1854; and every local and personal Act providing for the election of commissioners in any towns or places for purposes similar to the purposes of the said Acts. (Ap., xl.) And thus the provisions of the Municipal Elections Act of 1859 in regard to nominations were made to apply to all municipal elections in Ireland.

Uniformity of Nominations destroyed by Municipal Elections (Ireland) Act, 1879.]

But the Municipal Elections (Ireland) Act passed in 1879 (42 & 43 Vic., c. 53) made the provisions of the Municipal Elections Act, 1875 (38 & 39 Vic., c. 40), with some slight modifications, apply to every municipal borough in which the Municipal Reform Act, 1840 (3 & 4 Vic., c. 108) was then in force. Thus the uniformity in the mode of carrying out nominations for municipal elections in Ireland was destroyed, and they are now to be carried out in one way for a certain number of "boroughs," and in another way for all others, viz. :—

    I. In those municipal "boroughs" in Ireland in which the Municipal Reform Act, 1840 (3 & 4 Vic., c. 108) is in force (and also in the township of Rathmines and Rathgar)* nominations are to be carried out under the provisions of the Municipal Elections Act, 1875 (38 & 39 Vic., c. 40).†

    II. In those municipal "boroughs," "towns," or "townships" in which the Municipal Reform Act, 1840, is not in force, nominations are to be carried out according to the provisions of the Municipal Elections Act of 1859 (22 Vic., c. 59) with the exception of the township of Rathmines and Rathgar).

---

* The Rathmines and Rathgar Improvement Act, 1885 (48 & 49 Vic., c. cli., local and personal), s. 18, incorporates some of the provisions of the Municipal Elections Act, 1875, which are thus brought into force in that township.

† As interpreted and modified by the Municipal Elections (Ireland) Act, 1879.

Nominations in Boroughs under 3 & 4 Vic., c. 108.]

Class 1.—In those municipal boroughs in which the Municipal Reform Act, 1840, is in force, the following course is to be adopted, viz. :—

* Nine days at least before the election the town clerk is to publish a notice† as follows or to the like effect, by causing the same to be placed on the door of the town hall, and in some other conspicuous parts of the borough or ward for which the election is to be held.—(38 & 39 Vic., c. 40, sched. 1, s. 1, sub-secs. 1, 2) Ap. lxxi.-ii.

Form of Notice of Election to be Published.]

NOTICE.

Borough of   election of (‡councillors, aldermen, auditors,§ or assessors, *as the case may be*) for the   ward (or several wards) of the borough.

TAKE NOTICE.

1. That an election of (*here insert the number of councillors, aldermen, or assessors, as the case may be*) for the   ward (or several wards) of the said Borough will be held on the   day of   .

2. Candidates must be nominated by writing, subscribed by two enrolled burgesses as proposer or seconder, and by eight other enrolled burgesses as assenting to the nomination.

3. Candidates must be duly qualified for the office to which they are nominated, and the nomination paper must state the surname

---

* Means nine clear days, exclusive of day upon which notice is published, and day of election, and of Sundays.—*Howes v. Turner* (1876), 45 L. J. N. S. C. P., 550.

† Municipal Elections (Corrupt and Illegal Practices) Act, 1884 (47 & 48 Vict., c. 70, s. 14) provides that any bill, placard, or poster having reference to a municipal election, shall bear upon the face of it the name and address of the printer and publisher thereof, under a penalty of £100. This Act, however, does not apply to Ireland.

‡ The term councillor shall extend to and include an alderman.— (42 & 43 Vic., c. 53, sec. 2, sub-s. 2).

§ The Local Government (Ireland) Act, 1871 (34 & 35 Vic., c. 109, s. 11), abolishes the election of *auditors* in all places in Ireland except in Cork, Kilkenny, and Waterford.

and other names of the person nominated, with his place of abode and description, and may be in the following form, or to the like effect :—

NOMINATION PAPER.

Borough of   election of councillors, auditors, aldermen, or assessors for   ward, in the said borough (*or* the said borough), to be held on the   day of   18 .

We, the undersigned, being respectively enrolled burgesses, hereby nominate the following person as a candidate at the said election :—

Surname.	Other Names.	Abode.	Description.

(Signed),   A.B., of*
              C.D., of*

We, the undersigned, being respectively enrolled burgesses, do hereby assent to the nomination of the above person as a candidate at the said election.

Dated this   day of   18 .
       (Signed),   E.F., of*
                     G.H., of*
                     I.J., of*
                     K.L., of*
                     M.N., of*
                     O.P., of*
                     Q.R., of*
                     S.T., of*

4. Each candidate must be nominated by a separate nomination paper, but the same burgesses or any of them may subscribe as many nomination papers as there are vacancies to be filled for the borough (*or* ward) but no more.

5. Every person who forges a nomination paper, or delivers any nomination paper knowing the same to be forged, will be guilty of misdemeanour, and be liable to imprisonment for any term not exceeding six months with or without hard labour.

---

* The number on the burgess roll of the burgess subscribing, with the situation of the property in respect of which he is enrolled on the burgess roll.

6. Nomination papers must be delivered by the candidate himself, or his proposer or seconder, to the town clerk at his office before five o'clock in the afternoon of   day, the   day of   next.

7. The mayor will attend at the town hall on   day, the   day of   , from two to four o'clock in the afternoon, to hear and decide objections to nomination papers.

8. *Forms of nomination papers may be obtained at the town clerk's office; and the town clerk will, at the request of any enrolled burgess, fill up a nomination paper.

    Dated this   day of   18   .
                     A. B.,   Town Clerk.†
                                (Ap. lxxvi.)

When a defective Notice will render the Election void.]

Where the notice of election published by the town clerk made it appear that the last day for handing in nomination papers was the 23rd of October, when it was really the 22nd October, and the nomination papers of two candidates were in consequence delivered too late, the court ordered a new election, holding that the notice published by the town clerk was so defective as to be calculated to mislead the candidates, and so prevent a fair election.—(*Howes v. Turner*, 1876, L. R., 1 C. P. D., 670).

Time of Delivery of Nomination Papers.]

Nomination papers must be delivered to the town clerk seven days at least before the day of election, and before five o'clock in the afternoon of the last day on which any such nomination paper may by law be delivered.

Notice to be given to Persons nominated.]

The town clerk, on receiving the nomination paper, is to forthwith send notice of such nomination to each person nominated.

---

* The candidate need not necessarily be nominated by one of the printed forms supplied by the town clerk; it is only essential that the nomination should be made in accordance with the prescribed form.

† See footnote, *post*, p. 111.

The same Electors cannot subscribe more Nomination Papers than there are vacancies.]

If an elector subscribe nomination papers for more persons than he is entitled to, those nomination papers first subscribed and delivered, to the extent of the number of vacancies to be filled, will be valid; and any subscribed and delivered subsequently, invalid, *e.g.* :—At a municipal election where there were four vacancies to be filled, a burgess subscribed four nomination papers, which were delivered in due time, and subsequently he subscribed a fifth nomination paper, which was also delivered in due time. In each case he subscribed as one of the eight assenting burgesses required by the Act. It was held that the first four nomination papers were valid and the fifth invalid.—(*Burgoyne* v. *Collins*, (1882), L. R., 8 Q. B. D., 450). It is a matter of some doubt whether in a case of this sort the nomination papers which are delivered first, or those which are subscribed first, are to be taken as the valid ones.*

Nomination Paper must be delivered by the Candidate himself or his Proposer or Seconder.]

The nomination paper must be delivered to the town clerk by the candidate himself, or his proposer or seconder personally (38 & 39 Vic., c. 40, sec. 1, sub-s. 3, Ap. lxxii.)

It was held in the case of *Monks* v. *Jackson*, 1876, that the enactment with regard to the delivery of a nomination paper by the candidate, or his proposer or seconder, is not merely directory, but mandatory, and that consequently the delivery of a nomination paper by an agent would not be a compliance with the requirements of the statute.—(L.R., 1 C. P. D., 683).

Who may object.]

Each candidate, and the person appointed by him, shall, during the time appointed for the attendance of the mayor

* See Parker, p. 112.

for the purposes of this section, have, respectively, power to object to the nomination paper of every person nominated at the same election.—(38 & 39 Vic., c. 40, s. 1, sub-s. 3).

Decision of Returning Officer in regard to Nomination Papers.]

The decision of the returning officer (which is to be given in writing), if disallowing any objection to a nomination paper, is final; but, if allowing, the same is subject to reversal on petition, questioning the validity of the election.—(Sec. 1, sub-s. 3).

It is clear, therefore, that if he improperly allows an objection, his decision can be reversed, and the election declared invalid.—(*Badge* v. *Andrews*, 1878, L. R., 3 C. P. D., 511).

His decision not always final, if he disallows an objection.]

But even when he disallows an objection, his decision is only final, provided that the objection is one upon which he is entitled to adjudicate:—for example, in the case of *Howes* v. *Turner*, 1876, the mayor disallowed an objection in regard to a nomination paper which was delivered after the proper time for delivering same had expired, and the court held that his decision was not final, and was capable of being reversed (L. R., 1 C. P. D., 671); and in the case of *Monks* v. *Jackson*, 1876, it was held that the decision of the returning officer, disallowing an objection in regard to a nomination paper not having been delivered by the proper person was not final.—(35 L. T., N. S., C. P., 95.)

When an assenting burgess has subscribed more nomination papers than there are vacancies to be filled, the returning officer has no right to decide as to which of these nomination papers are valid, and which are not.—(*Burgoyne* v. *Collins*, 1882, L.R., 8 Q.B.D., 450).

Not entitled to decide objections in regard to qualifications of Candidate.]

He is not entitled to decide any objections in regard to the qualifications of a candidate,* which can only be settled before an election tribunal.—(*Howes* v. *Turner*, 1876, L.R., 1 C.P.D., 670).—See *Mayo* case, 1874 (2 O. & H., 194); *Tipperary* case, 1875 (3 O. & H., 21).

"He is not to hold a court of enquiry, but to compare the burgess roll and the nomination paper."—(*Gothard* v. *Clarke*, 1880, L.R., 5 C.P.D., 253).—See also *Henry* v. *Armitage*, 1883, L.R., 12 Q.B., 257.

In regard to form of nomination paper, his decision disallowing an objection is final.]

It has been pointed out that his decisions should be almost entirely confined to objections with regard to the nomination paper itself, or to the form of it, and it is only in regard to the disallowance of such objections that his decision is final. — (*Howes* v. *Turner*, 1876, L.R., 1 C.P.D., 680).

He should decline to consider objections in regard to matters not within his jurisdiction.]

He should decline to entertain objections on matters not within his jurisdiction, and neither formally allow or disallow them.

Different effect of disallowing an objection and refusing to entertain it.]

The returning officer's refusal to adjudicate upon any objection would have practically the same effect, as far as regarded the nomination of the candidates, as if he disallowed it; there would, however, be this difference—that an unsuccessful candidate, on whose behalf the objection was made, would be in a position to file a petition against the election, without being hampered with the apparently final decision of the returning officer.

---

* He is not entitled to refuse to put in nomination a candidate who is notoriously disqualified. In the *Tipperary* case it was held that Mr. Mitchell was rightly put in nomination, although declared disqualified by the House of Commons. —3 O. & H., 21.

Signature of Nominators must precede that of Assentors.]

The nomination paper must be filled up before being signed.—(*Harmon* v. *Park*, 1881, L.R., 7 Q.B.D., 369).

Those nominating the candidate must sign the nomination paper before it is signed by the assentors.

In the case of *Harmon* v. *Park*, a nomination paper, which, after it had been delivered to the town clerk, was altered (in the absence and without the consent of the proposer, seconder, or assenting burgesses) by a duly enrolled burgess, who struck out the name of the proposer, thinking that he was not duly qualified, and substituted his own name, was held to be invalid.—(L.R., 7 Q.B.D., 369).

If nomination paper withdrawn to amend some unimportant particular.]

It would seem, however, that if a nomination paper, after being duly handed in, is taken away for a short time for the purpose of altering it in some unimportant particular (for instance, for the purpose of having the name of "Fredk" changed into " Frederick"), and subsequently returned, even after the time for the delivery of the nomination papers had expired; this will not necessarily invalidate the nomination.—(*Howes* v. *Turner*, 1876, L. R., 1 C. P. D., 670).

Town Clerk should not let any nomination papers when delivered to him out of his possession.]

It is obvious, however, that once a nomination paper is delivered to the town clerk, he ought not to let it out of his possession; and if a candidate discovers in time that the nomination paper that has been put in for him is faulty, he can remedy this by having a fresh one put in, as, if one nomination paper is bad, and the other good, the validity of the good one will not be affected by the fact of a bad one having been put in.—(See *Northcote* v. *Pulsford*, 1875, L. R., 10 C. P., 484).

If there are different nominations for the same person only one is to be published.]

If the same person is nominated by two different nomination papers, the returning officer should be careful not to mistake them for distinct nominations for different persons, and publish them as such.*

Duty of Returning Officer in regard to double nominations.]

In the case *Northcote* v. *Pulsford*, 1875 (L.R., 10 C. P., 484), the Court held that "it is obviously the duty of the returning officer to inquire whether nominations which might apply to one or to different persons, are of the same or of different persons."

Town Clerk to supply nomination papers to enrolled burgesses.]

The town clerk is to supply any enrolled burgess with as many nomination papers as may be required.

Endorsement on nomination paper by Town Clerk.]

The town clerk, on receiving a nomination paper, should endorse upon it the date and hour upon which, and the name of the person by whom, it is delivered to him.

Proceedings at Nominations.]

The mayor is to attend† at the town hall on the day next after the last day for the delivery of nominations to the town clerk between the hours of two and four in the

---

* See *post*, p. 182.

† Parker, referring to the proceedings at nominations for Parliamentary elections, says (p. 113):—
"A returning officer may give into custody any person disturbing the proceedings, and may order him to be taken before the magistrate to give securities for his good behaviour, for it is his duty to adopt means to prevent the business from being interrupted.—(*Spilsbury* v. *Micklethwaite*, I. Taunt., 146). He is bound to take sufficiently prompt and efficient measures for securing order and regularity.—(*Coventry*, P. & K. 345, C. & R. 289.)"

He would seem to have the same powers when sitting to adjudicate on nomination papers, at municipal elections.

afternoon,* and is to decide on the validity of every objection—which is to be in writing—made to a nomination paper. No one unless the candidate nominated by each nomination paper, and one other person duly appointed by or on behalf of the candidate is (except for the purpose of assisting the mayor), entitled to attend such proceedings.—38 & 39 Vic., c. 40, s. 1, sub-s. 3). Ap. lxii.

Attendance of Agents at.]

The appointment by or on behalf of candidates of persons to attend the proceedings is to be made in writing under the hand of the candidate; or, in case he is absent from the United Kingdom, then under the hand of his proposer or seconder, and is to be delivered to the town clerk before five o'clock in the afternoon of the last day on which nomination papers may by law be delivered (38 & 39 Vic., c. 40, s. 1, sub-s. 3). Ap. lxxii.

Returning Officer not liable for a decision given bonâ fide.]

It has been held that where a returning officer had *bonâ fide* given a decision under 38 & 39 Vic., c. 40, s. 1, sub-s. 3, on the validity of an objection made to a nomination paper, a complaint of such decision as erroneous is not a complaint of the "conduct of such returning officer" within the meaning of 35 & 36 Vic., c. 60, s. 13,† sub-s. 6.—(*Harmon* v. *Park*, 1880, L. R., 6 Q.B.D. 323).

Conclusiveness of Burgess Roll.]

The Municipal Elections Act, 1875, enacts that:—

"A person shall not be entitled to sign or subscribe any nomination paper, or to vote, unless his name is on the burgess roll for the time being in force in the borough, or on the ward list for the time being in force for the ward for which such election shall be held; and every person whose name is on such burgess roll or ward list, as the case may be, shall be entitled to sign or subscribe any nomination paper, and to demand and receive a

---

* It is obvious—that as he must hear objections up to four o'clock—he can give his decisions some time after that hour, especially as they have to be written.

† The section of the Corrupt Practices (Municipal Elections) Act, 1872, here referred to, does not apply to Ireland.

ballot paper and to vote: provided that nothing in this section shall entitle any person to do any of the acts aforesaid who is prohibited from doing such acts, or any of them, by law, or relieve such person from any penalties to which he may be liable for doing any such act."—(38 & 39 Vic., c. 40, s. 5.)

Those subscribing must be on the Ward List of the Ward for which they nominate the Candidate.]

If the borough is divided into wards, the names of the proposer, seconder, and assentors must be on the ward list of the ward for which they nominate a candidate.

Nomination of a Candidate by disqualified persons.]

Aliens, minors, or persons convicted of bribery may, if their names are in the burgess roll or ward act, subscribe a nomination paper, but their doing so will disqualify the candidate on petition. There does not seem to be any penalty attached to those who, being disqualified, subscribe nomination papers.

All the names of the Candidates must be given.]

The nomination paper is to state the surname* and other names of the person nominated, with his place of abode and description.—(38 & 39 Vic., c. 40, s. 1, s.-s. 2).

In a nomination paper at an election for town councillors the name of a candidate, which was "Robert Vickers Mather," was inserted thus:—"Robert V. Mather"; and it was held not to be such a statement of the "surname and other names of the persons nominated" as to satisfy the requirements of section 1 of the Act (38 & 39 Vic., c. 40), and the form given in the second schedule.—(*Mather* v. *Brown*, 1876, L. R., 1 C. P. D., 683).

A recognised abbreviation of the Christian name of person nominated does not invalidate the nomination paper.]

It was held that a nomination paper at the election of

---

* In the case of compound surnames, the first part of such name should be printed first. In case the candidate is an Irish peer, or is commonly known by some title, he may be described by his title as if it was his surname, as in Parliamentary elections.—(See B.A., Sched. II). Ap. lii.

a town councillor, pursuant to this section, sufficiently states the Christian name "William" of the person nominated by "Wm."—(*Henry* v. *Armitage*, 1883, L. R., 12 Q. B., 257).

The court in this case considered that "Wm." was a way of writing "William," and therefore a statement of that name and no other name; that every abbreviation of a Christian name would not do, but that this was an abbreviation which would be understood by every one, and about which no doubt could arise.

A similar decision was given with case of *Reg.* v. *Bradley*, 1861, 30 L. J., Q. B., 180.

Signatures of the nominating and assenting burgesses sufficient.]

It might be well, perhaps, if nominating and assenting burgesses would subscribe their names to the nomination papers in exactly the same way as their names appear on the burgess roll; their not doing so, however, will not invalidate the nomination—their ordinary signatures, with the number on the burgess roll, being sufficient to identify them, and a returning officer would therefore be wrong in rejecting a nomination paper on the ground that the signatures of the nominators and assentors on the nomination paper and their names on the burgess roll did not exactly correspond. See *Bowden* v. *Besley*, 1888, 4 T.L.R., 590; *Gledhill* v. *Crowther*, 1889, 60 L.T., N.S., C.P., 866.

Description of property of those subscribing nomination paper need not be identical with that given on the Burgess Roll.]

And it is not necessary that the situation of the property which qualifies them should be described on the nomination paper in the same manner as that in which it is stated on the burgess roll; it is only necessary that it should be described sufficiently, so as to be readily recognised.—(*Soper* v. *Basingstoke*, 1877, L. R., 2 C. P., 444); *Henry* v. *Armitage*, 1883, L. R., 12 Q. B., 257).

Numbers of Burgesses on Burgess Roll must be accurately given.]

It has been held, however, that the number on the burgess roll of a burgess nominating a candidate at a municipal election must (in order to satisfy the requirements of 38 & 39 Vic., c. 40, sect. 1, sub-s. 2, and schedule 1, form 2), be correctly stated in a nomination paper; where a wrong number was inserted, the nomination paper was rejected by the returning officer, and his decision was upheld by the Court on a petition.—(*Gothard* v. *Clarke*, 1880, L. R., 5 C. P. D., 253).

The reason that so much importance is attached to the numbers of the burgesses being accurately given is, that these numbers afford a ready means to persons interested of ascertaining, by reference to the register, if those subscribing a nomination paper are qualified.

A separate nomination paper for each candidate.]

The nomination of each candidate must be by a separate nomination paper, and if more than one candidate is nominated by the same nomination paper all the nominations on such paper will be invalid.

Returning Officer bound to put in nomination candidate duly nominated.]

If a candidate is duly nominated the returning officer is bound to put him in nomination.—(See *Davies* v. *Lord Kensington*, 1874, L. R., 9 C. P., 729; *Mayo* case, 1874, 2 O. & H. 191; *ante*, footnote, p. 100).

Nomination of a person absent from the United Kingdom.]

M.E.A., 1875 (38 & 39 Vic., c. 40), s. 2, enacts that:

"The nomination of a person who is absent from the United Kingdom shall be void, unless his written consent, given within one month of the day of his nomination before two witnesses, be produced at the time of his nomination."—Ap. lxxiii.

For a candidate to be duly nominated, his presence, or even his assent (if he is residing within the United Kingdom), is not necessary. In a Parliamentary election, anyone proposing a candidate without his consent would be held liable for the election expenses of that candidate ; but in a Municipal election any voter or burgess can propose another, provided the latter is at the time resident within the United Kingdom, without his assent, and incurs no penalty by doing so.

Withdrawal of Candidates.]

However, M.E.A., 1875 (38 & 39 Vic., c. 40), s. 7, enacts that :

"Where more candidates are nominated at any municipal election than there are vacancies to be filled at such election, any of such candidates may withdraw* from his candidature by notice signed by him and delivered to the town clerk not later than two o'clock in the afternoon of the day next after the last day for the delivery of nomination papers to the town clerk ; provided that such notices shall take effect in the order in which they are delivered to the town clerk, and that no such notice shall have effect so as to reduce the number of candidates ultimately standing nominated below the number of the vacancies to be filled."—Ap. lxxiv.

Publication of names of persons nominated.]

M.E.A., 1875 (38 & 39 Vic., c. 40), s. 1, sub-sec. 3, enacts that :

"The town clerk shall, at least four days before the day of election, cause the surnames and other names of all persons duly nominated, with their respective places of abode and descriptions, and the names of the persons subscribing their respective nomination papers as proposers and seconders, to be printed and placed on the door of the town hall, and in some conspicuous parts of the borough or ward for which such election is to be held."—Ap. lxxiii.

---

* The Municipal Elections (Corrupt Practices) Act, 1884, 47 & 48 Vic., c. 70, s. 11, provides against anyone inducing a candidate to withdraw by promise or payment of money, etc., but this Act does not apply to Ireland.

Computation of Time.]

M.E.A., 1875 (38 & 39 Vic., c. 40), s. 11, enacts that :

"In reckoning time, for the purpose of the Act, Sunday, Christmas Day, Good Friday, and any day set apart for a public holiday, fast, or public thanksgiving, shall be excluded."—Ap. lxxv.

Bank Holidays are to be computed as ordinary days.

Municipal Elections Act, 1875, to be construed with Municipal Corporations Act, 1840.]

The Municipal Elections (Ireland) Act, 1879 (42 & 43 Vic., c. 53), s. 2, sub-sec. 1, enacts that:

"The Municipal Elections Act, 1875, shall be construed, as far as is consistent with the tenor thereof, with the Municipal Reform Act, 1840 (3 & 4 Vic., c. 108), and the Acts amending same, and the Acts for the time being in force relating to elections of councillors, aldermen, and assessors in boroughs."—Ap. lxxviii.

Penalties for offences in regard to nomination papers.]

M.E.A. 1875 (38 & 39 Vic., c. 40), s. 1, sub-s. 4, Ap. lxxiii., brings section 3 of the Ballot Act into force in relation to penalties for offences in regard to nomination papers, which enacts that :—

"Every person who forges,* or fraudulently defaces,† or fraudulently destroys any nomination paper, or delivers to the returning officer (or town clerk)‡ any nomination paper knowing the same to be forged, shall be guilty of a misdemeanour, and shall be liable, if he is a returning officer, or an officer or clerk in attendance at a polling station, to imprisonment for any term not exceeding two years, with or without hard labour, and if he is any other person, to imprisonment for any term not exceeding six months, with or without hard labour. Any attempt to commit any of these offences shall be punishable in the manner in which the offence itself is punishable. In any indictment or other prosecution for any of these offences in relation to the nomination papers, the property of such papers may be stated to be with the returning officer."—(B.A. s. 3), Ap. xxxiii.

---

* *i.e.*, fabricates.

† Erasing the names on the papers, or covering them with ink so as to obliterate, or otherwise making them illegible.—See *Owen*, p. 28.

‡ The word "returning officer" is to be taken to include town clerk in reference to delivery of nomination papers in this section.—M.E.A., 1875 (sec. 1, sub.-s. 4).

Class II.

Nominations in boroughs in which 3 & 4 Vic., c. 108, is not in force.]

The mode in which nominations in "boroughs" to which the Municipal Reform Act, 1840 (3 & 4 Vic., c. 108) is not in force* are to be carried out, is determined by the Ballot Act, 1872, part II., sec. 23, sub-s. 2, which enacts that:

> "The provisions of the Municipal Corporation Act, 1859, following; that is to say, section 5 and section 6, and section 7, except so much thereof as relates to the form of nomination papers, and section 8, except so much thereof as relates to assessors, shall extend and apply to every municipal borough in Ireland, and shall be substituted for any provisions in force in relation to the nomination at municipal elections. Provided always, that the term "councillor" in these sections shall, for the purposes of this section, include alderman, commissioner, municipal commissioner, town commissioner, township commissioner, or assessor of any municipal borough."—Ap. xxxix.

Town Clerk to publish notice.]

The Municipal Corporations† Act, 1859 (22 Vic., c. 35), s. 5, provides that:

> "Seven days at least before the day fixed for the election of any councillor or councillors, the town clerk shall prepare, sign, and publish a notice as follows, or to the like effect:—

Borough of
In the county of } To wit.

Election of councillors for the (ward of , in the) borough of , in the county of .

Take Notice.

1. That an election of (three) councillors will be held for the said ward (or borough) on , the day of , A.D. , in the said ward (or borough).

2. That any person entitled to vote may nominate for the said office himself (if duly qualified), or any other person or persons so qualified, not exceeding three in number.

---

* Towns under the Towns Improvement (Ireland), Act 1854; Townships under Local Acts (unless Rathmines); and the nine boroughs under 9 Geo. IV., c. 82, come under this second class.

† The Municipal Elections Act, 1859, is called the **Municipal Corporations Act, 859,** in the Ballot Act.

3. That every such nomination must be in writing, and must state the Christian names and surnames of the persons nominated, with their respective places of abode and descriptions.*

4. That any nomination paper must be signed by the party nominating, and may be in the following form, or to the like effect :—

Election of councillors for the (ward of   , in the) borough, of   , to be held on the   day of   A.D.   .

Nomination Paper.

Christian name and Surname of person nominated.	Place of abode of person nominated.	Description of person nominated.	Christian name and Surname of Nominator.	Address of Nominator.

Dated the   day of   18

(Signed),

5. That all nomination papers must be delivered to the town clerk on or before the   day of   next.

(Signed),†   A. B., Town Clerk.

(Ap. xxvi–vii–viii.)

Notice of nomination—how to be published.]

The town clerk is to cause such notice of nomination to be placed on the door of the town hall and in some other conspicuous parts of the borough or ward for which any such election is to be held.

* It does not seem necessary that the address of the person given in the nomination paper should be the same as that given on the register.

† A printed signature to the notice will be sufficient. See *Sligo* case, Power, Rodwell, and Davis Reports, 208.

Nomination papers to be lodged two whole days before the day of election.]

Sec. 6 (22 Vic., c. 35), provides that:

"The nomination papers shall be sent to the town clerk at least two whole days (Sunday excluded) before the day of election; and the town clerk shall at least one whole day (Sunday excluded) before the said day of election, cause the Christian names and surnames of the persons so nominated, with such statement of their respective places of abode and descriptions, and with the names of the party nominating them, respectively, to be printed and placed on the door of the town hall, and in some other conspicuous parts of the borough or ward for which such election is held."—Ap. xxvi.

Form of Notice.]

The Notice may be in the following form:—

Election of councillors for the (ward of———in the) borough of———.

I, the undersigned, being the town clerk for the said town or township of   , hereby give notice, that the Christian and surnames of the persons nominated for election as commissioners for the said township, and their respective places of abode, and description, and the names of the parties nominating them, as follows, viz.:—

——— (WARD).

Surnames.	Other Names.	Places of Abode of Persons Nominated.	Descriptions of Persons Nominated.	Names of Persons by whom Nominated.

The poll will take place on———, the—— day of———, 18 –, at———.

Signed,

Town Clerk.

Town Hall, ———,
———day of———18—.

Town Clerk to supply as many nomination papers as may be required.]

Sec. 7 (22 Vic., c. 35), enacts that:

"The town clerk shall provide as many nomination papers as may be required, and at the request of any person entitled to nominate, shall fill up a nomination paper in due form; provided, nevertheless, that such paper shall be signed by the person nominating."—Ap. xxvi.

Town Clerk to receive nomination papers up to 12 o'clock at night.]

The nomination papers are to be sent to the town clerk at least two whole days (Sunday excluded) before the day of election. No hour is specified up to which on the third day the town clerk is to receive nomination papers; but it has been decided* that he is bound to receive them up to 12 o'clock at night on the third day before the day of election (Sunday excluded). He need not remain in his office after the usual office hours for the purpose of receiving nomination papers, but if a nomination paper is sent or delivered to him, so that he receives it up to 12 o'clock at night on the third day before the election, he is bound to publish it.

Persons nominating candidates must be qualified voters in the wards for which they nominate candidates.]

It has been decided that the person who nominates a candidate must be duly qualified to vote in the ward for which he nominates the candidate—that is, his name must be on the burgess or voters' roll for that particular ward (The *Queen* v. *Parkinson*, 1867, L.R., 3 Q.B. 11), and if he nominates a candidate for a ward in which he (the nominator) is not qualified to vote, the nomination and election of that candidate will be void.

---

* It was held in the *Kingstown* case, 1885, that the day does not terminate till 12 o'clock at night.—(18 Ir., L. R., Q. B. 179).

Town Clerk not authorized to deal with invalid nomination papers.]

The town clerk does not seem to be invested with any authority by statute to deal with or reject invalid nomination papers*; but if a candidate not duly qualified is elected, and takes part in the proceedings of the body of which he has been elected a member, he runs a serious risk in those boroughs or towns to which the Commissioners Clauses Act of 1847 applies, incorporated by the sec. 24, Towns Improvement (Ireland) Act 1854, Ap. xix.

Penalty for acting as a Commissioner without being qualified.]

Sec. 15 of that Act enacts that:

"Every person who shall act as a commissioner, being incapacitated or not duly qualified to act, or before he has made or subscribed such declaration† as aforesaid, or after having become disqualified, shall for every such offence be liable to a penalty of fifty pounds (penalty may be recovered by any person) ; and such penalty may be recovered by any person, with full costs of suit, in any of the superior courts ; and in every such action the person sued shall prove that at the time of so acting he was qualified, and had made and subscribed the declaration aforesaid, or he shall pay the said penalty and costs without any other evidence being required from the plaintiff than that such person had acted as a commissioner in the execution of this or the special Act."‡—(10 Vic., c. 16, s. 15), Ap. iv., v.

Nomination of a Candidate without his consent.]

There seems to be no penalty attached to a person nominating a candidate without his consent; nor does a candidate so nominated appear to have any means of withdrawing. It is obvious that this power, of nominating a person without his consent, might be used unfairly. For example, supposing that "A" being a conservative and "B" a

---

* It is submitted, however, that the town clerk should not publish the nomination of a person whose name is not upon the register.

† Declaration required by s. 12 of same Act, Ap. lv.

‡ "Special Act" means the "Towns Improvement (Ireland) Act, 1854," in relation to those towns which have adopted the latter Act.—See 17 & 18 Vic., c. 103, s. 24, Ap. xxiii.

liberal candidate;—the conservatives were to nominate another liberal "C," it might have the effect of splitting the liberal votes between "B" and "C," and thus securing the return of "A."

Duties of Town Clerk.]

After receiving the nomination papers and publishing the names, &c., of those nominated, the town clerk does not seem to have any further duties to discharge in regard to an election, unless to receive and take charge of the ballot papers, &c., handed over to him by the returning officer at the termination of the election. The statutes do not seem to recognise or authorise his presence at elections; and, unless specially engaged by the returning officer to assist him, he seems to have no right to be present.*

Uncontested Elections.]

The procedure laid down in sec. 1 of the Ballot Act, 1872, with regard to an uncontested election (where no more candidates are nominated than there are vacancies to be filled up), does not apply to municipal elections.

Sec. 20 (7) of the Ballot Act enacts, that an uncontested municipal election is to be conducted in the way in which it would have been conducted if this Act had not been passed; but by s. 23, sub-s. 2, it enacts that sec. 8 (which deals with uncontested elections) of the Municipal Corporation† Act, 1859 (22 Vic., c. 35), (except so much thereof as applies to assessors), shall extend and apply to every municipal borough in Ireland.

This section (viz.:—sec. 8, 22 Vic., c. 35) is also incorporated in the Municipal Election Act, 1875, and thus,—by the effect of the Municipal Elections (Ireland) Act, 1879—applies to all boroughs under 3 & 4 Vic., c. 108. Hence the procedure in regard to uncontested elections is assimilated in

---

* It is customary, however, for him to act as assessor to the returning officer.
† The Municipal Elections Act, 1859, is called the Municipal Corporation Act, 1859, in the Ballot Act.

all municipal elections in Ireland, and is governed by this section, which requires the returning officer to publish the names of the persons elected not later than 11 o'clock on the day of election, and is as follows:—

"At any election of councillors to be held for any borough or ward:—

"1. If the number of persons so nominated shall exceed the number to be elected, the councillors to be elected shall be elected from the persons so nominated, and from them only.

"2. If the number of persons to be nominated shall be the same as the number to be elected, such persons shall be deemed to be elected; and the mayor or alderman and two assessors, as the case may be, shall publish a list of the names of the persons so elected not later than eleven of the clock in the morning of the said day of election.

"3. If the number of persons so nominated shall be less than the number to be elected, such persons shall be deemed to be elected. Such of the retiring councillors highest on the poll at their election, or, if the poll were equal or there were no poll, such as shall be nominated by the mayor shall be deemed to be re-elected to make up the number required to be elected; and the mayor or alderman and two assessors, as the case may be, shall publish a list of the names of all the persons so elected respectively, not later than eleven of the clock in the morning of the said day of election.

"4. If no persons be so nominated, the retiring councillors shall be deemed to be re-elected; and the mayor or alderman and two assessors, as the case may be, shall publish a list of the names of all the persons so elected, not later than eleven of the clock in the morning of the said day of election."—(Ap. xxvi.)

But there seems nothing to prevent the returning officer, in the event of there being no contest, from declaring the candidates elected as soon as the time for handing in nomination papers has expired.

CHAPTER XI.

PREPARATIONS FOR TAKING THE POLL.

Duties of returning officer in a contested election.]

In the event of a contest, the returning officer has important duties to perform in regard to taking the poll. He is to—provide (B.A., s. 8)—

1. Polling stations.
2. Ballot papers.
3. Stamping instruments.
4. Ballot boxes.
5. Copies of register of voters, &c.*
6. —Appoint presiding officers (B.A., r. 21) to preside at each station.
7. Appoint and pay poll clerks† (and counting assistants, if necessary).

And do such other acts and things as may be necessary for effectually conducting an election in the manner provided by the Ballot Act.—(B.A., s. 8). Ap. xxxiv.

Expenses of elections.] ‡

All expenses properly incurred by the returning officer, in relation or incident to municipal elections, are chargeable to the borough fund or rates.—Municipal Reform Act, 1840 (3 & 4 Vic., c. 108); Commissioners Clauses Act, 1847 (10 Vic., c. 16), s. 34.

---

* It is clear that he ought to provide a sufficient quantity of forms of declarations of "inability to read."
† The duties of poll clerks are of a responsible character, and they are paid from £1 1s. to £3 3s. each for the day, as the returning officer may think right. Presiding officers do not receive any remuneration.—See p. 92.
‡ See footnote *ante*, p. 81.

Polling Stations.]

The returning officer is to provide at every polling place a sufficient number of polling stations for the accommodation of the electors entitled to vote at such polling place.—(B.A., r. 15). Ap. xliii.

He may hire rooms for the purpose.*

In boroughs in which the Municipal Reform Act, 1840 (3 & 4 Vic., c. 108) is in force, the council of the borough has power to divide it (or the wards of it) into polling districts in such a manner as in the opinion of the council is most convenient for taking the votes of the burgesses at the poll; and the lists of burgesses (for these boroughs) are to be made out in such manner as to divide the names in conformity with such polling districts.—M.E.A., 1875 (38 & 39 Vic., c. 40), s. 10.

In towns or boroughs in which Municipal Reform Act, 1840 (3 & 4 Vic., c. 108), is not in force, the returning officer is authorized to distribute the polling stations in the way he thinks most convenient, etc.—(See B. A., r. 15).

The Municipal Reform Act, 1840 (3 & 4 Vic., c. 108), s. 65, enacts that no election under this Act shall be held in a church, chapel, or other place of public worship.†

In townships or boroughs not under the Municipal Reform Act, 1840 (3 & 4 Vic., c. 108), the returning officer is required to provide at least one polling compartment at each polling station (to enable electors to vote, properly screened from observation), for every 150 electors‡ entitled to vote at such polling station, and he is to give public notice of the situation of the polling station, and the

---

* A room hired in an occupied house will not render the owner of it liable for rates (B.A. s. 6).—App. xxxiv. The Returning Officer has no power, as in Parliamentary elections, to take a room compulsorily. It is a somewhat startling fact that in Ireland there is nothing to prevent the poll being taken in a public house. In England this is prohibited, unless with the consent of the candidates in writing.—16 Vic., c. 28, s. 4; and 16 & 17 Vic., c. 68, s. 6.

† A similar enactment by 2 & 3 Wm. IV., c. 45, s. 68.

‡ When voters were prevented from voting on account of an excessive number being allotted to a booth, the election was avoided.—*Belfast* case, 1842, *B. & A.*, 561.

description of voters entitled to vote at each station, and of the mode in which electors are to vote.—(B. A., rr. 16, 19).

The enactment, that at least one polling compartment shall be provided for every 150 voters at each polling station, does not apply to boroughs under the Municipal Reform Act, 1840; and the number of polling compartments in such boroughs to be furnished at each polling station is left to the discretion of the returning officer; and a notice* of the situation, division, and allotment of the polling places, and a description of the persons entitled to vote thereat, is to be published at least four days before the election.—M. E. A., 1875 (38 & 39 Vic., c. 40, s. 4).

This section (4) also provides that the returning officer shall furnish each presiding officer with the necessary number of ballot papers, which seems an unnecessary provision, having regard to the provisions of the Ballot Act, 1872 (sec. 8).

Irregularities in distribution of Polling Stations.]

It was held in the *Greenock* case, 1869, that irregularities in dividing the borough into polling districts, and assigning to voters their proper polling booths, will not render an election void, when it does not appear that these faulty arrangements were made otherwise than in good faith, or have affected the fairness of the election.—(1 O. & H., 249).

Several polling stations may be constructed in the same room or booth.—(B. A., r. 17). Ap. xlii.

---

* Notice may be given in this form:—

"Allotment of Polling Station to Voters.
" Polling Station No.———

" Notice is hereby given, that this polling station is allotted to voters numbered on the ward (or borough) list of   from Nos. 100 to 550, both inclusive.

Dated this——day of————18   .
"————Returning Officer."

Construction of Polling Compartments.]

A polling compartment,* or station, may be constructed in a simple way, as shewn in the following illustration:—

Sides (marked A and B), 6′ 6″ high × 3′ wide × 1¼″ thick; the back (marked C), 6′ 6″ high × 2′ 6″ wide × 1¼″ thick, with a shelf placed four feet from the ground (marked D), 2′ 6″ long × 1′ in depth × 1¼″ thick.

Pieces of wood of these dimensions can be procured and kept in stock, and a polling compartment may be easily erected, without any delay, at any time by screwing them together.

* Polling compartments and ballot boxes, &c., provided for Parliamentary, may be used for municipal elections, and *vice versá*, (B.A., s. 14). Ap. xxxvi.

Voter not to be out of view of Presiding Officer.]

It is pointed out by Cunningham (p. 90), that :—

" The compartment should be so placed relatively to the position of the ballot box that the voter, from the moment of his receiving a ballot paper to his depositing it in the ballot box, should not be for an instant out of the view of the presiding and other officers, so that he may not have an opportunity of exhibiting his vote."

Faulty arrangements at Polling Station.]

In the *Drogheda* case, 1874, some of the polling stations were on the first floors of private houses, which comprised two rooms, between which there was no internal communication, but in order to pass from one to the other, a person should cross a small landing upon which the doors of the two rooms stood at right angles to, and at a small distance from, each other.

" The presiding officer, with the authorized agents, sat in the front room, out of view of the back room or the landing. In the back room was placed a table, with a pencil on it, upon which the voter might mark his ballot paper. When the voter received his ballot paper in the front room, he was ordered by the presiding officer to proceed to the back room to mark his paper. The voter having done so, returned to the front room, and placed his paper in the ballot box there. On the landing between the two rooms was stationed a policeman, who was instructed to prevent more than one voter at a time entering either room, to prevent anyone from interfering with the voter, and to preserve order; but he received no instructions as to preventing voters while crossing the landing from showing their mark on the ballot paper, or as to how to act in case of such occurrence."

It was held that these faulty arrangements, which were made by the returning officer in perfect good faith under the idea that he was strictly carrying out the provisions of the Ballot Act, and which did not seem to have led to any infringement of the secrecy of the ballot, did not render the election void.—(2 O. & H., 206).

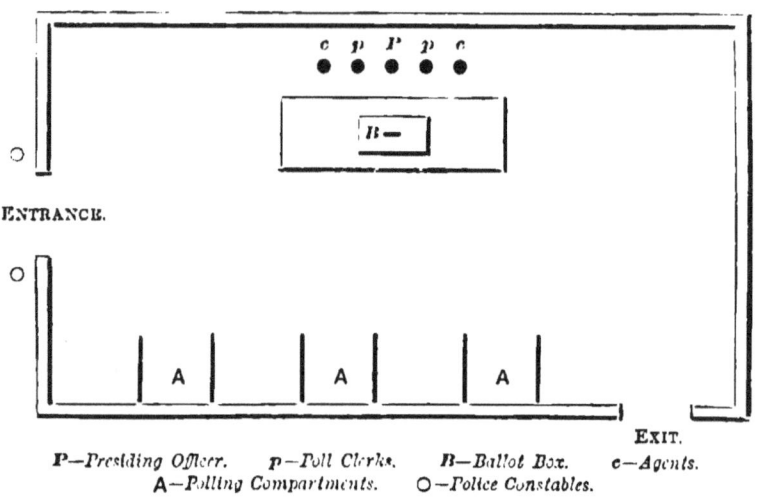

PLAN of POLLING STATION, to be followed as far as practicable.

P—*Presiding Officer.*   **p**—*Poll Clerks.*   **B**—*Ballot Box.*   **c**—*Agents.*
A—*Polling Compartments.*   O—*Police Constables.*

In boroughs or towns not under 3 & 4 Vic., c. 108, a polling compartment must be provided for every 150 voters. This station would, therefore, accommodate 450 voters.

But in boroughs under 3 & 4 Vic., c. 108, the number of polling compartments to be provided is left to the discretion of the returning officer.

The name of the ward should be placed in a conspicuous manner outside the polling place in order that the electors should have no difficulty in finding their way to the wards in which they are to vote.

Directions to voters.]

Forms of directions for the guidance of the voter, in voting, are to be printed in conspicuous characters, and placarded outside every polling station and in every compartment of every polling station, as follows:—

"The voter may vote for   candidate .

"The voter will go into one of the compartments, and, with the pencil provided in the compartment, place a cross on the right-hand side, opposite the name of each candidate for whom he votes thus X

"The voter will then fold up the ballot paper so as to show the official mark on the back, and leaving the compartment will, without showing the front of the paper to any person,* show the official mark on the back to the presiding officer, and then in the presence of the presiding officer put the paper into the ballot box, and forthwith quit the polling station.

"If the voter inadvertently spoils a ballot paper, he can return it to the officer, who will, if satisfied of such inadvertence, give him another paper.

"If the voter votes for more than   candidate , or places any mark on the paper by which he may be afterwards identified, his ballot paper will be void and will not be counted.

"If the voter takes a ballot paper out of the polling station, or deposits in the ballot box any other paper than the one given him by the officer, he will be guilty of a misdemeanour, and be subject to imprisonment for any term not exceeding six months, with or without hard labour."—(B. A. sched. ii.) Ap. liii.

Attendance of Constables.]

The returning officer is empowered to provide a sufficient attendance of police constables at the polling places by 13 & 14 Vic., c. 69, s. 97, which is incorporated with the Ballot Act (B. A., sec. 24, and Sched. iii.)

Declaration of Secrecy.]

Rule 54 (B.A.) provides that:—

"Every returning officer, and every officer, clerk, or agent authorised to attend at a polling station, or at the counting of the votes, shall, before the opening of the poll, make a statutory declaration of secrecy, in the presence, if he is the returning officer, of a justice of the peace, and if he is any other officer or an agent, of a justice of the peace, or of the returning officer; but no such returning officer, officer, clerk or agent as aforesaid shall, save as aforesaid,

---

* It has been pointed out that the voter incurs no penalty by showing his ballot paper after he has voted.

be required, as such, to make any declaration or take any oath on the occasion of any election."

The statutory declaration of secrecy must be made before the opening of the poll; and in order to avoid confusion on the morning of the day of election, it is desirable that the agents and those entitled to attend, should make the statutory form of declaration of secrecy on the previous day, and with this in view, it is advisable to publish a notice as follows :—

NOTICE.

Statutory Declaration of Secrecy.

Borough (or township or town) of   .
Presiding officers, clerks, and agents (and constables)* authorised to attend at any polling stations, or at the counting of the votes, at the forthcoming elections to be held on   day of   18   are requested to attend here on   (next), the   instant, between the hours of   o'clock and   o'clock, for the purpose of making the required statutory declarations of secrecy.

(Signed)
              Returning Officer.
Town Hall,   , 18   .

FORM OF STATUTORY DECLARATION OF SECRECY.

I solemnly promise and declare that I will not, at this election for   , do anything forbidden by sec. 4† of the Ballot Act, 1872, which has been read to me.

4. "Every officer, clerk, and agent in attendance at a polling station shall maintain and aid in maintaining the secrecy of the voting in such station, and shall not communicate, except for some purpose authorised by law, before the poll is closed, to any person any information as to the name or number on the register of voters of any elector who has or has not applied for a ballot paper or voted at that station,‡ or as to the official mark, and no such

---

* Strictly speaking, the police constables on duty at the polling booths should make the declaration of secrecy, because, although stationed outside, their services may be called into requisition within the booths.

† The section must be read to the declarant by the person taking the declaration.

‡ See *post*, pp. 144–5.

officer, clerk, or agent, and no person whosoever, shall interfere with or attempt to interfere with, a voter when marking his vote, or otherwise attempt to obtain in the polling station information as to the candidates for whom any voter in such station is about to vote or has voted, or communicate at any time to any person any information obtained in a polling station as to the candidate for whom any voter in such station is about to vote or has voted, or as to the number on the back of the ballot paper given to any voter at such station. Every officer, clerk, and agent in attendance at the counting of the votes shall maintain and aid in maintaining the secrecy of the voting, and shall not attempt to ascertain at such counting the number on the back of any ballot paper, or communicate any information obtained at such counting as to the candidate for whom any vote is given in any particular ballot paper. No person shall directly or indirectly induce any voter to display his ballot paper after he shall have marked the same, so as to make known to any person the name of the candidate for or against whom he has so marked his vote.

"Every person who acts in contravention of the provisions of this section shall be liable, on summary conviction before two justices of the peace, to imprisonment for any term not exceeding six months, with or without hard labour."—Ap. xxxiii.

Declaration of Secrecy by Returning Officer.]

It is to be observed that the returning officer must make the declaration of secrecy before a justice of the peace, but all the others can make it before him, whether he is a justice of the peace or not.

Tickets of Admission to Polling Station.]

The returning officer should issue an admission order to everyone authorised to attend, who has made the declaration of secrecy, in order that the police constables may know whom to admit.

Election not avoided by Officials omitting to take Declaration of Secrecy.]

In the *Drogheda* case, 1874, neither the returning officer or the sub-sheriff took declarations of secrecy; but there was no reason whatever to believe that this circumstance led to the infringement of the secrecy of the ballot, and it was held not to invalidate the election.—(2 O. & H., 206).

Candidate entitled to be present.]

A candidate may undertake the duties of, or assist his agent, and is entitled to be present at the polling stations and at the counting of the votes, or at any place at which his agent may, in pursuance of the Ballot Act, attend (B. A., r. 51); but he has a right to be present, even if he do not either himself undertake the duties of an agent or assist his agent in the performance of such duties; and, unless he interferes with the polling or misconducts himself in some other way, the presiding officer has no authority to exclude him.—(B. A., s. 9; *Clementson* v. *Mason* 1875 (L. J. N. S., C. P. 171).

—— Need not take Declaration of Secrecy.]

A candidate is not required to make the declaration of secrecy.

BALLOT PAPERS.

Sec. 2 (B.A.) provides that—The votes are to be given by ballot. The ballot of each voter shall consist of a paper (in the Act called a ballot paper) showing the names and description of the candidates. Each ballot paper is to have a number printed on the back, and to have attached a counterfoil with the same number printed on the face.— Ap. xxxii.

Rule 22 (B.A.),* enacts that:—

Every ballot paper is to contain a list of the candidates described, as in their respective nomination papers, and arranged alphabetically in the order of their surnames, and (if there are two or more candidates with the same surname) of their other names; it is to be capable of being folded

* Ap. xlii.

up, and is to be in the following form or as near thereto as circumstances will admit.—(B.A. Sched. II.) thus :—

FORM OF BALLOT PAPER.

Form of front of ballot paper.

COUNTERFOIL. No. NOTE.— *The counterfoil is to have a number to correspond with that on the back of the Ballot Paper.*			
	1	**BROWN** (John Brown, of 52, George St., Bristol, merchant).	
	2	**JONES** (William David Jones, of High Elms, Wilts, Esq.)	
	3	**MERTON** (Hon. George Travis, commonly called Viscount Merton, of Swanworth, Berks).	
	4	**SMITH** (Henry Sydney Smith, of 72, High Street, Bath, attorney).	

Form of back of ballot paper.

No.
    Election for   township [*or* borough *or* ward].
                  18 .

Note.—The number on the ballot paper is to correspond with that in the counterfoil.

Directions as to printing ballot paper.

" Nothing is to be printed on the ballot paper except in accordance with this schedule."

" The surname of each candidate, and if there are two or more candidates of the same surname, also the other names of such candidates, shall be printed in large characters, as shown in the form, and the names, addresses, and descriptions, and the number on the back of the paper, shall be printed in small characters."—Ap. liii.

The ballot papers are to be numbered consecutively and bound up in the form of cheque books; and a sufficient number provided for the electors in each ward *(allowance being made for ballot papers being spoilt).

The returning officer is to provide each polling station with materials for voters to mark the ballot papers, with instruments for stamping thereon the official mark, and with copies of the register of voters, or such part thereof as contains the names of the voters allotted to vote at such station. (B.A., r. 20), Ap. xlii.

Things with which Polling Stations are to be furnished.]

A presiding officer should see that his polling station is furnished with :—

    A ballot box (with key attached).

    Official stamp and seal.

    A certified copy of that portion of the register containing names of the electors who are entitled to vote at his polling station.

    "Directions for Guidance of Voters," one for each compartment, and several to be posted in and about the polling station.

    Ordinary ballot papers (white), which are to be counted and the number of same entered on the "Ballot Paper Account."

    A supply of coloured "ballot papers for tendered votes," which are also to be counted and the number of same entered on the ballot paper account.

---

* An election would be declared void if a returning officer failed to provide a sufficient supply of ballot papers, see *Hackney* case, 1874, 2 O. & H., 88.

A sufficient supply of forms of "declarations of inability to read."
———————————————— " declarations of secrecy."
Lists on which to record the "Votes marked by the presiding officer" and "the tendered votes."
A copy of the "statutory questions to be put to voters," and "form of oath to be administered."
Pens, ink, paper, sealing wax, pencils, blotting paper, brown paper, red tape, a swearing book, and seven large envelopes endorsed, respectively, with—

1. "Ordinary and tendered, unused, and spoilt ballot papers." 2. "Tendered ballot papers." 3. "Marked copies of the register of voters." 4. "Counterfoils of (ordinary and tendered) ballot papers." 5. "Tendered votes list." 6. "List of votes marked by the presiding officer." 7. "Declarations of inability to read."

Each envelope to be also endorsed with the name of the polling station, and the borough or ward, the date of election, and the name of the presiding officer.*

Ballot box.]

Every ballot box is to be so constructed that the ballot papers can be introduced therein, but cannot be withdrawn therefrom without the box being unlocked (B.A., r. 23), and to be capable of being sealed up so as to prevent the introduction of additional ballot papers after the close of the poll. (B. A., s. 2.) Ap. xxxii.

Official mark.]

The Returning Officer is to keep the official mark secret; it is not to be used for an election at the same place until after an interval of seven years has elapsed. (B. A., r. 20), Ap. xlii.

---

* The presiding officer who is in charge at the termination of the poll should endorse the packets with his name.

The machinery of the Ballot Act is so perfect that it would be almost impossible for fabricated ballot papers to be put into the ballot box without the fraud being discovered —for example, suppose that an elector went (early in the day) to a polling station and having obtained a ballot paper took it into one of the compartments for polling, and there made a copy of it, and the official mark on it (say on tracing paper), and from this copy got a quantity of forged ballot papers prepared, and distributed amongst a number of voters, arranging with them, to surreptitiously introduce the spurious papers into the ballot box by enclosing them in genuine papers, the fraud would inevitably be discovered when the returning officer came to verify the ballot paper account furnished by the presiding officer.

Day of Poll.]

The provision in Rule 14 (B. A.) regarding the day on which the poll is to take place,* does not apply to municipal elections, for which the day is fixed by the local or general Act which is in force for the particular borough.

The Municipal Reform Act, 1840 (3 & 4 Vic., c. 108), s. 52, enacts that corporations are not to become extinct by reason of elections not being held on the appointed days, and provides that if an election does not take place on the appointed day, it may be held on the following day, provided that it is not Sunday.

Hours of Polling.]

Under the Towns Improvement (Ireland) Act, 1854, (17 & 18 Vic., c. 103) the poll was to be opened at 9 o'clock, A.M., and closed at 4 o'clock, P.M.; and under the Commissioners' Clauses Act, 1847 (10 Vic., c. 16), sec. 30 (incorporated by the Towns Improvement (Ireland) Act, 1854), the presiding

---

* Doubtful whether, if an election be held on the wrong day, this will avoid election. See *Tralee*, 1890 (28 Ir. L. R. 10); *Longford*, 1870 (2 O. & H. 7.)

officer had power to close the poll at any time if one hour elapsed during which no voting paper was tendered at such polling station, but the poll must now, in every municipality be opened at 8 o'clock, A.M., and kept open continuously till 8 o'clock, P.M., and no longer.* (Elections Hours of Poll Act, 1885.) (48 Vict., c. 10.) Ap. lxxx.

Irregularity in opening or closing Polling Stations.]

It has been held, however, that the fact of the poll not having been opened in proper time, or having been kept open after the proper time, will not invalidate the election, provided that it can be shown that such irregularity has not affected the result of the election.

In the *Drogheda* (1874) case (2 O. & H. 202), Mr. Justice Barry held that the election ought not to be declared invalid by reason of the polling stations being substantially not open until a quarter to 9 o'clock, A.M., as this occurrence had not the remotest effect on the result of the election. In the *Hackney* (1874) case the election was declared void because the result of the election was materially affected—one polling station being closed all day and three others for part of the day. (2 O. & H. 77.)

Judge Grove remarked in this case (*id.* p. 85):—

"It seems to me that the object of the Legislature in this provision, is this—an election is not to be upset because the clerk of one of the polling stations was five minutes too late . . . . . . the objection must be something calculated really to affect the result of the election."

A municipal election in Belfast (1873) was declared void on the ground that votes were received after the prescribed hour, although the outer door of the house in which the poll was taken was closed at the proper hour, and no votes were afterwards received except from electors who were inside before the door was closed. (*Gribbin* v. *Kirker*, Ir. R. 7 C. L. 30).

* See footnote p. 132.

In this case a considerable number of voters, sufficient to affect the result of the election, polled after the prescribed hour.

An election may be declared void without its being necessary to show that the irregularity has actually affected the result of the election; it is only necessary to show that it might have affected it. It was held in the *Worcester* (1880) case that the presiding officer may have the door of the polling station closed before the time, if there are sufficient voters within to occupy him in taking the votes till 8 o'clock, P.M. (3 O. & H. 189.)

No ballot papers should be given out after 8* o'clock, P.M.; but ballot papers given out by the presiding officer before 8 P.M. should be received.

CHAPTER XII.
THE POLL.

Ballot Box to be shown empty.]
The presiding officer at any polling station, just before the commencement of the poll, is to show the ballot box empty to any persons who may be present in the station (so that they may see that it is empty), and then lock it up, and seal it so as to prevent its being opened without breaking the seal, and place it in his view for the receipt of ballot papers, and keep it so locked and sealed. (B. A., r. 23), Ap. xliii.

Voter to state his name and address.]
When a person presents himself at the polling station to vote, he should state his name and address to the presiding officer or poll clerk.†

---

* Hours of polling are fixed in England by Greenwich mean time, and in places in Ireland are fixed by Dublin mean time, not by local time (43 & 44 Vic., c. 9, s. 1).

† This is not provided for by the Act, but as the returning officer can only ask the prescribed questions, he would seem to be precluded from asking the voter his name and address.

Ballot paper to be marked on both sides with the official mark.]

Immediately before a ballot paper is delivered to an elector it is to be marked on both sides with an* official mark, and the number, name, and description of the elector, as stated in the copy of the register, is to be called out, by the presiding officer or poll clerk, and the number of such elector is to be marked on the counterfoil† and a mark placed in the register against the number of the elector, to denote that he has received a ballot paper, but without showing the particular ballot paper‡ which he has received. (B. A., r. 24).—Ap. xliii.

Vote to be marked secretly—mandatory.]

The elector having received the ballot paper, shall forthwith proceed into one of the compartments in the polling station, and there *secretly* mark his vote on the ballot paper, and fold it up so as to conceal his vote, and shall then put it, so folded up, into the ballot box in the presence of the presiding officer—after having shown him§ the official mark on the back of it (B. A., s. 2 and r. 25.)—Ap. xxxii., xliii.

The enactment as to the ballot paper being marked *secretly* is held to be mandatory (see Lord Coleridge's judgment, quoted pp. 164-5), and therefore any infringement of it might render the election void.

The object of requiring the voter to show the official mark is, of course, to prevent any forged ballot paper being put into the ballot box.

---

* As to the liability of the presiding officer with regard to ballot papers not being stamped with the official mark, see *post*, p. 180.

† If the Presiding Officer puts the wrong number on the counterfoil, this will not render the vote void on scrutiny. *Stepney* 1886, 54 L. T., N. S. 686.

‡ This is an additional precaution, lest the agents might see the number on the back of it.

§ As to how far the presiding officer is responsible for ascertaining whether the official mark is on the paper before he allows it to be deposited in the ballot box, see p. 180.

Offences in regard to Ballot Papers.]

Sec. 3 (sub-sects. 2, 4, 6), B. A., enacts that—

Every person who—

"(2.) Forges or counterfeits or fraudulently defaces or fraudulently destroys any ballot paper or the official mark on any ballot paper; or

"(3.) Without due authority supplies any ballot paper to any person; or

"(4.) Fraudulently puts into any ballot box any paper other than the ballot paper which he is authorised by law to put in; or

"(5.) Fraudulently takes out of the polling station any ballot paper; or

"(6.) Without due authority destroys, takes, opens, or otherwise interferes with any ballot box or packet of ballot papers then in use for the purposes of the election;

"Shall be guilty of a misdemeanour, and be liable, if he is a returning officer or an officer or clerk in attendance at a polling station, to imprisonment for any term not exceeding two years, with or without hard labour, and if he is any other person, to imprisonment for any term not exceeding six months, with or without hard labour.

"Any attempt to commit any offence specified in this section shall be punishable in the manner in which the offence itself is punishable."—Ap. xxxiii.

Must vote at allotted Booth.]

No person shall be admitted to vote at any polling station except the one allotted to him. (B. A., r. 18. See *Oldham case*, 1869, 1 O. & H., 163; *post*, p. 180.)

Every person whose name is on Register is entitled to receive a Ballot Paper.]

Any person whose name is on the register of voters for the time being in force is entitled to demand or receive a ballot paper and to vote, even if by mistake his name has been placed on the list.

"Nothing," says Judge Lush, "shall take place at the polling booth but a reference to the Register to ascertain whether the person who presents himself is the person on the Register or not." (*Worcester*, 1880, 3 O. & H., 186.)

Sect. 88 of the Representation of the People (Ireland) Act, 1868 (13 & 14 Vic., c. 69),* enacts that—

"No inquiry shall be permitted at the time of polling as to the right of any person to vote, nor any objection thereto, made or received by any returning officer or his deputy except only as follows (that is to say):—That the returning officer or his respective deputy shall, if required, on behalf of any candidate, put to any voter at the time of his tendering his vote, and not afterwards, the following questions, or either of them :—

"1. Are you the same person whose name appears as A. B. on register of voters now in force for the city (town or borough as the case may be)?

"2. Have you already voted, either here or elsewhere, at the election for the city (town or borough, as the case may be)?"

The returning officer or his deputy shall, if required, on behalf of any candidate at the time aforesaid, administer an oath, or (in the case of a Quaker, Moravian, or Separatist) an affirmation to any voter in the following form :—

"You do swear (or affirm, *as the case may be*) that you are the same person whose name appears A. B. on the register of voters now in force for the city (or town or borough, *as the case may be*), and that you have not before voted, either here or elsewhere, at the present election for the city of   (or town or borough of   , *as the case may be*).

"So help me God."—Ap. xi.

The presiding officer, or poll clerk, appointed by the returning officer, may ask the questions and administer the oath.—(B. A., s. 10.)

It is to be observed that no person is to be required to answer these questions or take the prescribed oath except on a demand made by a personation agent on behalf of a candidate; and without such demand being made, the person presenting himself to vote may decline to answer the questions or to take the oath or affirmation, and the presiding officer would not on this ground be entitled to decline to give him a ballot paper.

---

* Sections 88 to 97 of this Act are brought into force in municipal elections by the Ballot Act, sec. 24.

Sec. 89 (13 & 14 Vic., c. 69) enacts:

"That, save as aforesaid, it shall not be lawful to require any voter at any election to take any note or affirmation, either in proof of his freehold, occupation, or of his residence, age, or other qualification or right to vote, or of his qualification continuing, or of his not owing any cesses, rates, or taxes whatsoever, any law or statute, local or general, to the contrary notwithstanding, nor to reject any vote tendered at such election by any person whose name shall be upon the register of voters in force for the time being, except by reason of its appearing to the returning officer or his deputy, upon putting such questions as aforesaid or either of them, that the person so claiming to vote is not the same person whose name appears on such register as aforesaid, or that he had previously voted at the same election, or except by reason of such person refusing to answer the said questions or either of them, or to take the said oath, or to make the said affirmation; and no scrutiny shall hereafter be allowed by or before any returning officer with regard to any vote given or tendered at any such election, any law, statute, or usage to the contrary notwithstanding."—Ap. xi.

It is important that the questions should be put in due form, and strictly in accordance with the language used in the Act.*

The answers to the questions must be direct and positive: equivocal or evasive answers will not do; but Cunningham points out that, supposing the person at first gives an evasive answer or declines to answer, yet if he subsequently presents himself to vote and offers to answer the questions and take the oath if required, the presiding officer ought to put the questions to him again, and if he answers them satisfactorily, allow him to vote.

The presiding officer cannot refuse to allow a person to vote whose name is on the register, provided‡ that he, if required, answers the prescribed questions satisfactorily, and

---

* The questions must be put in the very words of the Act.—*Canterbury*, 1835, K. & O., 326.

† See p. 95.

‡ Even if he knows that he is disqualified.

If persons inherently or by law disqualified—such as aliens, felons, minors, paid agents, and persons proved guilty of corrupt practices—vote, their names will be struck off on scrutiny; and they will be liable to whatever penalties are attached to their voting.

takes the oath or affirmation—if he do refuse, he may render himself liable to a criminal prosecution for the breach of a public duty, even though he knows that the voter is disqualified.—*Pryce* v. *Belcher*, 1847, C.B., 866.

There is only one proviso, therefore, with regard to a person's being allowed to vote if his name be on the register—and that is, that he answer, if required, the questions, and takes the oath permitted by law to be asked of and to be administered to voters at the time of polling.—(B. A., r. 27.)

And no person whose name is not on the list—even though he has the required qualification—is entitled to demand a ballot paper or to vote. The reason for such a provision is obvious, as the presiding officer has no authority to go into the qualifications of any person, or to take evidence, or to ask any questions (unless as to the identity of a voter or as to whether he has voted before); and a person whose name was not on the list would have no register number, and, therefore, the presiding officer would not be able to comply with the requirements of the statute by putting the register number of the voter on the counterfoil of the ballot paper.

Conclusiveness of the Register how shown.]

The Ballot Act, 1872, enacts that:—

"At any election for a county or borough a person shall not be entitled to vote unless his name is on the register of voters for the time being in force for such county or borough; and every person whose name is on such shall be entitled to demand and receive a ballot paper and to vote," &c.—(B. A., s. 7), Ap. xxxiv.

But part II., sec. 20, sub-sec. 7 (*C.*) (Ap. xxxviii.), provides that this provision shall not apply to municipal elections.

The register is made conclusive in boroughs under the Municipal Reform Act, 1840, by sec. 5 of the Municipal Elections Act, 1875 (38 & 39 Vic., c. 40), which enacts that—

"A person shall not be entitled to vote unless his name is on the burgess roll for the time being in force for the ward for which such election shall be held."

And by section 10 of the Corrupt Practices (Municipal Elections) Act, 1872 (35 & 36 Vic., c. 60), which applies to all municipalities in Ireland—

"Subject to the provisions of this section, a register shall, for all purposes, be conclusive as to the right of the persons included therein to vote at an election for the purposes whereof such register is in force," &c.

Hence—as the language in these sections is substantially the same—the conclusiveness of the register in Parliamentary and municipal elections as regards the boroughs under the Municipal Reform Act, 1840 (3 & 4 Vic., c. 108), is on precisely the same footing.

In case of *Stowe* v. *Jolliffe*, 1874, it was held that sec. 7 of the Ballot Act makes the register conclusive not only on the returning officer, but also on every tribunal which has to inquire into elections, except only in the case of "persons prohibited from voting by any statute or by the common law of Parliament,"—persons who from some inherent, or for the time irremovable, quality in themselves have not, either by prohibition of statutes or at common law, the status of Parliamentary electors—such as peers,* women,† persons holding certain offices or employments under the crown, persons convicted of crimes which disqualify, or the like. The proviso is not pointed at disqualification by reason of the receipt of parochial relief or other alms since the date of the register, non-occupation, insufficient qualification, or the like. As to these, the register is conclusive, and their votes cannot be struck out by the election Judge on scrutiny.—(L. R. 9, C. P. 734.) See also *Worcester*, 1880, 3 O. & H. 186.

In the *Londonderry* case, 1886, it was held that Ballot Act, sec. 7, gives the right to vote to any person whose name is on the register and who does not come within the express

---

* Peers or persons holding office under the Crown are not disqualified from voting at municipal elections.

† Women are qualified to vote in Municipal Elections in Belfast, see *ante*, footnote, p. 44, and in Municipal Elections in England (45 and 46 Vic., c. 50, s. 63).

provision that he is prohibited from voting by statute or common law.—(4 O. & H., 103.)

Conclusiveness of Register in Boroughs or Towns not under the Municipal Reform Act, 1840.]

The register is made conclusive in municipal elections in towns or boroughs which have adopted the Towns Improvement (Ireland) Act, 1854, by the Local Government (Ireland) Act, 1871, sec. 26—" Such list shall be evidence that the persons therein named are entitled to vote," and by sec. 10, Corrupt Practices Act, 1872 (35 & 36 Vic., c. 60). It is to be observed that neither of these sections state that the list shall be conclusive as regards the persons whose names are omitted from it, to vote; but as a person qualified to vote whose name is omitted from the list could neither vote at the election, nor "tender his vote" and claim to have it counted on scrutiny; and as it does not appear that an election tribunal has any power to inquire into questions of qualification, unless in the case of persons inherently disqualified, it is submitted that the voter's list is equally conclusive in towns or boroughs under the Towns Improvement (Ireland) Act, 1854—as the burgess roll is in boroughs under the Municipal Reform Act, 1840. If it were proved, however, that a number of electors, sufficient to turn an election,—whose qualifications were clear and indisputable,—were omitted from the list of voters, an election court would probably order a new election.

If, therefore, A. B. has not the proper franchise or rating qualification, or has not occupied the premises for the qualifying period, &c.; yet if his name is on the register he is entitled to vote, and his vote cannot be questioned *quo warranto*, on petition; if, on the other hand, the name of X. Y. (who is fully qualified) is omitted from the list—his right to vote cannot be established on petition. The register being conclusive, not only on the presiding officer, but also on any tribunal which has to inquire into elections.

Voting in two wards.]

A burgess of a borough divided into wards, was on the roll for two wards and voted in each ward. It was held that it must be taken that he had properly made his selection to vote in the ward in which he first voted, and that his vote for this ward was good, and not vitiated by his voting subsequently in the other ward.—*Queen* v. *Harrald*, 1873, L. R., 8 Q. B. 418; *Queen* v. *Tugwell*, 1868, L. R., 3 Q. B. 704. See also *Stepney*, 1886, 54 L. T., N. S. 685.

Son voting in his Father's name.]

When a son, honestly believing that he was entitled to vote, voted in his father's name (the latter being the voter on the register), the vote was struck off on scrutiny, but he was not held guilty of personation.—See *Berwick-on-Tweed*, 1881, 44 L. T., N. S. 290; *Athlone*, 1880 (3 O. & H., 57); *post*, p. 143, footnote.

Deaf and Dumb Persons.]

Deaf and dumb persons whose names are on the register are to be allowed to vote if they can, by signs or writing, answer the questions, and take the oath.

Idiots, Lunatics, and Drunken Persons.]

Idiots, lunatics, or drunken persons are entitled to vote if their names are on the register, and if they are able to answer the questions authorized by statute to be put to them, and to take, if required, the statutory oath.

There is no other ground than their being unable or unwilling to answer the questions satisfactorily, or take the oath, upon which the presiding officer could refuse to give them a ballot paper.

Name wrongly given on register does not vitiate vote.]

A vote is not vitiated by a voter's name being wrongly given on the register so long as the identity of the voter is established.*—(*Oldham*, 1869, 1 O. & H., 153; *Canterbury*, 1835, K. & O., 327). Nor does a mistake in the description of a locality where a voter's house is situated invalidate the vote.—(*Canterbury*, 1835, K. & O., 327.)

The question, it is to be observed, is not " Are you A. B. ?" but "Are you the same person whose name appears as A. B. on the register?"

Votes marked by the Presiding Officer.]

"The presiding officer, on the application of any voter who is incapacitated by blindness, or other physical cause from voting in manner prescribed in this Act, or (if the poll be taken on Saturday) of any voter who declares that he is of the Jewish persuasion, and objects on religious grounds to vote in manner prescribed by this Act, or of any voter who makes the required declaration that he is unable to read is, in the presence of the agents† of the candidate, to cause the vote of such voter to be marked on a ballot paper in manner directed by such voter, and the ballot paper to be placed in the ballot box, and the name and number on the register of voters of every voter whose vote is marked in pursuance of this rule, and reason why it is so marked, shall be entered on a list, in this Act called ' the list of voters marked by the presiding officer.'"—(B. A., r. 26), Ap. xliii.

Declaration of inability to read.]

The declaration of inability to read is to be made by the voter at the time of polling, before the presiding officer, who is to attest it in the form hereinafter mentioned, and no fee is to be charged in respect of such declaration.

* The presiding officer is not to ask a voter to spell his name.—(*Canterbury*, K. & O., 131.)

† This implies that the agents are to be allowed to see how the elector voted, which seems contrary to the whole spirit of the Ballot Act. There is a very widespread opinion that the franchise ought not to have been extended to persons unable to read or write. A writer in the *Irish Times* suggests, with regard to a mode of taking the votes of illiterate persons, that a large photograph of each candidate should be placed outside each polling booth, on a distinctive coloured paper, and that each voting paper should bear the different colours—opposite the names and corresponding with those of the photographs—in the spaces made for the marks to be placed on. He adds: " The most uneducated mortal could make a mark on the coloured paper to correspond with the person he wished to vote for ; and in case of colour blindness (which, I believe, is of rare occurrence in Ireland) the photograph would be quite sufficient."

ELECTION OF COMMISSIONERS (OR TOWN COUNCILLORS).
Act 35 & 36 Vict., cap. 33.

DECLARATION OF INABILITY TO READ.

I, A. B., of   being numbered   on the register of voters for the   ward, township (or borough) of   do hereby declare that I am unable to read.

——— his mark.

Day of   18

I, the undersigned, being the presiding officer for the polling station for   ward in the township or borough of   do hereby certify that the above declaration having been first read to the above-named A. B., was signed by him in my presence with his mark.

Signed, ———,
Presiding officer for the polling station for
          ward, township or borough of

Day of   18 ."

(B. A., Sch. II.), Ap. liv.

The returning officer should supply a sufficient number of forms for making the declaration of inability to read, as he might possibly be liable to an action if the supply were not sufficient.

Tendered Votes.*]

"If a person representing himself to be a particular elector named on the register applies for a ballot paper after another person has voted as such elector, the applicant shall, upon duly answering the questions and taking the oath, permitted by law to be asked of and to be administered to voters at the time of polling, be entitled to mark a ballot paper in the same manner as any other voter, but the ballot paper (in this Act called a tendered ballot paper) shall be of a colour differing from the other ballot papers, and, instead of being put into the ballot box, shall be given to the presiding officer and endorsed by him, with the name of the voter and his number in the register of voters, and set aside in a separate packet,† and shall not be counted by the returning officer.

---

* Tendered votes may be counted on scrutiny.

† In the *Buckrose* case, 1886 (4 O. & H. 115) where the voter put the tendered ballot paper into the ballot box instead of returning it to the presiding officer (contrary to rule 27), the court held that the vote was bad, inasmuch as the voter himself disregarded the rule.

And the name of the voter and his number on the register shall be entered on a list,* in this Act called the tendered votes list." (B. A., r. 27), Ap. xliv.

Definition of Personation.]

"A person shall for all purposes of the laws relating to municipal elections be deemed to be guilty of the offence of personation who, at an election . . . . . . applies† for a ballot paper in the name of some other person, whether that name be that of a person living or dead, or of a fictitious person, or who having voted once at any such election, applies at the same election for a ballot paper in his own name."—(B. A., s. 24).

Punishment.]

"The offence of personation, or of aiding, abetting, counselling or procuring the commission of the offence of personation by any person, shall be a felony, and any person convicted thereof shall be punished by imprisonment for a term not exceeding two years, together with hard labour."

Returning officer to prosecute.]

"It shall be the duty of the returning officer to institute a prosecution against any person whom he may believe to have been guilty of personation, or of aiding, abetting, counselling, or procuring the commission of the offence of personation by any person at the election for which he is returning officer, and the costs and expenses of the prosecutor and the witness in such case, together with compensation for their trouble and loss of time, shall be allowed by the court in the same manner in which courts are empowered to allow the same in cases* of felony."—(B.A., s. 24), Ap. xxxix.

Any person applying for a ballot paper under this Act shall be deemed "to tender his vote," or "to assume to vote."—(B.A., s. 15), Ap. xxxvi.

The offence of personation shall be deemed to be a corrupt practice within the meaning of the Parliamentary Elections Act, 1868 (31 & 32 Vic., c. 125).—B. A., s. 24.

---

* In the *Stepney* case, 1886, it was proved by a voter that he had been personated, and that when he went to the poll and claimed his vote, the presiding officer gave him a tendered ballot paper, but omitted to endorse the applicant's name upon it. The court held that although the presiding officer had not complied with the directions of rule 27 (B. A.), yet upon scrut'ny the vote ought to be counted. —(4 O. & H. 43).

† Hence it is not necessary that a person should have been asked the questions to render him liable to be prosecuted for personation. To constitute personation, the vote must be tendered with a dishonest intention. See *ante*, p. 140.

Section 93 (13 & 14 Vic., c. 69), enacts:

"That if at the time any person tenders his vote at such election, or after he has voted, and before he leaves the polling booth, any such agent so appointed as aforesaid shall declare to the returning officer, or his respective deputy presiding therein, that he verily believes and undertakes to prove that the said person so voting is not in fact the person in whose name he assumes to vote, or to the like effect; then, and in every such case, it shall be lawful for the said returning officer, or his said deputy, and he is hereby required, immediately after such person shall have voted, by word of mouth to order any constable or other peace officer to take the said person so voting into his custody, which said order shall be a sufficient warrant and authority to the said constable or peace officer for so doing; but the said returning officer, or his deputy, shall cause the words 'protested against for personation' to be placed against the vote of the person so charged with personation when entered in the poll book."*—Ap. xiii.

The person so charged is to be taken at the earliest convenient time before two justices. He is to be let out on bail on finding sufficient security. He may be committed for trial.—(Secs. 94 and 95 *id.*), Ap. xiii.

Justices may award compensation to persons unjustly charged.—(Sec. 96, *id.*), Ap. xiv.

Giving information as to who had voted in violation of statutory declaration.]

In the *Bolton* (1874) case (reported in 2 O. & H. 141), the personation agents were furnished with a register of the voters to which tickets were attached opposite the name of each voter; as soon as a voter had voted the agent stealthily tore off the ticket and put it in his pocket, and subsequently conveyed it to some person outside the polling station, and by this means persons outside knew while the poll was going on who had voted and who had not voted.

---

* Poll books were of course abolished by the Ballot Act, and according to rule 38 (B. A.), this term "poll book" may be taken to mean either the ballot paper or the register of voters. Some difference of opinion exists as to whether the words "protested against for personation" should be written against the name of the person on the register of voters or on the tendered ballot paper.

They continued to do this after being requested to desist. The court held that they had committed a violation of the statutory declaration which they had made, and committed an offence within the meaning of the provisions of the Ballot Act, thereby rendering themselves liable to serious punishment.

Mr. Justice Mellor, in his judgment, said as to this:—

"There is no doubt that the legislature, when it passed the Ballot Act, did intend that that should be a perfectly secret mode of voting as far as any instrumentality or machinery which it could provide could make it so. . . . .

"It is clear that it was deliberately done, because when Mr. W. found that it was proposed to be done, he remonstrated and protested against it, warning them that it was contrary to the provisions of the Ballot Act, and therefore placing them in the condition of transgressing the law 'intentionally.'—(2 O. & H. 135.)

In the case of *Stannanought* v. *Hazeldine*, 1879, it was held, however, that to warrant a conviction under the 4th section of the Ballot Act, it must be proved that the information as to the voters was actually communicated to some person, and that proving merely that the means of acquiring such information was afforded to anyone was not sufficient (L. R. 4 C. P. D. 191).

It is difficult to understand why the agents found it necessary to adopt the plan above referred to, as by placing persons (who had not made the declaration of secrecy) outside at the entrance of the polling station, with copies of the register to identify and mark off the voters as they went in to vote, they could have more easily, and without any risk, accomplished their object;* or the candidate (not being obliged to make the declaration of secrecy) could have given the information without incurring any penalty.

* Of course in a large or thickly populated borough it might be difficult to get persons who would be able to identify all the electors.

It was held in the case of *Clementson* v. *Mason*, 1875 (L. R. 10, C. P. 213), that sec. 4 of Ballot Act requires secrecy till the poll is closed as to the names of those who have not offered to vote, the intention being to prevent pressure being put upon those electors who do not wish to vote.

A person who inadvertently violates the secrecy of the ballot is liable to punishment.—*Reg.* v. *Uncles*, 1873 (Ir. R. 8, C. L. 50).

Presiding Officer to keep order.

"The presiding officer shall keep order at his station, shall regulate the number of electors to be admitted at a time, and shall exclude all other persons except the clerks, the agents of the candidates, and the constables on duty.' *—(B. A., r. 21), Ap. xlii.

Penalty for Misconduct in Polling Station.]

Section 9 (B. A.) enacts that :—

"If any person misconducts himself in the polling station, or fails to obey the lawful orders of the presiding officer, he may immediately, by order of the presiding officer, be removed from the polling station by any constable in or near that station, or any other person authorised, in writing, by the returning officer to remove him ; and the person so removed shall not, unless with the permission of the presiding officer, again be allowed to enter the polling station during that day. Any person so removed as aforesaid, if charged with the commission in such station of any offence, may be kept in custody until he can be brought before a justice of the peace, provided that the powers conferred by this section shall not be exercised so as to prevent any elector who is otherwise entitled to vote at any polling station from having an opportunity of voting at such station."—(B. A., s. 9), Ap. xxxv.

Disturbance at Poll.]

If any disturbance or confusion occurs at a polling station, the presiding officer is justified in having the room cleared and order restored before proceeding with the poll.— (*Worcester*, 1880, 3 O. & H. 188).

Adjournment.]

The presiding officer has power (under B. A., s. 10), to adjourn the poll.

---

* This rule does not apply to candidates. (See *ante*, p. 126.)

Riot.]

In case of a riot* he should not close the poll, but adjourn it till the next day.† When once a poll is closed it cannot be re-opened.

The state of things which would justify the presiding officer in adjourning the poll is laid down in the *Dudley* case, 1874:—

"Such a state of things as placed the whole town in a state in which reasonable men, who were not very zealous partizans or men of extraordinary courage, had not a fair opportunity of voting. It is quite irrespective of any agency on the part of the candidates."—(2 O. & H. 121.)

To Vote without delay.]

The voter shall vote without undue delay, and shall quit the polling station as soon as he has put his ballot paper into the ballot box.—(B. A., r. 25), Ap. xliii.

Spoilt Ballot Papers.]

A voter who has inadvertently dealt with his ballot paper in such a manner that it cannot be conveniently used may, on returning it to the presiding officer and proving the fact of the inadvertence to the satisfaction of that officer, obtain another ballot paper in the place of the ballot paper so delivered up (in the Ballot Act called a spoilt ballot paper); the spoilt ballot paper is to be immediately cancelled (B. A., r. 28); it must not be destroyed, as the presiding officer has to account for the ballot papers entrusted to him.—(See p. 149.)

Duties of Presiding Officer after close of Poll.]

"The presiding officer at each station, as soon as practicable after the close of the poll, is, in the presence of agents of the candidates (if any are present), to make up into separate packets,

---

* See 5 & 6 Wm. IV., c. 36, s. 8.   † See *post* p. 156.

sealed with his own seal and the seals of such agents of the candidates as desire to affix their seals—

"1. Each ballot box in use at his station, unopened, but with the key attached; and

"2. The unused and spoilt ballot papers, placed together; and

"3. The tendered ballot papers; and

"4. The marked copies of the register of voters, and the counterfoils* of the ballot papers; and

"5. The tendered votes list, and the list of votes marked by the presiding officer, and a statement of the number of the voters whose votes are so marked by the presiding officer under the heads of 'physical incapacity,' 'Jews,' and 'unable to read,' and the declarations of inability to read; and shall deliver such packets to the returning officer."—(B. A., r. 29), Ap. xliv.

Judge Brett, in the case of *Stowe* v. *Jolliffe*, 1874 (L. R., 9 C. P., 446), stated that in his view of this rule the numbers do not denote what is to be put in one packet, but merely have reference to the divisions of the subjects, and the "marked register" should be put in a sealed packet to itself. And it has been pointed out† that this is obvious, from the fact that the "marked register" is to be open to public inspection subject to certain regulations (B. A., r. 42); but that the counterfoils‡ are only to be inspected by order of court having cognizance of election petitions.—(B. A., r. 41), Ap. xlvi.

In complying with this rule, therefore, the unused and spoilt ballot papers are to be placed together, but all the other things mentioned in this list are to be made up into separate packets.

"The packets shall be accompanied by a statement made by such presiding officer, showing the number of ballot papers entrusted to him, and accounting for them under the heads of ballot papers in the ballot box, unused, spoilt, and tendered ballot papers, which statement is in this Act referred to as the ballot paper account."—(B. A., r. 30), Ap. xliv.

* This involves severing the partly-used ballot book so as to keep the numbered counterfoils separate from the unmarked ballot papers.

† See Owen, p. 75.

‡ The counterfoils are most jealously guarded, as they are the keys of secrecy of the ballot.

The Poll.

FORMS FOR
PRESIDING OFFICER'S RETURNS TO RETURNING OFFICER.

No. 1.

BALLOT PAPER ACCOUNT.

Municipal Election for the Ward of———in the Borough (Township or Town) of————, Co. of————, held on the——day of——, 18—.

(Polling Station No.———)

Number of Ballot Papers entrusted to Presiding Officer.	How accounted for
Ballot Papers (white), . . .	Number in Ballot Box, . . Number spoilt, . . Number unused, . . Total, . . .
Ballot Papers for tendered votes (coloured), ...	Number of tendered Ballot Papers used, . . Number of coloured Ballot Papers unused, . . . Total, ...

Dated this——day of——, 18—.

(Signed)———,

Presiding Officer.

No. 2.

Municipal Election for the Ward of——— in the Borough (or Town or Township) of————, in the County of————, held on the——day of————, 18

(Polling Station No.———)

List of Votes marked by the Presiding Officer.

Name of Voter.	No. on Register of Voters.	Reason why marked.		
		Physical incapacity (state what).	Unable to read.	Jew.

Dated this —— day of ——, 18— .

(Signed)————,
Presiding Officer.

No. 3.

18—.

Municipal Election for the Ward of ————, in the Borough (or Town or Township) of————, in the County of————.

(Polling Station No.———)

Tendered Votes List.

Name of Voter.	No. in the Register of Voters.

Dated this——day of————, 18—.

(Signed)————,
Presiding Officer.

The following is a useful form* to provide for the use of the presiding officer, giving him a summary of the duties he has to discharge in taking the poll :—

* Forms of this nature can be procured from Messrs. Thom & Co. (Limited), Abbey-street, or Browne & Nolan, Nassau-street, Dublin.

Instructions to Presiding Officer.

1. You are to open the poll in your polling station at eight o'clock in the forenoon, and keep it continually open until the hour of eight o'clock in the afternoon, when you are finally to close it.

(Persons who have received ballot papers before eight o'clock, p.m., may be allowed to vote and deposit their papers in the ballot box within a reasonable time after eight o'clock, p.m.)

2. You are not to leave your polling station until relieved of charge of it by another duly appointed presiding officer; or by the returning officer.

3. You shall before the commencement of the poll, show the ballot box, empty, to such persons, if any, as may be present in your polling station, so that they may see it is empty, and shall then lock it up, and place your seal upon it, so as to prevent its being opened without breaking such seal, and shall keep it in your view for the receipt of ballot papers so locked and sealed.

4. *Who entitled to Vote.*—Every person whose name is on the register for the time being in force for the particular ward or borough, is entitled to receive a ballot paper and to vote at the polling station allotted to him, and no other person.

5. As each elector applies to you for a ballot paper, he is to state his name and address; when he applies look at the register to see if the name is on it; then call out the number, name, and description of the elector as he appears on the register, and place a mark on the register against the elector's name to denote that he has received the ballot paper, but without showing the particular ballot paper he has received.

6. You are then to stamp the ballot paper on *both* sides with the official mark, and hand it to the elector, marking

on the counterfoil the number of the elector as it appears on the register.

7. The elector, on receiving the ballot paper, is forthwith to proceed into one of the compartments in the station, and there secretly mark his vote on the paper, and fold it up so as to conceal his vote, but so as to leave the official mark on the back visible; he is then (keeping the paper still folded) to show you the official mark on the back of the paper; and having done so, place the paper, still folded, in the ballot box in your presence.

8. He is to vote without undue delay, and quit the station as soon as he has put the paper into the box.

9. *Spoilt Ballot Papers.*—If an elector has inadvertently dealt with a ballot paper so that it cannot be conveniently used—on proving to your satisfaction the inadvertence—you shall give him another in its place; the spoilt paper to be immediately cancelled, but preserved, as you will have to account for all the ballot papers you receive in the ballot paper account to be furnished to the returning officer. Endorse on the spoiled ballot paper and its counterfoil the word "*cancelled.*"

10. If required by the agent acting on behalf of any candidate, you are to put to the elector at the time he tenders his vote, *before* you hand him the ballot paper, but not *afterwards*, either or both of the following questions, that is to say:—

"1. Are you the same person whose name appears as A. B. on the register of voters now in force for the city (town, township, or borough, *as the case may be*) of ———?

"2. Have you already voted either here or elsewhere at this election for the city (town, township, *or* borough, *as the case may be*) of ———?"

You are not to put, or permit to be put, to any elector any other questions whatsoever. An inaccuracy in the name or address of a voter on the register will not disqualify him for voting.

11. If the voter refuses to answer these questions, or either of them, you are not to give him a ballot paper; but if he answers both questions satisfactorily, you are to deliver the ballot paper to him, unless, before you have done so, you shall be required by any candidate or his agent to administer to the voter the following oath, or (in case of a Quaker, Moravian, or Separatist), affirmation, that is to say:—

" You do swear (or affirm, *as the case may be*) that you are the same person whose name appears as A. B. on the register of voters now in force for the city (town, township, *or* borough, *as the case may be*) of   , and that you have not before voted either here or elsewhere at the present election for the city (town, township, *or* borough, *as the case may be*) of   .
So help you God."

You are not to administer, or permit to be administered, to any elector, any other oath or affirmation whatsoever.

12. If the voter, when so required by you, refuses to take the above oath or affirmation, you are not to deliver to him the ballot paper; but if he takes the oath or makes the affirmation, you will then deliver the ballot paper to him.

13. You may delegate to the poll clerks any of the following duties:—

To call out name and number of the voter as he receives a ballot paper—stamp ballot papers and deliver them to voters—enter on counterfoils register number of voters—ask statutory questions—administer prescribed form of oath—take declarations of inability to read; but you should yourself see that the official mark is on the back of the ballot paper before you allow it to be deposited in the ballot box; you must preserve order at your station; you cannot give authority to the poll clerks to order the arrest, exclusion, or rejection of any person from the polling station.

14. You may order the arrest or removal of any person who—
 (1.) Interferes with a voter while he is marking his vote.
 (2.) Endeavours to induce him to show how he has voted.
 (3.) Communicates any information as to who has, or who has not, voted.
 (4.) Endeavours to deposit anything not a genuine ballot paper in the ballot box.
 (5.) Attempts to take away a ballot paper from the polling station.

15. *Personation.*—If at the time any person applies to you for a ballot paper, and before you have delivered it to him, or after he has voted, and before he leaves your polling station, the agent nominated by any candidate for the purpose of detecting personation shall declare to you " that he verily believes and undertakes to prove that the person so applying or voting, is not the person in whose name he assumes to vote," or to the like effect, or that he has already voted at the same election—you are, nevertheless, to deliver the ballot paper to him, and permit him to vote if he has not previously voted; and immediately after, and before such person has left the polling station, you are, by word of mouth, to order a constable to take the said person into his custody, and shall cause the words " protested against for personation " to be placed on the register against the name of the person so charged with personation.

16. *Tendered Votes.*—If a person, representing himself to be a particular elector on the Register, applies for a ballot paper after another person has voted as such elector, he shall, upon duly answering the questions and taking the oath permitted by law (paragraphs 9 and 10), be entitled to mark a ballot paper as any other voter; but such paper, called a " tendered ballot paper," is to be of a colour

different from other ballot papers, and instead of being put into the ballot box, shall be given to you, and you are to endorse it with the name of the voter and his register number,, and set it aside in a separate packet, and enter the name and number of the voter on the " tendered votes list."

17. You shall, on the application of any voter who is incapacitated by blindness or other physical cause from voting in the prescribed manner, or, if the poll be taken on Saturday, of any voter who declares that he is of the Jewish persuasion and objects, on religious grounds, to vote in the prescribed manner; or, of any voter who makes the declaration hereinafter mentioned—that he is unable to read—you shall, in the presence of the agents of the candidates (but not in the presence of any other person unless he has taken the declaration of secrecy) mark the vote of such voter on a ballot paper, as directed by such voter, and place the ballot paper in the ballot box; and the name and number on the register of voters of every voter whose vote is so marked by you, and the reason why it is so marked, shall be entered on a list called the "list of votes marked by the presiding officer." The "declaration of inability to read" is to be made by the voter at the time of voting, and you shall attest it in the prescribed form.

18. You are to regulate (by instructions to the constable at the door) the number of persons to be admitted to your station at the one time; you are not to allow overcrowding.

19. *Preservation of order in the polling stations.*—If any person misconducts himself in the polling station, or fails to observe your lawful orders, he may immediately, by your order, be removed from the polling station by any constable in or near the station, or by any other person authorized *in writing* by the returning officer; and the

person so removed shall not, unless with your permission, again be allowed to enter the station during the day. The person removed, if charged with the commission in the station of any offence, may be kept in custody until he can be brought before a justice of the peace. But these powers are not to be exercised so as to prevent an elector, otherwise entitled to vote, having an opportunity of voting. By the exercise of discretion, forbearance, and good temper, combined with firmness, you will most probably be saved the necessity of resorting to this power.

20. If, notwithstanding the exercise of the power vested in you before alluded to, the proceedings of taking the poll shall be interrupted or obstructed by any riot or open violence at or near your polling station, or by the violent or forcible prevention, obstruction, or interruption of voters proceeding on their way to your polling station (the last-mentioned prevention, obstruction, or interruption being *shown by affidavit*), you shall not for such cause finally close the poll; but shall adjourn the taking of the poll until the following day, unless such day be a Sunday, and then to the following Monday, of which adjournment you must forthwith give notice to the returning officer; but before you adjourn the poll you ought, *if possible*, to communicate with the returning officer.

21. *Close of the poll.*—As soon as practicable after the close of the poll, in the presence of the candidates or their authorized agents, you shall make up into separate packets (or place in seven different envelopes)—

    (1.) The "unused (ordinary and tendered) and spoilt ballot papers" (placed together), having first counted them and entered them in the ballot paper account.

    (2.) The "tendered ballot papers" used.

    (3.) The "marked copies of the register of voters."

(4.) The " counterfoils of the (ordinary and tendered) ballot papers."
(5.) The " tendered votes list."
(6.) The " list marked by presiding officer."
(7.) The " declarations of inability to read."

You are to seal each of these packets with your own seal, and allow any of the agents, who desire to do so, to affix their seal thereto. Each packet or envelope should be endorsed with a statement of its contents, the name of the polling booth and borough, and the date of the election and your own name.

The ballot box is not to be opened, but made into a separate packet and sealed in such a way as to prevent the introduction of anything else into it, and the agents are entitled to affix their seals to it if they so desire.

NOTE.—The key is to be attached to the ballot box.

NOTE.—If any persons have been arrested by your instructions, report the names of these persons, and the facts in connection with their arrest, to the returning officer.

Ballot paper account.—These several packets you shall deliver to the returning officer, accompanied by a statement called " the ballot paper account," made by you, showing the number of ballot papers entrusted to you, and accounting for them under the heads of—(a) ballot papers in the ballot box ; (b) unused ; (c) spoilt ; and (d) tendered ballot papers.

CHAPTER XIII.

COUNTING THE VOTES.

The rules, laid down in the Ballot Act (1872) to be observed in counting the votes, apply to municipal elections.—(B.A., r. 64), Ap. xlix.

Agents may attend the counting of votes.]

The candidates may respectively appoint agents to attend the counting of the votes.—(B. A., r. 31), Ap. xliv.—(See appointment of agents *ante*, p. 81).

Notice of such appointment to be sent to the returning officer.]

The name and address of every agent is to be transmitted to the returning officer one clear day* at the least before the opening of the poll; and the returning officer may refuse to admit to the place where the votes are counted any agent whose name and address has not been so transmitted, notwithstanding that his appointment may be otherwise valid, and any notice required to be given to an agent by the returning officer may be delivered at or sent by post to such address.—(B. A., r. 52), Ap. xlviii.

Notice to be given to agents to attend the counting of votes.]

The returning officer is to give notice in writing to the agents of the candidates appointed to attend at the counting of the votes of the time and place at which he will begin to count same.—(B. A., r. 32), Ap. xliv.

Non-attendance of agent.]

The non-attendance of such agent or agents of the candidates as may be authorised to attend will not invalidate

* See footnote *ante*, p. 31.

the act or thing done, if such act or thing is otherwise duly done.—(B. A., r. 55), Ap. xlviii.

If agent dies.]

If an agent dies, or becomes incapable of acting, the candidate may appoint another agent in his place, and shall forthwith give to the returning officer notice in writing of the name and address of the agent so appointed.—(B. A., r. 53), Ap. xlviii.

No persons, except those duly appointed, to be present at counting of votes.]

No persons (except with the sanction of the returning officer) may be present at the counting of the votes, unless the returning officer, his assistants and clerks, and the agents of the candidates—(B. A., r. 33), Ap. xlv.

It is to be observed, however, that this rule (33) will not apply to candidates who may be present wherever their agents may, in pursuance of the Act, attend.—(B. A., r. 51). See *ante*, p. 126.

Additional assistants may be appointed.]

In a circular issued by the Irish Office containing an abstract of the principal provisions of the Ballot Act, 1872, for guidance of returning officers, it is stated that it is obvious that the returning officer ought not to sanction the presence at the counting of the votes of any person other than the candidates and their agents, and his assistants and clerks, except for the purpose of assisting in the counting.

The returning officer may appoint, in addition to the clerks, competent persons to assist him in counting the votes.—(B. A., r. 48). No one is to be allowed to be present at the counting of the votes (except the candidate), unless he has made the declaration of secrecy.

Votes to be counted as soon as possible after the close of the poll.]

The returning officer is required to make arrangements for counting the votes as soon as practicable after the close of the poll.—(B. A., r. 32). When the borough or township is a comparatively small one, and the counting of the votes will not occupy more than a few hours, and can be finished on the same day on which the poll is taken, the returning officer generally arranges to commence the counting immediately after the close of the poll. He can only do this, however, with the consent of the agents, as without their consent the votes cannot be counted during the hours between seven* o'clock at night and nine o'clock on the succeeding morning.—(B. A., r. 35). Therefore, in small towns or boroughs the returning officer, in giving the agents the required notice, might state that the votes would be counted immediately after the close of the poll, unless this arrangement was objected to by any of the agents.

Counting to be proceeded with continuously.]

The returning officer is, as far as practicable, to proceed continuously with the counting, except during the hours which are (if objected to) prohibited, and the time which may be allowed for refreshment.—(B. A., r. 35), Ap. xlv.

During intervals in the counting, ballot papers and other documents to be properly secured.]

If any interval occurs between the close of the poll and the counting of the votes, or during the counting of the votes, the returning officer is directed to place the ballot

---

* Under the Elections (Hours of Poll) Act, 1885 (48 Vic., c. 10), the poll must be kept open till 8 o'clock p.m. When the Ballot Act, 1872, was passed the poll was not to be kept open after 4 p.m., and, under certain circumstances, it might be closed sooner.—See Commissioners Clauses Act, 1847, s. 29, Ap. viii.

papers and other documents relating to the election under his own seal, and the seals of such of the agents of the candidates as desire to affix their seals, and to otherwise take proper precautions for the security of such papers and documents.—(B. A., r. 35), Ap.

It would be a matter of serious consequence if the ballot papers were tampered with or stolen, and the returning officer would do well to leave constables in charge of them.

Ballot papers to be mixed and counted together before Votes are counted.]

Before proceeding to count the votes* the returning officer is, in the presence of the agents of the candidates (B. A., r. 34), to—

1. Open each ballot box.
2. Take out and count the papers therein.
3. Record the number thereof.
4. Then mix together the whole of the ballot papers in the ballot box (or if there be more than one ballot box for a ward, he is to mix together all the ballot papers in the boxes for that ward).

He is then to proceed to count the votes.

The form given (p. 162) will be found to be a convenient one for the counting assistants to enter the votes for each candidate as they are read out by the returning officer, by making a stroke for each vote in the square opposite to the candidate's name for whom the vote is given.

* In counting the ballot papers it is a convenient plan to arrange them in heaps of five-and-twenty for each candidate.

[FORM.
L

162 *Municipal Elections in Ireland.*

The returning officer, while counting and recording the number of ballot papers, and counting the votes, is to keep the ballot papers with their faces upwards, and take all proper precautions for preventing any person from seeing the numbers printed on the back of such papers.*—(B. A., r. 34), Ap. xlv.

Agents not authorized to interfere with Ballot Papers.]

The agents are not authorized to interfere with the ballot papers or the assistants engaged in counting, but are entitled to inspect the face of bad and doubtful ballot papers.

Returning Officer must himself decide on the validity of Ballot Papers.]

The returning officer must himself decide on the validity of the ballot papers; he cannot delegate this part of his duty (which is judicial), to anyone else.

His decision final.]

The decision of the returning officer as to any question arising in respect of any ballot paper is final, subject to reversal on petition questioning the election or return.—(B.A., s. 2), Ap. xxxii.

Ballot Papers to be rejected.]

He is to reject, and not count, any ballot papers on the following grounds :—

1. Want of official mark.
2. Voting for more candidates than entitled to.
3. Writing or mark by which voter could be identified.
4. Unmarked or void for uncertainty.—(B. A., r. 36), Ap. xlv.

---

* Because, of course, anyone seeing the number on the back of the ballot paper would thus gain a knowledge of the number of the counterfoil, and with that knowledge could ascertain (if he had previously noted the particular ballot paper issued to the voter) the name of voter.

Principles laid down by Lord Coleridge for determining the validity of Ballot Papers.*]

Lord Coleridge, in delivering the judgment of the Court, in the case of *Woodward* v. *Sarsons*, 1875 (L. R., 10 C. P. 746-7-8), on the validity and invalidity of certain votes, said:—

"The (Ballot) Act is divided into the principal part, which contains certain sections, and two schedules which contain certain rules and forms; and by S. 28, 'the schedules and the notes thereto, and directions therein shall be construed and have effect as part of this Act.' The rules and forms, therefore, are to be construed as part of the Act, but are spoken of as containing 'directions.' Comparing the sections and the rules, it will be seen that for the most part, if not invariably, the rules point out the mode or manner of doing what the sections enact shall be done. And in schedule 2, the first note states that:—'the forms contained in this schedule, or *forms as nearly resembling the same as circumstances will admit*, shall be used." And on the ballot paper, as given with schedule, is '*directions* as to printing ballot paper,' and ' Form of *directions for the guidance of voters in voting*," &c.

Directory as distinguished from absolute enactments.]

"These observations lead us to the conclusion that the enactments as to the rules in the first schedule, and the forms in the second, are directory enactments, as distinguished from the absolute enactments in the sections in the body of the Act, and in such case, in order to determine the preliminary question, which is, whether there has been a material breach of the Act, and which must be determined before determining what effect such breach has upon a vote or on the election, the general rule is, that an absolute enactment must be obeyed or fulfilled exactly, but it is sufficient if a directory enactment be obeyed or fulfilled substantially.

"The second section enacts, as to what the voter shall do, that 'the voter having secretly marked his vote on the paper, and folded it up so as to conceal his vote, shall place it in an enclosed box.' This is all that is said in the body of the Act about what the voter shall do with the ballot paper. That which is absolute,

---

* A Select Committee of the House of Commons appointed to inquire into the working of the Ballot Act, recommended that this case and judgment should be sent to every returning officer.—Parliamentary Paper 162 of 1876.

therefore, is, that the voter shall mark his paper *secretly*. How*
he shall mark it, is in the directory part of the statute. By
rule 25, the elector, on receiving the ballot paper, shall forthwith proceed into one of the compartments in the polling
station, and *there mark his paper* and fold it up so as to
conceal his vote, and shall then put his ballot paper, so folded
up, into the ballot box.' This rule, it will be observed,
does not yet say how the paper is to be marked. But, in schedule
2, is given the 'Form of ballot paper,' and appended to the
form is a note which, by S. 28, is to be construed and have effect
as part of the Act. This note contains the 'Form of directions
for the guidance of the voter in voting.' The voter will go into
one of the compartments, and with the pencil provided in the compartment, place a cross on the right hand side opposite to the
name of each candidate for whom he votes, thus × .' This is the
only enactment throughout the statute as to the manner and form
in which the voter is to mark a ballot paper. And therefore, by
the general rule before mentioned, it would be necessary that the
absolute enactment, that the paper should be marked *secretly*,
should be obeyed exactly; but it would be sufficient that the
manner of marking the paper should be obeyed substantially. If
these two enactments be so obeyed, there is no breach of the Act.
The extent of the error which is to vitiate so as to annul the
ballot paper is further to be gathered from the statute itself. By
section 2, any ballot paper which has not on its back the official
mark, or on which votes are given to more candidates than the
voter is entitled to vote for, or on which anything (except the said
number on the back), is *written or marked, by which the voter can
be identified*, shall be void, and not counted. It is not every
writing or every mark besides the number on the back
which is to make the paper void, but only such a writing
or mark as is one by which the voter can be identified. So, in
rule 36, 'The returning officer shall report the number of
ballot papers rejected and not counted by him under the several
heads:—(1) Want of official mark; (2) Voting for more candidates
than entitled to; (3) *Writing or mark by which voter could be
identified*; (4) Unmarked, or void for uncertainty.' And then, in
schedule 2, in the note to the form before referred to, we have
this warning:—'If the voter votes for more than ——— candidates, or places *any mark* on the paper *by which he may be afterwards identified*, his ballot paper will be void, and will not be
counted.' The result seems to be, as to writing or mark on the
ballot paper, that if there be substantially a want of any mark,
or a mark which leaves it uncertain whether the voter intended to
vote at all or for which candidate he intended to vote or if there be

---

* It has been observed that the mistake made by the Court in the Scotch
(Wigtown) case, was regarding the directions to voters as mandatory

marks indicating that the voter has voted for too many candidates, or a writing or a mark by which the voter can be identified, then the ballot paper is void, and is not to be counted, or, to put the matter affirmatively, the paper must be marked so as to show that the voter intended to vote for some one, and so as to show for which of the candidates he intended to vote. It must not be marked so as to show that he intended to vote for more candidates than he is entitled to vote for, nor so as to leave it uncertain whether he intended to vote at all or for which candidate he intended to vote, nor so as to make it possible, by seeing the paper itself, or by reference to other available facts, to identify the way in which he has voted.

"If these requirements are substantially fulfilled, then there is no enactment and no rule of law by which a ballot paper can be treated as void, though the other directions in the statute are not strictly obeyed. If these requirements are not substantially fulfilled, the ballot paper is void, and should not be counted, and if it is counted, it should be struck off on scrutiny. The decision in each case is upon a matter of fact, to be decided first by the returning officer, and afterwards, by the election tribunal on petition."

Ballot Papers with peculiar marks held good.]

The following are illustrations of some of the peculiarly* marked ballot papers in the case of *Woodward* v. *Sarsons*,† which, in the absence of any evidence of pre-arrangement (of the marks on the ballot papers being intended as a means of identifying the voters), were held by the Court to be good.

(I.) Two or more crosses instead of one. (*Woodward* v. *Sarsons*, 1875, L. R., 10 C. P., 749), thus :—

1	SARSONS.	
2	WOODWARD.	X X

---

* It must be borne in mind that any mark on the ballot paper, by which the voter might be identified, would justify the Returning Officer in rejecting it.

† See 44 L. J., N. S., p. 296.

1	SARSONS.	
2	WOODWARD.	X

X

1	SARSONS.	XXX
2	WOODWARD.	

The Court considered that "there could be no doubt of the voter's intention to vote, and no doubt of the intention to vote emphatically for the one candidate."

(II.) A straight stroke in addition to the cross (*id.*), thus :—

1	SARSONS.	X |
2	WOODWARD.	

(III.) A mark like the letter P in addition to the cross (*id.*), thus:

1	SARSONS.	X ¶
2	WOODWARD.	

(IV.) A straight line in lieu of a cross (*id.*), thus :—

1	SARSONS.	/
2	WOODWARD.	

(V.) A star instead of a cross (*id.*), thus :—

1	SARSONS.	✳
2	WOODWARD.	

(VI.) A cross marked with a tremulous hand (*id.*), thus :—

1	SARSONS.	X
2	WOODWARD.	

(VII.) A blurred cross, and a better cross added (*id.*), thus :—

1	SARSONS.	X x
2	WOODWARD.	

(VIII.) A pencil line drawn diagonally across the paper through the name of the candidate not voted for (*id.*, 748), thus :—

1	SARSONS.	X
2	~~WOODWARD.~~	

(IX.) A cross on the left instead of the right hand side of the candidate's name (*id.*, 749), thus :—

1	X SARSONS.	
2	WOODWARD.	

1 X	SARSONS.	
2	WOODWARD.	

(X.) A cross placed near the left hand corner of the ballot paper (*id.*), thus —

X 1	SARSONS.	
2	WOODWARD.	

A ballot paper torn longitudinally, through the middle, as indicated by the dotted line, thus :—

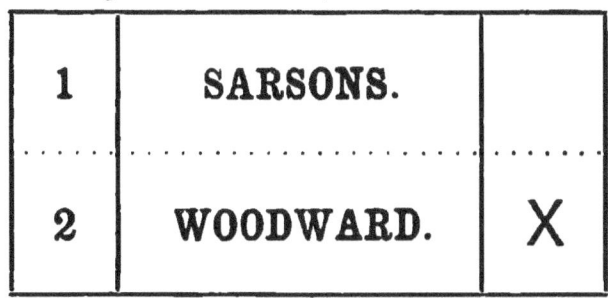

In the case of *M'Laren* v. *Home* 1881 (3 O. & H., 178), where a ballot paper was marked with a long cross, part of which was in the square allotted to one candidate and part in that of the other; the Court decided that it should be counted as a good vote for the candidate in whose square the intersection of the Cross appeared :—

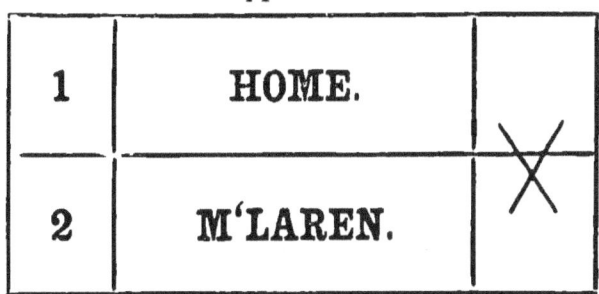

Marks on back of ballot papers will not invalidate them except intended as a means of identification.]

Marks on the back of a ballot paper (if it is well marked on the front), will not invalidate it—unless there is some evidence to show that these marks are intended as a means of identification—as the back of the ballot paper is not intended to be seen.

In the *Stepney case*, 1886 (4 O. & H., 35), the Court were divided in opinion as to the validity of a ballot paper which was marked with a cross (in the usual way), on the face of it, but also marked on the *back* with a cross, with the name "John Mitchell" written after it. The name of John Mitchell did not appear on the register of voters, and there was no evidence, that it was writing by which the voter could be identified.

A ballot paper with the figure 33 written on the back of it, was held good, in the absence of any evidence that the voter could be identified. (*Buckrose*, 1886, 4 O. & H., 111.)

A ballot paper marked in the usual way, on the face with a cross opposite one candidate's name, but with a cross upon the back opposite the other candidate's name was allowed good for the former. (*Id.*)*

Rejected Ballot Papers.]

In the following cases (*Woodward* v. *Sarsons*) the ballot papers were held to be bad :—†

(I.) When marked with the name of the candidate :—

1	**SARSONS.**	*Sarsons.*
2	**WOODWARD.**	

Lord Coleridge (in regard to this paper) said :—

"We disallow it with some hesitation; there is no cross at all; and we yield to the suggestive rule that the writing by the voter of the name of the candidate, may give too much facility, by reason of the handwriting, to identify the voter." (*Id.* 749.)

---

* These decisions are not in accord with that given in a previous (the *Wigtown*) case (2 O. & H., 219), where a ballot paper with two parallel strokes on the back in addition to the cross, on the face of it, was held to be bad. It is submitted that the later decisions are more reliable.

† It has been pointed out that no absolute rule exists for determining the validity of a ballot paper; any suspicious mark or deviation would entitle the Returning Officer to reject the paper.

(II.) When marked with the name of a voter.

(E. Prews was the name of a voter on the burgess roll.)

1	SARSONS.	X
2	WOODWARD.	

E. Prews.

The Court decided in the *Wigtown* case, 1874 (2 O. & H., 216), that a ballot paper marked on the face of it, with the name "A. C. Allan, Clothier," was invalid (although it did not appear that this was the name of a voter); holding that a name put on a voting paper might lead to the identification of the voter afterwards, and that it was not the duty of the returning officer at the time to inquire or know anything about the name.

(III.) When marked with initials in addition to the cross (*id.* 750); thus :—

1	SARSONS.	
2	WOODWARD.	C. W. X

In the *Buckrose case*, 1886 (4 O. & H., 111.), it was decided that ballot papers marked as follows should be rejected, viz. :—

(a) With a cross on the left of one candidate's name, and a

straight line on the right hand side of the other candidate's name, thus :—

$\overset{1}{\text{X}}$	M'ARTHUR.	
2	SYKES.	/

(*b*.) With a line opposite to one candidate's name, and a cross opposite to that of the other, thus :—

1	M'ARTHUR.	/
2	SYKES.	X

It is obvious why the Court rejected these ballot papers, as a stroke or straight line being held to be a good mark, the marks on these papers are consequently equivalent to "votes for more candidates than there are vacancies."

(*c*.) With a cross immediately upon the name of a candidate in such a way as to make it appear possible the elector intended to strike the name out.*

1	M'ARTHUR.	
2	SY✗KES.	

* It is difficult to understand why the Court held this ballot paper invalid, as it seems obvious that the intention of the elector was to vote for Sykes, and that he merely fell into the error of marking the paper with a cross on, instead of opposite, to the name.

Ballot paper marked with a circle.]

A ballot paper marked with a circle instead of a cross was held bad in the *Wigtown* case, 1874.—(2 O. & H., 215.)

Mr. Justice Denman, in delivering judgment in the *Stepney* case, 1886, said :—

"The question here is, whether a ballot paper is good in which the voter, instead of making the cross or a mark of the ordinary kind straight with his pen, deliberately makes a circle. If a man does that, he really must do it either with some sinister object, or it is so perversely and absurdly in deviation from the directions of the Ballot Act, as to make it a case in which he ought really to be held to have thrown away his vote. If he does it with the sinister object of having his vote known, then he has forfeited his vote, because he has violated the Ballot Act. If he does it purposely—and one cannot understand a man supposing that a cross is a circle—he has done it perversely, and done it in such a way as again to legitimately forfeit his vote. If he does it purposely, knowing that his vote may be thrown away, then he really has not indicated his intention to vote for the candidate against whose name he has placed the mark; so that, in any case, there is no good ground for holding that a circle is a cross within the meaning of the Ballot Act."—(4 O. & H., 37.)

But, in a case heard shortly afterwards (*Buckrose*, 1886, 4 O. & H., 111), a circle was held to be a good mark (in the absence of any evidence of its being intended as means of identification), on the ground that it is a mark which can be employed to sufficiently indicate the candidate for whom an elector intended to vote.

When vote is uncertain for any candidate ballot paper must be rejected.]

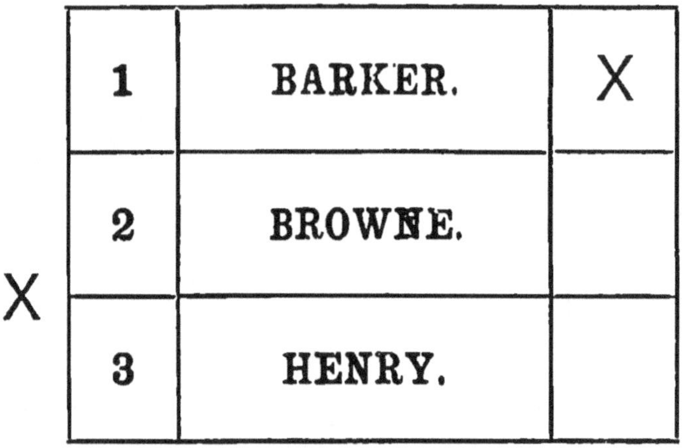
1
BARKER.
X
2
BROWNE.
X
3
HENRY.

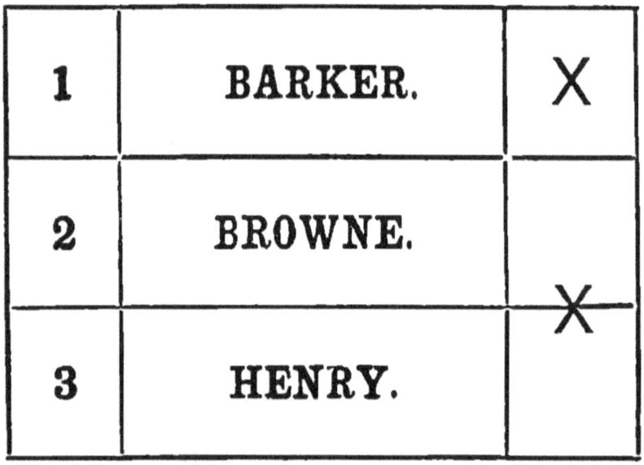
1
BARKER.
X
2
BROWNE.
X
3
HENRY.

In the above illustrations the vote as regards Barker is good, but as regards the other candidates void, for "uncertainty;" consequently the ballot paper must be rejected altogether by the returning officer.

Authorities, however, are not agreed on this point.

Mr Parker holds (p. 194) :—

"That a ballot paper which is certain as to some voters, may be counted as to those votes, though it is uncertain as to others."

* Carleton (p. 49), on the other hand, forcibly points out—

"That the power of the returning officer is to reject, not '*votes*,' but 'ballot papers.' For example, if there are two seats to be filled up and three candidates, and the voter has unmistakably voted for one of them, but has so put his other mark as to leave it uncertain for which of the other two he voted, in such case—however hard it may be toward the candidate who got the certain vote, and however it may be dealt with on petition - the returning officer ought to reject the ballot paper *altogether*; otherwise he could not comply with the statute (Sch. 1, Part I., R. 36), which requires him to report the number of *ballot papers*—not *votes*—rejected, not counted, and does not contemplate the case of a ballot paper *partly* admitted and *partly* rejected."

Ballot papers void for uncertainty.]

A ballot paper having the cross put at the top, outside the parallelogram containing the candidates' names and the space for the cross, was held bad, as being void for uncertainty (*Berwick-on-Tweed*, 1880, 3 O. & H. 178) ;† thus :—

X   *Ballot Paper.*

1	HOME.	
2	M'LAREN.	

* Carleton on Elections, 10th Ed.

† It was argued that it indicated an intention on the part of the elector to vote for the candidate whose name stood first on the ballot paper.

The judges, however, were not agreed as to this ballot paper being a bad one. But a similarly marked ballot paper was declared void in the *Stepney* case, 1886 (4 O. & H. 37) and in the *Buckrose* case, 1886 (4 O. & H. 111.)

Ballot Paper.

		X
1	ISAACSON.	
2	DURANT.	

——marked on the back.]

A ballot paper marked on the *back* with a cross (which could be seen through the paper) opposite the name of one of the candidates was rejected (*Buckrose* case, 1886, 4 O. & H. 111). The Court held that the mark must be on the face of the paper, and that a cross on the back is not a compliance with the Act. (See also *Berwick-on-Tweed*, 1880, 3 O. & H. 182.)

——marked with peculiar ink, etc.]

It was held that a ballot paper marked with a cross with ink not being of a peculiar character, instead of a pencil, is good (*Wigtown*, 1874, 2 O. & H. 223); but it has been pointed out that if the returning officer finds any peculiar ink or pencil has been used and occurs through a number of ballot papers, or observes anything in relation to same which would lead him to suppose that there was any pre-arrangement, he should reject those ballot papers.

A ballot paper marked, without discolouring the paper, for instance, with a blunt knife or finger nail,* is a good mark, provided that it appears that such mark was intentionally made (*M'Laren* v. *Home*, 1881, 44 L. T. N. S. Q. B. 289).

——marked by presiding officer with register number of voter.]

In the *Barnstable* municipal election, 1875 (32 L. T. N. S. 602), where the presiding officer marked on the face of the ballot paper the number of the voters appearing on the burgess roll, which would enable any of the persons present at the counting of the votes to identify the way in which the party had voted, the ballot papers so marked were rejected by the returning officer; but the Court held, on petition, that he was wrong in rejecting them. This decision, however, is at variance with that given in the case of *Woodward* v. *Sarsons* (1875, L. R. 10 C. P. 734).

The decision of the Court in the latter case is probably more reliable.

Ballot papers of illiterate voters wrapped up in declaration of inability to read.]

When the ballot papers of illiterate voters were placed by the presiding officer in the ballot box, each wrapped up in the corresponding " declaration of inability to read," instead of being made up into a separate packet, sealed with the seal of the presiding officer, and so delivered to the returning officer (pursuant to B. A., Sch. 1, Part I., rr. 26, 29), (by which proceeding these voters could have been, but were not in fact, identified), it was held that, notwithstand-

---

* The want of intelligence and idiosyncrasies exhibited by voters in regard to voting is sometimes extraordinary. The writer has been informed of a case where an elector, on retiring into the polling compartment to mark the ballot paper delivered to him by the presiding officer, marked instead the *example of a ballot paper* hung up in the compartment, and deposited the ballot paper he had received, unmarked in the ballot box.

ing this mistake on the part of the presiding officer, the votes were properly counted (*Woodward* v. *Sarsons*, L. R. 10 C. P. 734).

Voting at wrong polling station.]

A vote of an elector who tendered it at a wrong polling station was struck off, on the ground that the fault was his as well as the poll clerk's (*Oldham*, 1869, 1 O. & H. 163).

Presiding Officer liable for breach of ministerial duties.]

Want of the official mark can only occur from the fault or carelessness of the presiding officer or the poll clerk.

When the presiding officer * omitted to mark a number of ballot papers with the official mark, in consequence of which—(such votes being held void by the returning officer)—the candidate lost the election, it was held that the presiding officer was *primâ facie* liable to such candidate for the omission (*Pickering* v. *James*, 1873, L. R., 8 C. P. 489).

It was, however, decided in this case that a presiding officer could not be held responsible for any acts of commission or omission on the part of the poll clerk in the performance of the duties which he might (with certain specified exceptions) delegate to him, inasmuch as he does not appoint the poll clerk, and hence the relation of master and servant does not exist between them (*id.*)

The Court was divided in opinion in this case whether the Ballot Act does, or does not, impose on the presiding officer the duty of ascertaining before the voter deposits a voting paper in the ballot box whether the official mark is on such paper (*id.*) In a later case (*Ackers* v. *Howard*, 1886,

---

* If this omission was the fault of the poll clerk, he could not have been held responsible. In the *Oldham* case (1 O. & H. 163), it was held to be the duty of the voter under the Ballot Act to see that the ballot paper it had on the official mark, and to show that mark to the presiding officer.

16 Q. B. D. 739), the Judges held that it was the intention of the Legislature that this duty should be imposed on the presiding officer.

Ballot Papers not marked with the Official Stamp.]

Under section 2 of the Ballot Act, 1872, a ballot paper not marked with the official mark on the back should be rejected (*Wigtown*, 1874, 2 O. & H. 216).

A ballot paper not having upon the face of it the official mark, but conforming in other respects with requirements of the Ballot Act, is valid. See case of *Ackers* v. *Howard*, 1886 (16 Q. B. D. 739,) where this point was very fully considered.

Stamping Instrument to perforate.]

It is desirable to use a stamping instrument which will perforate the paper, and thus render it impossible for the ballot paper to have the official mark on one side only The use of such an instrument is authorized by B. A., s. 24.

Omission to enter number of voter on counterfoil.]

In the *Pickering* v. *Startin* case, 1873 (28 L. T., N. S. C. P. 112), the Court were undecided whether it would avoid an election on petition if a presiding officer, or poll clerk acting for him, omitted to enter the number of the voter on the counterfoil.

In the *Arklow Petition* case (1890),* where the defeated candidate petitioned against the election, on the ground that women (not being qualified to vote in that town) were allowed to vote, it appeared on scrutiny that the counterfoils were not marked with the voter's number on the register, so that the Judges were unable to determine whether women had voted or not; the election was declared void, the returning officer being made liable for the costs.

* Not reported.

Name of candidate entered twice on ballot papers.]

When a candidate at a municipal election was twice nominated, one nomination being good and the other bad, and his name appeared in the ballot papers twice, once in respect of each nomination, it was held that the votes given to him under each name were valid, and that he was entitled to have the total of the votes so given counted for him (*Northcote* v. *Pulsford*, 1875, 10 L. R. C. P. 476).

In case of equality of votes.]

The provisions contained in sec. 2 (B. A.), prohibiting the returning officer from giving an original vote, and authorizing him to give a casting vote, do not apply in the case of municipal elections (see B. A., s. 20 (7) *a*.) He is, therefore, not precluded from voting if he is a registered voter,* and under that portion of section 30, of the Commissioners' Clauses Act (1847), which is not repealed by schedule 6 of the Ballot Act, the returning officer—or where the borough is divided into wards—the presiding officer, has power to determine, by lot, which of two candidates, with an equal number of votes, is to be declared duly elected.

In boroughs under 3 & 4 Vic., c. 108, the mayor and assessors, or aldermen and assessors, or any two of them, shall name, from amongst those persons for whom the number of votes shall be equal, so many as shall be necessary to complete the requisite number to be chosen aldermen or councillors as the case may be (3 & 4 Vic., c. 108, s. 58.)

In municipal elections in England and Wales under 5 & 6 Will. IV., c. 76, sec. 35, the officer returning has a right to give a casting vote.

* He could not (unless in some exceptional cases, see *ante*, p. 72, footnote), be legally a mayor or chairman, and hence could not be a returning officer without being a registered voter.

Endorsement on rejected ballot papers.]

The returning officer is to endorse* "rejected" on any ballot paper which he may reject as invalid, and shall add to the endorsement "rejection objected to," if an objection be in fact made by any agent to his decision. The returning officer is to report to the town clerk the number of ballot papers rejected, and not counted by him classified in a list under the several heads of—

1. Want of official mark ;
2. Voting for more candidates than entitled to ;
3. Writing or mark by which voter could be identified ;
4. Unmarked or void for uncertainty ;

and shall, on request, allow any agents of the candidates, before such report is sent, to copy it.—(B. A., rr. 36 and 64(*b*).)

AFTER THE COUNTING OF THE VOTES.

Upon the completion of the counting, the returning officer is to seal up in separate packets the counted and rejected ballot papers. He is not to open the sealed packet of tendered ballot papers, or marked copy of the register of voters and counterfoils ;† but to proceed, in the presence of the agents of the candidates, to verify the ballot paper account given by each presiding officer by comparing it (1) with the number of ballot papers recorded by him (the returning officer), (see B. A., r. 34), (2), the number of unused and spoilt ballot papers in his possession, and (3) the tendered votes list ; and shall re-seal each sealed packet after examination.

The returning officer shall report to the town clerk the result of such verification, and shall, on request, allow any agents of the candidates, before such report is sent, to copy it.—(B. A., r. 37.)

---

* Not necessarily on back of ballot paper.—*Ackers* v. *Howard*, 1886, 16 Q. B. D., 742. His omission to endorse rejected ballot papers in this way will not, however, avoid the election.

† Counterfoils, being the keys of the secrecy of the ballot, are not to be opened, but to be kept sealed, as they are sent by the presiding officer.

Form of Returning Officer's Report.

Election of ———

For the Borough of ———

Held the —— day of ———, 18—.

Ballot Boxes.	Ballot Papers in each Box.	Ballot Papers rejected.		Votes obtained by each Candidate.	
		Causes of rejection.	Number.	Candidates' Names.	Votes obtained.
No. 1,	200	Want of official mark,	2	Jones, Henry,	90
No. 2,	130	Voting for more candidates than entitled to,	12	M'Guffin, William,	76
No. 3,	170	Writing or mark by which voter could be identified,	14	Murphy, John,	150
		Unmarked,	10	Robinson, Patrick,	50
		Void for uncertainty,	12	Smith, Joseph,	110
Total Ballot Papers in Ballot Boxes,	500	Total Ballot Papers rejected,	50		

I hereby report that I have verified the Presiding Officer's Ballot Paper accounts, and that the above is a correct statement of the number of Ballot Papers in each Ballot Box and the number of Ballot Papers rejected by me, and the number of votes obtained by each candidate at this Election.

Dated the —— day of ———, 18—.

(Signed), ———,
Returning Officer.

To the Town Clerk.

The returning officer shall forward to the town clerk of the municipal borough in which the election is held—

(1.) All the packets of ballot papers in his possession, together with
(2.) His own reports, as to rejected ballot papers, and as to the result of his verification.
(3.) The ballot paper accounts furnished by the presiding officers.
(4.) "The tendered votes lists."
(5.) "The list of votes marked by the presiding officers" (which consists of a list with the name and number of the illiterate voters, &c.) (B.A., r. 26), and statements relating thereto.
(6.) "The declarations of inability to read."
(7.) The packets of counterfoils.
(8.) The marked copies of the registers sent by each presiding officer.[*]

Each packet is to be endorsed with a description of its contents, the date of the election, and the name of the borough for which such election was held. These documents are to be kept by the town clerk among the records of the borough. (B. A., rr. 38, and 64 (b.))

The town clerk is to retain for one year, amongst the records of the borough all documents relating to an election forwarded to him in pursuance of the Ballot Act by the returning officer, and unless otherwise directed by a competent court, shall, at the expiration of that period cause them to be destroyed. (B. A., rr. 39, 64 (b.))

The publication of a notice by the returning officer of the number of votes obtained by each candidate is now held to be a declaration that those who obtained the majority of votes were elected.

If a candidate is duly nominated and obtains a majority

---

[*] Leigh (p. 106) points out that the lists (if any) made out by the presiding officers of persons protested against for personation should also be forwarded.

of votes, the returning officer is bound to declare him elected, even though he knows that he is disqualified. See *Reg. v. Mayor of Bangor*, 1886, 18 Q. B. D., 349.*

The returning officer shall as soon as possible give public notice† of the names of the candidates elected, and, in the case of a contested election, of the total number of votes given for each candidate, whether elected or not. (B. A., r. 45.) Ap. xlvii.

The presiding officer‡ is directed to declare the result of the poll and also to send a notice to each person elected, informing him of the fact of his being elected. (10 Vic., c. 16, s. 30,) Ap. vii.

When it was alleged on petition that the counting was performed incorrectly by the returning officer, the Court ordered the votes to be recounted. (*Renfrew*, 1874, 2 O. & H. 213.

CHAPTER XIV.

ELECTION OF MAYOR, ALDERMEN, ASSESSORS,§ CHAIRMAN.

Time of Election and Duration of Office.]

The mayor is to be elected by the council from the aldermen or councillors on the 1st December in every year, and to enter upon his office on 1st January following, and is to continue in office for one year, or until his successor shall have accepted the office of mayor, and shall have made and subscribed the necessary declaration.—(6 & 7 Vic., c. 93, s. 5).

Equality of Votes for.]

In the case of an equality of votes at an election of mayor, the alderman, who shall have been elected by the greatest number of votes, shall have a second or casting vote.— (3 & 4 Vic., c. 108, s. 83).

---

* On appeal to the House of Lords the decision in this case was confirmed, 58 L. T. N. S. 502.

† The result of the election should be posted immediately on the outer door of the building in which the counting takes place.

‡ It is submitted that, although this section is not repealed by the Ballot Act, this duty should now be discharged by the Returning Officer.

§ This chapter deals with the election of these officers in boroughs under the Municipal Reform Act, 1840 (3 & 4 Vic., c. 108), where not modified by subsequent Local Acts.

Vacancy.]

In case the person elected mayor shall decline to accept the office, or, having agreed to accept the same, shall, after his election, die or become incapable of discharging the duties of such office, or cease to be an alderman or councillor of the borough, the council shall within ten days elect another fit person to be mayor for the ensuing year or the residue thereof, as the case may be.—(3 & 4 Vic., c. 108, s. 83).

Form of Declaration to be made.]

Mayor, aldermen, councillors, municipal commissioners, or assessors, are not to act until they have made a declaration of acceptance of office, as follows :—

" I, A. B., having been elected mayor (or alderman, councillor, municipal commissioner, or assessor) for the borough of—— —— (or for the ward of—— —— in the borough of———), do hereby declare that I take the said office upon myself, and will duly and faithfully fulfil the duties thereof according to the best of my judgment and ability." *

And in the case of the party being required to be qualified by estate :—

" And I do hereby declare that I am seized or possessed of real or personal estate (*or both, as the case may be*) to the amount of £1,000 (*as the case may require*) over and above what will satisfy my just debts."

Or when a qualification by reason of the occupancy of a house is allowed :—

"That I now occupy, and have for twelve calendar months last past, occupied a house rated for the relief of the poor at the net annual value of not less than £25 (or   pounds, *as the case may be*), situate within the borough."—(3 & 4 Vic., c. 108, s. 85.)

Fine for Non-acceptance of Office.]

Every person duly qualified who shall be elected to the office of alderman, councillor, auditor, or assessor shall accept the office or pay a fine of £50, to be placed to the credit of the borough fund, or in the case of mayor, a fine of £100.—(*Id.*, s. 86.)

---

* The form may be made a general one, by adding the following words, viz. :—
" And I further declare that I am fully qualified to fill the office of ———, according to the laws governing same."

Fines for Resignation of Office.]

Fine for resignation of mayor's office, without the consent of the council, £100; for resignation of that of alderman, councillor, auditor, or assessor, without consent of the council, £50.—(*Id.*, s. 87.)

Sections 88 & 89 deal with the disqualifications of mayor, aldermen, assessors, and auditors, and the penalties to which they are subject for acting if disqualified.

In the event of a person residing for six months within the borough, his qualification for these offices is identical with his qualification to vote.

Aldermen—how elected.]

Aldermen are elected in the same way as councillors.

Term of Office.]

An alderman's ordinary term of office is six years. One-half of the whole number of aldermen go out of office every third year.

The half to go out are those who have been aldermen for the longest time without re-election.—(3 & 4 Vic., c. 108, ss. 61-2).

Any alderman, on going out of office, may be re-elected.

If incapable of acting.]

The mayor may, in case of the illness or incapacity to act of any alderman, appoint another alderman to act in his place.—(3 & 4 Vic., c. 108, s. 72).

Auditors and Assessors.]

Two auditors and two assessors* are to be elected on 3rd day of November in each year—no burgess is eligible for these offices who is a councillor, town clerk, or treasurer.—(3 & 4 Vic., c. 108, s. 70).

Election to take place in the same manner as in the case of councillors.—M. E. Act, 1875 (38 & 39 Vic., c. 40), s. 1.

* Under the Municipal Reform Act, 1840, two ward assessors are also appointed.

Auditors are still elected in Cork, Kilkenny, and Waterford. In all other places by the Local Government Board (Ireland) (34 & 35 Vic., c. 109), s. 11, Ap. xxix.

Chairman.]

In boroughs under 9 Geo. IV., c. 82, the chairman is elected annually, on the 1st day of August, by a majority of the commissioners who shall have taken the oath. His qualification is the same as that of other commissioners.

In case the chairman is unable to attend, he may appoint a deputy-chairman; or in case he is absent, and has not appointed a deputy, the council may elect a chairman.—(9 Geo. IV., c. 82, s. 28).

In towns under the Towns Improvement (Ireland) Act, 1854, the chairman is elected under the 37th section of the Commissioners Clauses Act, 1847 (10 Vic., c. 16), which enacts :—

"At the first meeting of the commissioners they shall, by the majority of the votes of the commissioners present, elect one of their body to be their chairman until the next annual meeting of the commissioners, when, and at every subsequent annual meeting, the commissioners shall, in like manner, elect a chairman for the ensuing year; and in case the chairman die, or resign, or cease to be a commissioner, or otherwise become disqualified to act as such, the commissioners present at the meeting next after the occurrence of such vacancy, shall choose some other of their body to fill such vacancy, and the chairman so elected shall continue in office so long only as the person in whose place he was elected would have been entitled to continue chairman; and if at any meeting of the commissioners the chairman be not present, one of the commissioners present shall be elected chairman of such meeting by the majority of the votes of the commissioners present at such meeting."—Ap. ix.

Sec. 38 (*id.*) enacts that if—

"There be an equality of votes in the election of the chairman, it shall be decided by lot which of the commissioners having an equal number of votes shall be chairman.'

And also :—

"That at every annual meeting the chairman going out of office at that meeting shall, if present and willing to act, be the chairman of such meeting."—Ap. ix.

CHAPTER XV.
OCCASIONAL VACANCIES.
In towns or boroughs under 9 Geo. IV. c. 82.]

In towns or boroughs, under 9 Geo. IV. c. 82, casual, or as they are sometimes called, extraordinary vacancies, are filled up by the board or council, not by the constituency at large. The person elected to fill the office continues in it, for the unexpired term which his predecessor would have held it.

The chairman is required to call an extraordinary meeting of the commissioners to fill up the vacancy.—(9 Geo. IV., c. 82, s. 17).

Municipal Reform Act, 1840.]

In boroughs in which the Municipal Reform Act, 1840 (3 & 4 Vict., c. 108,) is in force, the Municipal Elections (Ireland) Act (42 & 43 Vict., c. 53), 1879, s. 2 enacts that:—

"In the event of any extraordinary vacancy occurring in the office of any alderman, councillor, or assessor, the election to supply such vacancy shall take place not later than 14 days after notice shall have been given to the mayor or town clerk by any two burgesses, and the mayor shall fix the day for holding such election, whether the borough be divided into wards or not."*

And sec. 3 (*id.*) repeals so much of the ss. 81 & 82 of 3 & 4 Vic., c. 108, as relates to the fixing of the day of election by the alderman.

Towns Improvement (Ireland) Act, 1854.]

In towns under the Towns Improvement (Ireland) Act, 1854 (17 & 18 Vic., c. 103), the Commissioners Clauses Act, 1847 (10 Vic., c. 16), s. 19 enacts:—

"If any of the commissioners die or resign, or be disqualified, or cease to be a commissioner from any other cause than that of going out of office by rotation, the remaining commissioners,

---

* A *mandamus* may be obtained to compel a Council to hold an election to fill a vacancy.—See 2 T. L. R. (1886), 431.

if they think fit, may, within one month from the happening of such vacancy, elect another commissioner in his place; and every commissioner so elected shall continue in office only so long as the person in whose place he is elected would have been entitled to continue in office."

The election or co-option of a commissioner must be made at a special meeting, but the acceptance of the resignation of a member is ordinary business, and may be done at an ordinary meeting.—See *Queen (Cochrane) v. Byrne*, 1888 (22 Ir. L. R. 330).

When an occasional vacancy occurs in a town council the commissioners must elect a candidate to fill it by voting openly.—(*Queen v. Hazley*, 1887, 11. Ir. L. R. 360).

CHAPTER XVI.*
CORRUPT PRACTICES.

Corrupt Practices defined.]
The Corrupt Practices (Municipal Elections) Act, 1872 (35 & 36 Vic., c. 60),† s. 3 enacts:—

"That the terms 'bribery,' 'treating,' 'undue influence,' and 'personation,' shall respectively include anything committed or done before, at, after, or with respect to an election, which if done before, at, after, or with respect to an election of members to serve in Parliament, would render the person committing or doing the same liable to any penalties, punishments, or disqualifications, for bribery, treating, undue influence, or personation, as the case may be, under any Act for the time being in force with respect to elections of members to serve in Parliament."‡—Ap. lx.

The Public Bodies Corrupt Practices Act, 1889§ (52 & 53 Vict., c. 69).—sec. 1, sub-sec. 2, enacts that:—

" Every person who shall by himself, or by and in conjunction with any other person, corruptly give, promise, or offer any gift,

---
* This chapter is only intended to give a general outline of the subject.
† This Act applies to every municipality in Ireland.
‡ This has the effect of making the provisions of all previous and subsequent Acts in force in relation to these corrupt practices at Parliamentary elections applicable to municipal elections.
All Acts for the prevention of corrupt practices prior to the Corrupt Practices Prevention Act, 1854 (17 & 18 Vic., c. 103) have been repealed by that Act.
§ This Act applies to every municipality in Ireland.

loan, fee, reward, or advantage whatsoever to any person, whether for the benefit of that person, or of another person, as an inducement to or reward for or otherwise on account of any member, officer, or servant of any public body as in this Act defined, doing or forbearing to do anything in respect of any matter or transaction whatsoever, actual or proposed, in which such public body as aforesaid is concerned, shall be guilty of a misdemeanour." Ap. lxxxii.

Sec. 7 enacts:—

"'The expression 'advantage' includes any office or dignity, and any forbearance to demand any money or money's worth or valuable thing, and includes any aid, vote, consent, or influence, or pretended aid, vote, consent, or influence, and also includes any promise or procurement of or agreement or endeavour to procure, or the holding out of any expectation of any gift, loan, fee, reward, or advantage, as before defined."—Ap. lxxxiv.

Bribery defined.]

The Corrupt Practices Prevention Act, 1854 (17 & 18 Vic., c. 103), s. 2 defines bribery, viz.:—

" The following persons shall be deemed guilty of bribery and shall be punishable accordingly:

" 1. Every person who shall, directly or indirectly, by himself, or by any other person on his behalf, give, lend, or agree to give or lend, or shall offer, promise, or promise to procure or to endeavour to procure, any money, or valuable consideration, to or for any voter, or to or for any person* on behalf of any voter, or to or for any other person in order to induce any voter to vote, or refrain from voting, or shall corruptly do any such act as aforesaid, on account of such voter having voted or refrained from voting at any election.

" 2. Every person who shall, directly or indirectly, by himself or by any other person on his behalf, give or procure, or agree to give or procure, or offer, promise, or promise to procure or to endeavour to procure, any office, place, or employment to or for any voter, or to or for any person on behalf of any voter, or to or for any other person, in order to induce such voter to vote, or refrain from voting, or shall corruptly do any such act as aforesaid, on account of any voter having voted or refrained from voting at any election.

" 3. Every person who shall, directly or indirectly, by himself, or by any other person on his behalf, make any such gift, loan, offer, promise, procurement, or agreement as aforesaid, to or for any person, in order to induce such person to procure, or endeavour

---

* Hence need not be a voter.

to procure, the return of any person to serve in Parliament, or the vote of any voter at any election.

"4. Every person who shall, upon or in consequence of any such gift, loan, offer, promise,* procurement, or agreement, procure or engage, promise, or endeavour to procure the return of any person to serve in Parliament, or the vote of any voter at any election.

"5. Every person who shall advance or pay, or cause to be paid, any money to or to the use of any other person with the intent that such money or any part thereof shall be expended in bribery at any election, or who shall knowingly pay or cause to be paid any money to any person in discharge or re-payment of any money wholly or in part expended in bribery at any election.

"Sec. 3. The following persons shall be deemed guilty of bribery and shall be punishable accordingly :

"1. Every voter who shall, before or during any election, directly or indirectly, by himself or by any other person on his behalf, receive, agree, or contract for any money, gift, loan, or valuable consideration, office, place, or employment, for himself or for any other person, for voting or agreeing to vote, or for refraining or agreeing to refrain from voting, at any election.

"2. Every person who shall, after any election, directly or indirectly, by himself or by any other person on his behalf, receive any money or valuable consideration on account of any person having voted or refrained from voting, or having induced any other person to vote or refrain from voting, at any election.

"And any person so offending shall be guilty of a misdemeanour, and shall also be liable to forfeit the sum of ten pounds to any person who shall sue for the same, together with full costs of suit."

Corrupt payment of Rates.]

Section 49 of the Representation of the People (England) Act, 1867 (30 & 31 Vict., c. 102), s. 49 enacts that—

"Any person, either directly or indirectly, corruptly paying any rate on behalf of any ratepayer for the purpose of enabling him to be registered as a voter, thereby to influence his vote at any future election, and any candidate or other person, either directly or indirectly, paying any rate on behalf of any voter for the purpose of inducing him to vote or refrain from voting, shall be guilty of bribery, and be punishable accordingly; and any person on whose behalf, and with whose privity any such payment is made, shall also be guilty of bribery, and be punishable accordingly."

* Bribery, although nothing is received.

A similar provision exists in the Representation of the People (Scotland) Act, 1868 (31 & 32 Vic., c. 48), but the corresponding Irish Act does not contain any such provision. However, this is not important, as the payment of rates, or the giving of any valuable consideration for the purpose of influencing persons to vote for the candidate on whose behalf the payment is made, is bribery at common law.—See *Bushby*,* p. 130.

The payment, however, of a voter's rates for the purpose of enabling him to have his name placed on the register, in order that he may vote in accordance with what are known to be his political views, is not bribery.—*Oldham*, 1869 (1 O. & H., 166).

Corrupt practices avoid an election.]

The Corrupt Practices (Municipal Elections) Act, 1872 (35 & 36 Vic., c. 60), s. 5 enacts :—

An election shall be avoided if any corrupt practices or offences against this Act are committed by agents with the candidate's knowledge and consent.

If it be shown that an agent (within the scope of his authority) bribes a voter without the knowledge or consent, or even in direct contravention to the instructions of the candidate, it will avoid the election (*Harwick* (1880) case 3 O. & H. 69), but will not render the candidate liable for penalties. To render the candidate liable, it must be shown that the agent bribed with his knowledge and authority.

Mr. Justice Denman said in his judgment in the *Ipswich* case, 1886 :—

"It is important that it should be understood as a matter of law that if any agent of a candidate chooses to expend money illegally in the promotion of that candidate's return, whether the money came from a great political club, or from a subscription

* "Bushby's Practice of Elections," by Hardcastle.

of well-wishers, or from an enthusiastic supporter, such expenditure will be fatal to the candidate who succeeds by its help." —(4 O. & H. 74).

A single act of bribery avoids election.]

Judge Keating held, in the *Norwich* case, 1871, that a single act of bribery avoids election.

" It seems hard at first sight that a single act of bribery should avoid an election; but when an act of bribery is committed the whole election of the party bribing is tainted. It is no longer an election : it is utterly void."—(2 O. & H. 41).*

But it has been laid down that for a single isolated case to upset an election, very strict proof is necessary.—(*Hastings*, 1869, 1 O. & H. 218, per Blackburn, J.)

Sec. 6 (35 & 36 Vic., c. 60) provides for an election being avoided on the ground of general corruption.

Voters not to be employed as paid canvassers.]

Sect. 7 (*id.*) prohibits any person, whose name is on the register of voters for any borough (or ward thereof), from being retained or employed for payment or reward by or on behalf of a candidate at an election for such borough (or ward thereof) as a canvasser, for the purposes of the election.

Penalty for.]

If any person is retained or employed by or on behalf of a candidate at an election in contravention of this prohibition, such person, and also the candidate or other person by whom he is retained or employed, shall be deemed to be guilty of an offence against this Act, and shall be liable, on summary conviction before two justices of the peace, to a penalty not exceeding ten pounds. (*id.*)

Paid canvassers prohibited from voting.]

An agent or canvasser who is retained or employed for payment or reward for any of the purposes of an election, shall not vote at the election, and if he votes he shall be

* See also *Birkbeck* v. *Bullard*, 1886 (54 L.T.N.S., 625).

guilty of an offence against this Act, and shall be liable, on summary conviction before two justices of the peace, to a penalty not exceeding Ten Pounds (*id.*)

The vote of a paid agent of candidate, who had retired before the poll commenced, was held to be invalid.—(2 O. & H., 20).

Retainer to voter not bribery.] See *ante*, p. 84.

Conveyance of voters to and from the poll.]

Sec. 8 (C. P. (M. E.) A., 1872, 35 & 36 Vic., c. 60) makes payment by a candidate or his agent, for the conveyance of voters to or from the poll a corrupt practice, and renders any person guilty of this offence liable, on summary conviction before two justices of the peace, to a penalty not exceeding five pounds.

The conveyance of voters to or from the poll in carriages (not kept on hire) lent gratuitously for the purpose, is not illegal.

A promise to pay a voter's travelling expenses is not bribery, provided there is no condition imposed upon him that he shall vote for a particular candidate; payment on this condition would be bribery.*—*Dublin*, 1869 (1 O. & H. 273).

In the *Bolton* case, 1874, where a candidate's agent sent voters railway tickets to bring them to the poll and back, and asking them to come and vote for the candidate, it was held not to amount to bribery, as it did not contain a conditional promise.—(2 O. & H., 145.)†

It has been held that an offer to sell a vote, unless proved to have been accepted, is not a corrupt act.—*Mallow* case, 1870 (2 O. & H., 21).

---

* Or if it were shown that the intention of the payment of his travelling expenses was to induce him to vote.—See *Packard v. Collings*, 1886, 54 L. T. N. S. 619.

† At Parliamentary Elections, all payments for travelling expenses are illegal —(46 & 47 Vic., c. 51, s. 7).

Instances of what may constitute bribery.]

A wager may constitute bribery if made with a corrupt motive, to induce an elector to vote for a particular candidate.

It has been held that payment of 5s. for the loss of a hat at a public meeting was not an illegal payment.—*Stepney*, 1886 (4 O. & H., 39).

Payment of voters for " colourable " services is bribery.*— (3 O & H., 153).

The vote of an elector who received the money paid to his children, who were employed by the candidate as messengers, was struck off on scrutiny.—*Stepney*, 1886 (4 O. & H., 38).

In the *Lisburn* case (W, & B., 225) it was held that the payment of money, to induce a person to personate his father (who was dead) and vote, was bribery.

Bribery may consist in paying excessive prices for *bonâ fide* services in order to influence a voter.—See *Westminster*, 1889 (1 O. & H., 90).

The offer of a bribe to a person *primâ facie* entitled to vote, but who subsequently becomes disqualified, has been held to be bribery.—*Guildford*, 1869 (1 O. & H., 14).

Martin, *B.*, in the *Westminster* case, 1869 (1 O. & H., 95), pointed out in regard to bribery—" That the question is not whether the voter was actually influenced, but whether the alleged briber intended to influence the voter."

Payment to recompense workmen for wages lost through coming to vote is bribery.—*Staleybridge*, 1869 (20 L.T.N.S., 75 ; 1 O. & H. 67); *Hastings*, 1869 (1 O. & H., 219).

In the *Gravesend* case, 1880, it was held that promising an advantage to an elector was bribery, even though no

---

* The employment and payment of voters by a candidate or his election agent is made a corrupt practice at Parliamentary elections under 46 & 47 Vict., c. 51, s. 52 (2).

condition was attached to it.—(3 O. & H., 84); see also *Launceston*, 1874 (2 O. & H., 129).

General bribery, without its being traced to the candidate or his agents, will invalidate an election.—*Guildford*, 1869 (1 O. & H., 15).

Bribery at common law equally as by Act of Parliament will avoid an election.—*Lichfield*, 1869 (20 L.T., N.S., 14).

If voters pair.]
It is not illegal for two voters to pair; but if, under the impression that one has broken his promise and voted, the other votes—his vote, in the absence of fraud, is good.—*Northallerton*, 1869 (1 O. & H., 169).

Time of giving bribe unimportant.]
Immaterial at what period money was given or offered, provided that it was with a view of influencing the election. —*Sligo*, 1869 (1 O. & H., 302).

Treating.]
"IV. Every candidate at an election who shall corruptly by himself, or by or with any person, or by any other ways or means on his behalf, at any time, either before, during, or after any election, directly or indirectly give or provide, or cause to be given or provided, or shall be accessory to the giving or providing, or shall pay, wholly or in part, any expenses incurred for any meat, drink, entertainment, or provision, to or for any person, in order to be elected, or for being elected, or for the purpose of corruptly influencing such person or any other person to give or refrain from giving his vote at such election, or on account of such person having voted or refrained from voting, or being about to vote or refrain from voting at such election, shall be deemed guilty of the offence of treating, and shall forfeit the sum of fifty pounds to any person who shall sue for the same, with full cost of suit; and every voter who shall corruptly accept or take any such meat, drink, entertainment, or provision, shall be incapable of voting at such election, and his vote, if given, shall be utterly void and of none effect "—(17 & 18 Vict., c. 102, sec. 14).*

---

* This only provides for a penalty on the candidate who corruptly treats, and the person accepting the treat; but 46 & 47 Vic., c. 51 (An Act for the better prevention of Corrupt and Illegal Practices at Parliamentary Elections, 1883), s. 1, makes any person guilty of treating or undue influence at a Parliamentary election liable to punishment.

It is to be observed that the meat, drink, or entertainment must be *corruptly* given.—(*Carrickfergus*, 1869, 1 O. & H., 265).

In the *Norfolk* case, 1869 (1 O. & H., 243) Judge Blackburn said:—

"I have found that the notion has prevailed that for a candidate to give anything in the way of meat or drink was fatal to an election. That is a salutary notion, and acts as a protective machinery to the candidate; but I cannot lay down the law to the full extent that that goes. But I can say that whenever a candidate or agent gives any meat or drink he does what is a foolish and imprudent thing, because it becomes a question what the intention was in doing such a thing; and if the judge finds that the intention was to influence and affect voters, it vacates the election."

The Corrupt Practices Prevention Act, 1854 (17 & 18 Vic., c. 102), s. 23, enacts:—

"And whereas doubts have also arisen as to whether the giving of refreshment to voters on the day of nomination or day of polling be or be not according to law, and it is expedient that such doubts should be removed: Be it declared and enacted, that the giving or causing to be given to any voter on the day of nomination or day of polling, on account of such voter having polled or being about to poll, any meat, drink, or entertainment by way of refreshment, or any money or ticket to enable such voter to obtain refreshment, shall be deemed an illegal act, and the person so offending shall forfeit the sum of forty shillings for each offence, to any person who shall sue for the same, together with full costs of suit."

It has been held that the giving of refreshments on the nomination or polling days does not avoid the election unless it can be shown to have been given *corruptly*.—See *Westminster*, 1869 (1 O. & H., 91); *Bradford*, 1869 (1 O. & H., 37); *Bodmin*, 1869 (1 O. & H., 122).

Treating is not an entertainment given to equals, but an entertainment given by a superior to an inferior with the object of securing the goodwill of the inferior.—*Birkbeck* v. *Bullard*, 1886 (54 L.T.N.S., 626).

In the *Kidderminster* case, 1874 (2 O. & H., 173), the respondent, in the course of a speech, said :—

"When we have won the election, we will have an entertainment together."

It was held to be a corrupt promise, constituting bribery, and the election declared void.

Refreshments to Women.]

Treating may consist of giving refreshments to women with a view of their influencing the votes of their brothers, fathers, or sweethearts.—*Tamworth*, 1869 (1 O. & H., 86).

Undue influence defined.]

" Every person who shall, directly or indirectly, by himself, or any other person on his behalf, make use of, or threaten to make use of, any force, violence, or restraint, or inflict or threaten the infliction, by himself or by or through any other person, of any injury, damage, harm, or loss, or in any other manner practise intimidation upon or against any person in order to induce or compel such person to vote or refrain from voting, or on account of such person having voted, or refrained from voting at any election, or who shall, by abduction, duress, or any fraudulent device or contrivance, impede, prevent, or otherwise interfere with the free exercise of the franchise of any voter, or shall thereby compel, induce, or prevail upon any voter, either to give or to refrain from giving his vote at any election,* shall be deemed to have committed the offence of undue influence, and shall be guilty of a misdemeanour, and in *Scotland* of an offence punishable by fine or imprisonment, and shall also be liable to forfeit the sum of fifty pounds to any person who shall sue for the same, together with full costs of suit."—(17 & 18 Vic., c. 102, s. 5.)†

Clerical Influence.]

As to what constitutes undue clerical influence and spiritual intimidation, see Judge Keogh's remarks in the *Galway* (1869) case (1 O. & H., 306), and Judge Fitzgerald's remarks in *Longford* (1870) case (2 O. & H., 13, 16).

---

* This was recognised as a vital principle when Parliament was in its infancy. 3 Edward I., c. 5, enacts—" Because elections ought to be *free*, the king . . . commandeth upon great forfeiture that no man, by force of arms, nor by malice or menacing, shall disturb any to make free election."

† See note, p. 198.

Threatening to give up a Pew.]
It was held to be intimidation for a pew-holder to threaten to give up renting a pew in chapel unless the minister voted in the way he (the pew-holder) wished *Northallerton*, 1869 (1 O. & H., 168).

Watching Voters.]
Parker says (p. 335):—

"Watching the voters in and out of the polling station, and keeping an eye upon them, in the hope that by doing so they might be induced to vote for a particular candidate, or at all events not to vote against him, has been held not to be such an interference with the free exercise of the franchise as to fall within the *section* (*Lichfield*, 3 O. & H., 137). The contrary might, however, be held if the practice were repeated and continued.—(*Id.* 138)."

Fraudulent Devices.]
In the *Gloucester* case (1873), where a number of cards were issued to the electors, printed like ballot papers, having a × after the name of a particular candidate, with a note to the effect that the vote of any elector who did not mark his ballot paper in a similar manner would be lost: it was held this did not constitute a fraudulent device within the meaning of sec. 5 of the Corrupt Practices Act, 1854 (2 O. & H., 60). See, also, *Stepney*, 1886 (4 O. & H., 56).

The court stated, however, that candidates should be careful, in issuing circulars to voters, not to use any ambiguous language calculated to deceive or to trick the voters into the belief that their votes would be lost unless they voted for some particular candidate.

In a case where an agent publicly stated on several occasions that the voting according to the Ballot Act was a "farce," and that he had discovered a plan by means of which he would be able to ascertain, after the election, how each voter had voted, and distributed 10,000 copies of a newspaper amongst the electors, containing an article in support of his alleged discovery, the judges were divided in opinion as to whether the action taken by him amounted to a "fraudulent device" to prevent or impede free exercise of the franchise.—(*Down*, 1880, 3 O. & H., 122).

Personation.]
(See *ante*, pp. 143-4).

Disqualifications.]
Any corrupt practice proved to have been committed at an election by, or with the knowledge or consent of a candidate, makes him personally guilty, and subject to the following disqualifications during seven years (and if he has been elected renders his election void), viz.:—

"(1) He shall be incapable of holding or exercising any municipal office or franchise, and of having his name placed on the register, or voting at any municipal election.

"(2) He shall be incapable of acting as a justice of the peace and of holding any judicial office.

"(3) He shall be incapable of being elected to, and of sitting or voting in Parliament.

"(4) He shall be incapable of being registered or voting as a Parliamentary voter.

"(5) He shall be incapable of being employed by any candidate in any Parliamentary or municipal election.

"(6) He shall be incapable of acting as overseer or as guardian of the poor."—(35 & 36 Vic., c. 60, s. 4), Ap. lx.

Any person found guilty of any corrupt practice at an election shall (whether he was a candidate or not), be subject during seven years from the date of the conviction or judgment to these disqualifications (*id.*), and his vote shall be struck off in counting (*id.*, sec. 10), Ap. lx. & lxii.

Costs of Prosecution.]
"The costs and expenses of a prosecutor and his witnesses in the prosecution of any person for either of the corrupt practices of bribery, undue influence, or personation at an election, together with compensation for trouble and loss of time, shall, unless the court before which such person is prosecuted otherwise directs, be allowed, paid, and borne in the same manner in which they may be allowed, paid, and borne in cases of felony.

"The clerk of the peace of the county in which a borough is situate, or in the case of a borough which is a county of a city or a county of a town, or in which there is a clerk of the peace, the clerk of the peace of such county of a city or county of a town or borough, shall, if he is directed by an election court acting under the provisions of this Act, to prosecute any person for either of the corrupt practices of bribery, undue influence, or personation at the election in respect of which the court acts, or to sue or proceed against any person for penalties for bribery, treating, undue influence, or any offence against this Act at such election, prosecute, sue, or proceed against such person accordingly."—(35 & 36 Vic., c. 60, sec. 9), Ap. lxii.

CHAPTER XVII.

CONTROVERTED ELECTIONS.

Grounds upon which an Election may be questioned.]

An election may be questioned by petition on the grounds—

(*a.*) That the election was as to the borough or ward whole avoided by general bribery, treating, undue influence, or personation; or

(*b.*) That the election was avoided by corrupt practices or offences against the Corrupt Practices (Municipal Elections) Act, 1872 (35 & 36 Vic., c. 60), committed at the election; or

(*c.*) That the person whose election is questioned was at the time of election disqualified; or

(*d.*) That he was not duly elected by a majority of lawful votes.*—C. P. M. E. A., 1872 (35 & 36 Vic., c. 60, s. 12), Ap. lxii.

An election shall not be questioned on any of these grounds except by an election petition (*id.*)

Who may present a Petition.]

Any person who voted or was qualified to vote may present a petition.—(34 & 35 Vic., c. 109, s. 20), Ap. xxix.

* See *ante*, p. 186.

Within what time.]

The petition must be presented within one month after the election (*id.*)

The petition must be in the prescribed form, and be delivered to the prescribed officer of the court.

Copy of Petition to be served on Town Clerk, and on Member whose return is petitioned against.]

The petitioner shall within three days* after lodging the petition deliver a copy of it to the clerk of the governing body, and to any member of such governing body in respect of whose election it has been presented.

An unsuccessful candidate cannot properly be made a respondent.—*Lowering* v. *Dawson* (1875), L. P. 10, C. P. 726.

Petitioner to give security for payment of costs.]†

At the time of the delivery of the petition to the prescribed officer, or within three days afterwards, the petitioner shall give security for the payment of all costs, charges, and expenses that may become payable by him to any person summoned as a witness on his behalf, or to any member whose election is complained of.

Amount of security.]

The amount of the security shall be one hundred pounds; it shall be given either by recognizance to be entered into by not more than four sureties, or by a deposit of money in manner prescribed, or partly in one way and partly in the other.—(34 & 35 Vic., c. 109, s. 20), Ap. xxix.

Powers of Court.]

"As soon as conveniently may be after the presenting of such petition and the giving of such security, but not sooner than ten days thereafter, the court or one of the judges thereof shall proceed to inquire into and decide upon the matters and

---

* "In reckoning time for the purposes of this Act, Sunday, Christmas Day, Good Friday, and any day set apart for a public feast or thanksgiving, shall be excluded."—(35 & 36 Vic., c. 60, s. 25), Ap. lxx.

† An overloaded petition will be visited with costs even if successful.—*Birkbeck* v. *Ballard*, L.T.N.S., 626.

allegations contained in such petition, and shall have power to take evidence upon oath, and to compel the attendance of witnesses, and shall have all and the same powers, jurisdiction, and authority as in other cases coming within the jurisdiction of the court, and shall either confirm the election or order a new election, or make such order and give such relief in the premises as to them or him may seem right, and such decision and orders shall in all respects be final and conclusive upon all parties."—(*Id.*)

How Vacancy is to be filled up in Towns.]

"Where the court or judge has declared that the election of any member of the governing body of any town was void, such member shall cease to act as such, and there shall be a vacancy in such governing body, which vacancy shall be filled by the election of a new member by the persons qualified to vote at such election, according to the provisions of the special Act in respect of the election of members."—(34 & 35 Vic., c. 109, s. 20). Ap. xxx.

Rules to be made by Court.]

"The court may from time to time make, revoke, and alter general rules and orders in regard to the practice, procedure, and costs of petitions," &c.—(34 & 35 Vic., c. 109, s. 21). Ap. xxx.

It has been held that there is no power to amend a municipal election petition after the expiration of twenty-one days from the election by adding a charge of treating.

Sec. 15, sub-secs. 4 to 12 of the Corrupt Practices Municipal Election Act, 1872 (35 & 36 Vic., c. 60), deals with the regulations to be observed by the court on the trial of a petition.—(Ap. lxiii.)

Sec. 16, sub-secs. 1 to 4, with the examination and expenses of witnesses at the trial of the petition.—(Ap. lxiv.)

Sec. 17, sub-secs. 1 to 5, with the abatement and withdrawal of petition.—(Ap. lxv.)

Sec. 18, sub-secs. 1, 2, with the withdrawal and substitution of respondent on a petition.—(Ap. lxvi.)

Sec. 19, sub-secs. 1 to 3, with the costs.—(Ap. lxvii.)

Sec. 20, sub-secs 3, 4, with provisions for the reception of the court upon trial of a petition.—(Ap. lxvii.)

Sec. 21, sub-secs. 1 to 5, with respect to the jurisdiction and general rules—(Ap. lxviii.)

Sec. 22 with the expenses of the court.—(Ap. lxix.)

Acts done by Candidate whilst result of Petition is pending not invalid.]

Sec. 23 enacts:—

"Where a candidate who has been elected to an office at an election is by a certificate of the court, or by a decision of the superior court, declared not to have been duly elected, acts done by him in execution of such office before the time when the certificate or decision is certified to the town clerk, shall not be invalidated by reason of his being so declared not to have been duly elected." —(Ap. lxix.)

How vacancy to be filled up in Boroughs.]

Sec. 24:—

"Where upon a petition the election of any person to an office has been declared void, and no other person has been declared elected in his room, a new election shall forthwith be held to supply the vacancy in the same manner as in the case of an extraordinary vacancy in the office, and for the purposes of any such new election any duties to be performed by a mayor, alderman, or any officer shall, if such mayor, alderman, or officer has been declared not elected, be performed by a deputy, or other person who might have acted for him if he had been incapacitated by illness."— (Ap. lxx.)

Elector not to be required to state for whom he has voted.]

Sec. 26 re-enacts sec. 12 of the Ballot Act, 1872, viz. :—

"No person who has voted at an election by ballot shall in any proceeding to question the election be required to state for whom he has voted."—(Ap. xxxvi., lxx.)

25th Section of Ballot Act unnecessary.]

The 25th section of the Ballot Act, 1872, which enacts that one vote shall be struck off, on a scrutiny, for each voter proved to have been corrupted by a candidate or his agents, etc., is quite unnecessary; as pointed out by Leigh (p. 117). He says:—

"This section was framed to meet a system of scrutiny of a totally different character to the one now in the Ballot Act. By the scheme originally embodied in the Bill it was proposed that the ballot should be entirely secret, without power of following the votes by means of counterfoils, and the only means whereby a petitioner claiming the seat could acquire it without a fresh election was by help of the provisions of the 25th section. When the House of Lords introduced the present system of counterfoils, afterwards adopted by the Government, this section became wholly unnecessary."

Inspection of rejected ballot papers.]

An inspection of rejected ballot papers, in the custody of the town clerk, may be obtained by an order from a county (or civil bill) court having jurisdiction in the borough, or any part of it, or from any tribunal in which an election may be questioned.—(B.A., rr. 40, 64).

An appeal from such civil bill court may be had in like manner as in other cases in such court.

The order for inspection will only be granted by the court on being satisfied by evidence on oath* that the inspection or production of such ballot papers is required for the purpose of instituting or maintaining a prosecution for an offence in relation to ballot papers, or for the purpose of a petition questioning an election.—(B.A. r. 40) Ap. xlvi.

Any power given to a court by this rule may be exercised by a judge of such court at chambers.—(*Id.*)

Inspection of Counterfoils and Counted Ballot Papers—how to be obtained.]

No person shall, except by the order of a tribunal having cognizance of petitions complaining of undue elections, open the sealed packet of counterfoils after the same has been once sealed up, or be allowed to inspect any counted ballot papers in the custody of the town clerk; such order may be made subject to such conditions as to persons, time, place, and mode of opening or inspection as the tribunal may think expedient: provided that on making or carrying into effect any such order care shall be taken that the mode

---

* See *Stowe* v. *Joliffe*, 1874. L.R. 9 C.P., 446.

in which any particular elector has voted shall not be discovered until he has been proved to have voted, and his vote has been declared by a competent court to be invalid.—(B.A., rr. 41, 64), Ap. xlvi.-ix.

Regulations for the Inspection, and Fees for copies of Documents.]

The regulations for the inspection of documents and the fees for the supply of copies of documents of which copies are directed to be supplied, shall be prescribed by the council of the borough, with the consent of the Chief Secretary or the Lord Lieutenant of Ireland; and subject, as aforesaid, the town clerk in respect of the custody and destruction of the ballot papers and other documents coming into his possession in pursuance of this Act, shall be subject to the directions of the council of the borough.—(B.A., rr. 64 (b), 66), Ap. xlix.-l.

Where an order is made for the production by the town clerk of any document in his possession relating to any specified election, the production by such clerk or his agent of the document ordered, in such manner as may be directed by such order, or by a rule of the court having power to make such order, shall be conclusive evidence that such document relates to the specified election; and any endorsement appearing on any packet of ballot papers produced by such town clerk or his agent shall be evidence of such papers being what they are stated to be by the endorsement. The production from proper custody of a ballot paper purporting to have been used at any election, and of a counterfoil marked with the same printed number and having a number marked thereon in writing, shall be *prima facie* evidence that the person who voted by such ballot paper was the person who at the time of such election had affixed to his name in the register of voters at such election the same number as the number written on such counterfoil.—(B.A., rr. 43, 64). Ap. xlvii.-ix.

TABLE showing the Acts in force in the different BOROUGHS, TOWNS, and TOWNSHIPS in IRELAND.

The Towns Improvement (Ireland) Act, 1854 (17 & 18 Vic., c. 103).			Local Acts.	Municipal Reform Act, 1840 (3 & 4 Vic., c. 108), Sched: le A.	Municipal Commissioners (3 & 4 Vic., c. 108).	9 Geo. IV., c. 82.
Antrim.	Coleraine.	Mallow.	Blackrock (co. Dub.)	Belfast.	Carrickfergus.	Armagh.
Ardee.	Cookstown.	Maryborough.	Bray.	Clonmel.		Bandon.
Arklow.	Cootehill.	Midleton.	Clontarf.	Cork.		Downpatrick.
Athlone.	Dromore.	Monumellick.	Dalkey.	Drogheda.		Dungannon.
Athy.	Dundalk.	Mullingar.	Drumcondra.	Dublin.		Fethard.
Aughnacloy.	Dungarvan.	Naas.	Enniskillen.	Kilkenny.		Monaghan.
Bagnalstown.	Ennis.	Navan.	Galway.	Limerick.		Omagh.
Balbriggan.	Enniscorthy.	Nenagh.	Kilmainham.	Londonderry.		Wicklow.
Ballina.	Fermoy.	New Ross.	Kingstown.	Sligo.		Youghal.
Ballinasloe.	Gilford.	Newbridge.	Newry.	Waterford.		
Ballybay.	Gorey.	Newtownards.	Pembroke.	Wexford.		
Ballymena.	Granard.	Parsonstown.	Rathmines.			
Ballymoney.	Holywood.	Portadown.				
Ballyshannon.	Keady.	Queenstown.				
Banbridge.	Kells.	Rathkeale.				
Bangor.	Killarney.	Roscommon.				
Belturbet.	Killiney.	Skibbereen.				
Boyle.	Kilrush.	Strabane.				
Callan.	Kinsale.	Tandragee.				
Carlow.	Lane.	Templemore.				
Carrickmacross.	Letterkenny.	Thurles.				
Carrick-on-Suir.	Limavady.	Tipperary.				
Cashel.	Lisburn.	Tralee.				
Castlebar.	Lismore.	Trim.				
Castleblayney.	Listowel.	Tuam.				
Cavan.	Longford.	Tullamore.				
Clonakilty.	Loughrea.	Warrenpoint.				
Clones.	Lurgan.	Westport.				

* And Local Acts.

Acts of Parliament the whole or portions of which affect Municipal Elections in Ireland.

An Act to make provision for the Lighting, Cleansing, and Watching of Cities, Towns Corporate, and Market Towns in Ireland in certain cases, 1828. (9 Geo. IV., c. 82).

An Act for the more effectual Relief of the Destitute Poor in Ireland, 1838. (1 & 2 Vict., c. 56).

An Act for the regulation of Municipal Corporations in Ireland, 1840. (3 & 4 Vict., c. 108).

An Act to explain and amend certain enactments contained respectively in the Acts for the regulation of Municipal Corporations in *England* and *Wales*, and in *Ireland*, 1842. (5 & 6 Vict., c. 104).

An Act for the further amendment of an Act for the more effectual Relief of the Destitute Poor in Ireland, 1843. (6 & 7 Vict., c. 92).

An Act to amend and explain the Municipal Reform Act, 1840 (1843). (6 & 7 Vict., c. 93).

The Commissioners Clauses Act, 1847. (10 Vict., c. 16).

The Towns Improvement Clauses Act, 1847. (10 & 11 Vict., c. 34).

An Act to amend the Laws which regulate the Qualification and Registration of Parliamentary Voters in *Ireland*, and to alter the Law for rating Immediate Lessors of Premises to the Poor Rate in certain Boroughs, 1850. (13 & 14 Vict., c. 69).

An Act further to explain and amend the Acts for the Regulation of Municipal Corporations in England and Wales and Ireland, 1852. (15 & 16 Vict., c. 5).

An Act to amend the Laws relating to the Valuation of Rateable Property in Ireland, 1852. (15 & 16 Vict., c. 63).

Corrupt Practices Prevention Act, 1854. (17 & 18 Vict., c. 102).

The Towns Improvement (Ireland) Act, 1854. (17 & 18 Vict., c. 103).

The Municipal Elections Act, 1859. (22 Vict., c. 35).

The Representation of the People (Ireland) Act, 1868, (31 & 32 Vict., c. 112).

An Act to amend the Law relating to the legal condition of Aliens and British subjects, 1870. (33 & 44 Vict., c. 14).

An Act to abolish forfeiture for Treason and Felony, and to otherwise amend the Law relating thereto, 1870. (33 & 34 Vict., c. 20).

The Local Government (Ireland) Act, 1871. (34 & 35 Vict., c. 109).

The Ballot Act, 1872. (35 & 36 Vict., c. 33).

The Debtor's (Ireland) Act, 1872. (35 & 36 Vict., c. 57).

The Corrupt Practices (Municipal Elections) Act, 1872. (35 & 36 Vict., c. 60).

The Municipal Elections Act, 1875. (38 & 39 Vict., c. 40).

The Municipal Privilege Act (Ireland), 1875. (39 & 40 Vict., c. 76).

The Public Health (Ireland) Act, 1878 (41 & 42 Vict., c. 52).

The Municipal Elections (Ireland) Act, 1879. (42 & 43 Vict., c. 53).

The Town Councils and Local Boards Acts, 1880. (43 Vict., c. 17).

Statutes (definition of time) Act, 1880. (43 & 44 Vict., c. 9).

The Bankruptcy Act, 1883. (46 & 47 Vict., c. 52).

The Municipal Voters Relief Act, 1885. (48 Vict., c. 9).

The Elections (Hours of Poll) Act 1885. (48 Vict., c. 10).

The Medical Relief Disqualification Removal Act, 1885. (48 & 49 Vict., c. 46).

The Public Bodies Corrupt Practices Act, 1889. (52 & 53 Vict., c. 69).

Special or Local Acts :—

The Rathmines Improvement Act, 1847. (10 & 11 Vict., c. ciiii.)
The Dublin Improvement Act. 1849. (12 & 13 Vict., c. 85).
The Galway Town Improvement Act, 1853. (16 & 17 Vict., c. cc.)
The Rathmines and Rathgar Improvement Act, 1862. (25 Vict., c. xxv.)
The Pembroke Township Act, 1863. (26 & 27 Vict., c. lxxii.)
The Blackrock Township Act, 1863. (26 & 27 Vict., c. cxxi.)
The Bray Township Act, 1866. (29 & 30 Vict., c. cclix.)
The Dalkey Township Act, 1867. (30 & 31 Vict., c. cxxxiv).
The New Kilmainham Township Act, 1868. (31 & 32 Vict., c. cx.)
The Clontarf Township Act, 1869. (32 & 33 Vict., c. lxxxv.)
The Township of Kingstown Act, 1869. (32 & 33 Vict., c. cxxxiii.)
The Enniskillen Borough Improvement Act, 1870. (33 & 34 Vict., c. cxliii.)
The Newry Improvement Act, 1871. (34 & 35 Vict., c. cxcviii.)
The Drumcondra, Clonliffe, and Glasnevin Township Act, 1878. (41 & 42 Vict., c. clvii.)
The Rathmines and Rathgar Improvement Act, 1885. (48 & 49 Vict., c. cli.)
The Municipal Corporation of Belfast Act, 1887. (50 & 51 Vict., c. cxviii.)
The Newry Improvement Act, 1889. (52 & 53 Vict , c. clvii).
The Municipal Registration (Dublin and Belfast) Act, 1891, (54 & 55 Vict., c.   )

ª In the revised edition of the Statutes this Act has been treated as a local and personal one.

APPENDIX.

ERRATA.

Appendix, p. xxxiv. Footnote:—
Read "The first portion of section 6" instead of "Section 6."

APPENDIX.

COMMISSIONERS CLAUSES ACT, 1847.
(10 VICT., c. 16.)

III. The following words and expressions, both in this and the special Act, and any Act incorporated therewith, shall have the several meanings hereby assigned to them, unless there be something in the subject or the context repugnant to such construction; (that is to say,)

> Words importing the singular number only shall include the plural number; and words importing the plural number only shall include the singular number:
>
> Words importing the masculine gender only shall include females:
>
> The word "Person" shall include a corporation, whether aggregate or sole:
>
> The word "Lands" shall extend to messuages, lands, tenements, and hereditaments or heritages of any tenure:
>
> The word "Month" shall mean calendar month:
>
> The expression "Superior Courts," where the matter submitted to the cognizance of the court arises in *England* or *Ireland*, shall mean Her Majesty's Superior Courts of Record at *Westminster* or *Dublin*, as the case may require, and shall include the Court of Common Pleas of the County Palatine of *Lancaster* and the Court of Pleas of the County of *Durham*; and where such matter arises in *Scotland* shall mean the Court of Session:
>
> The word "Oath" shall include affirmation in the case of Quakers, and any declaration lawfully substituted for an oath in the case of any other persons allowed by law to make a declaration instead of taking an oath:
>
> The expression "the Clerk" shall mean the Clerk of the Commissioners, and shall include the word "Secretary":
>
> The expression "the Town" shall mean the town or district named in the special Act within which the powers of the Commissioners are to be exercised.

With respect to the qualification of Commissioners, be it enacted as follows:—

VI. Where by the special Act the qualification of the Commissioners is made to depend upon their being rated in respect of property of a given amount, then if two or more persons be jointly rated in respect of any property, each of such persons shall, subject to the provisions herein and in the special Act contained, be eligible to be chosen a Commissioner, provided the property in respect of which such persons are rated be of a rateable yearly value, which, when divided by the number of persons so rated, will give to each a sufficient rateable yearly value according to the provisions of this and the special Act.

VII. The same property shall not at the same time give a qualification as Commissioner to one person as the owner, and to another as the occupier thereof.

VIII. No bankrupt or insolvent, or person not qualified as required by the special Act, shall be capable of being or continuing a Commissioner.

IX. Any person who at any time after his appointment or election as a Commissioner shall accept or continue to hold any office or place of profit, under the special Act, or be concerned or participate in any manner in any contract, or in the profit thereof or of any work to be done under the authority of such Act, shall thenceforth cease to be a Commissioner, and his office shall thereupon become vacant.

X. Provided always, that no person being a shareholder or member of any joint stock company established by Act of Parliament, shall be prevented from acting as a Commissioner by reason of any contract entered into between such company and the Commissioners; but no such Commissioner, being a member of such company, shall vote on any question relating to the execution of this or the special Act in which such company is interested.

XI. A person shall not be incapable of acting as a Justice of the Peace in the execution of this or the special Act, with reference to the levying of any penalty thereunder, by reason of his being a Commissioner.

XII. No person shall be capable of acting as a Commissioner, except in administering the declaration hereinafter mentioned, until he shall have made and signed, before one of the Commissioners, a declaration to the effect following:—

" I, A. B., do solemnly declare, that I will faithfully and impartially, according to the best of my skill and judgment, execute all the powers and authorities reposed in me as a Commissioner, by virtue of the [*here name the special Act*], and also that I [*here set forth a statement of the possession of the qualification required by the special Act in the terms thereof*]."

XIII. Any person who shall falsely or corruptly make and subscribe the declaration aforesaid, knowing the same to be untrue in any material particular, shall be deemed guilty of a misdemeanour, or in *Scotland* shall be deemed guilty of perjury.

XIV. Every person elected or appointed a Commissioner shall, at the meeting of Commissioners at which he first attends as a Commissioner, make and subscribe the declaration herein required; and any Commissioner, whether he himself have made such declaration or not, may administer such declaration.

XV. Every person who shall act as a Commissioner, being incapacitated or not duly qualified to act, or before he has made or subscribed such declaration as aforesaid, or after having become disqualified, shall for every such offence be liable to a penalty of fifty pounds; and such penalty may be recovered by any person, with full costs of suit, in any of the superior courts; and in every such action, the person sued shall prove that at the time of so acting he was qualified, and had made and subscribed the declaration aforesaid, or he shall pay the said penalty and costs without any other evidence being required from the plaintiff than that such person had acted as a Commissioner in the execution of this or the special Act; nevertheless all Acts as a Commissioner of any person incapacitated, or not duly qualified, or not having made or subscribed the declaration aforesaid, done previously to the recovery of the penalty, shall be as valid as if such person had been duly qualified.

XVI. Every Commissioner who for the space of six months after his appointment neglects to make and subscribe the declaration herein-before required, or who for six months in succession is absent from all meetings of the Commissioners, and to act in the execution of this and the special Act, shall be deemed to have refused to act, and shall cease to be a Commissioner.

And *with respect to the election and rotation of the Commissioners*, where the Commissioners are to be elected by the ratepayers or other like class of electors, be it enacted as follows:

XVII. Where by the special Act it is provided that the Commissioners shall be elected by the ratepayers within the town, or other like class of electors, the first body of Commissioners, whether appointed by the special Act, or elected under the provisions of this and the special Act, shall go out of office according to the prescribed rotation and at the prescribed times, and where no rotation or time of going out of office is prescribed, they shall go out of office by rotation in the following manner; (that is to say,) on the first *Thursday* in the month of *September* in the year following that in which the special Act is passed, one-third of such body of Commissioners shall go out of office, and on the first *Thursday* in *September* in the following year another third of such body of Commissioners shall go out of office, and on the first *Thursday* in *September* in the year following the remainder of such body of Commissioners shall go out of office, and on the first *Thursday* in the month of *September* in every subsequent year, one-third of the Commissioners, being those who have been longest in office, shall go out of office; and in each instance, the places of the retiring Commissioners shall be supplied by the election of a like number of Commissioners in the manner herein or in the special Act provided: Provided always, that if the prescribed number of Commissioners be some number not divisible by three, and the number of Commissioners to retire be not prescribed, the Commissioners shall in each case determine what number of Commissioners, as nearly one-third as may be, shall go out of office, so that no Commissioner shall remain in office longer than **three years** without being re-elected.

XVIII. Every Commissioner going out of office by rotation, or otherwise ceasing to be a Commissioner, may be re-elected; and after such re-election he shall, with reference to going out by rotation, be considered as a new Commissioner.

XIX. If any of the Commissioners die or resign, or be disqualified, or cease to be a Commissioner from any other cause than that of going out of office by rotation, the remaining Commissioners, if they think fit, may, within one month from the happening of such vacancy, elect another Commissioner in his place; and every Commissioner so elected shall continue in office only so long as the person in whose place he is elected would have been entitled to continue in office.

XXII. Where the appointment of the returning officer to act at the election of Commissioners is not provided for by the special Act, the chairman of the Commissioners shall be the returning officer; and if the Commissioners are to be elected for wards, the said chairman shall act as the presiding officer at the election for the ward for which he was elected a Commissioner, and he shall appoint some other Commissioner for each of the other wards to be the presiding officer at the election for such ward; and in case of the death of any such presiding officer, or of his declining or becoming incapable to act, the Commissioners shall appoint another of their body to be the presiding officer in the place of the person so dying or declining, or becoming incapable to act; and the clerk to the Commissioners shall, two days at least before each election, by advertisement, placards, or otherwise, give public notice of every such appointment.

*[XXIV. Where by the special Act the owners of property and ratepayers are entitled to vote in the election of the Commissioners, and no scale of voting is prescribed, every such owner and ratepayer shall have respectively the same number and proportion of votes according to the scale following; (that is to say,)

If the property in respect of which he is entitled to vote be rated upon a rateable value of less than fifty pounds, he shall have one vote:

If such rateable value amount to fifty pounds and be less than one hundred pounds, he shall have two votes:

If it amount to one hundred pounds and be less than one hundred and fifty pounds, he shall have three votes:

If it amount to one hundred and fifty pounds and be less than two hundred pounds, he shall have four votes:

If it amount to two hundred pounds and be less than two hundred and fifty pounds, he shall have five votes:

And if it amount to or exceed two hundred and fifty pounds, he shall have six votes.]

---

* Expressly excepted from incorporation by Towns Improvement Act, 1854, sec. 24.

XXV. Where by the special Act, the Commissioners are directed to be elected for wards, every person entitled to vote in the election of Commissioners shall vote for Commissioners for that ward only wherein the property or part thereof in respect of which his name appears in the rate book is situate; and if any person be rated in respect of property situate in more than one ward, he may vote for Commissioners for any one of such wards; but having so voted he shall not afterwards, at the same election, vote for a Commissioner for any other ward, and any vote so afterwards given by him shall be void.

*[XXVII. If the qualification of the electors of the Commissioners depend upon the rates payable by such electors, the Returning Officer may summon the overseers or inspectors of the poor, collectors, and other officers employed in the assessment or collection of the rates, to attend the election in order to assist in ascertaining that the persons presenting themselves to vote, or who have voted, are or were duly qualified to vote at such election; and such overseers or inspectors, rate collectors, or other officers, shall attend with the rates and such other documents necessary for the purpose aforesaid as may be in their custody or power, at such places and at such times as the Returning Officer may direct, and shall answer all such questions as any presiding officer at the poll shall put to them respecting the title of any person to vote at the election; and any overseer or inspector, rate collector, or other officer who shall wilfully neglect or fail to perform the duties hereby imposed upon him, shall for such neglect or failure be liable to a penalty not exceeding twenty pounds.]

†XXVIII.   *   *   *   *   *   *
The presiding officer shall, if he thinks fit, or if he be required so to do by any person entitled to vote at the said election, put to any voter at the time of his delivering in his voting paper the following questions, or either of them:

‡   *   *   *   *   *   *   *

2. Have you already voted at the present election? [or, *if the Town be divided into Wards*,] Have you already voted for Commissioners to be elected for this or any other ward at the present election?

And no person required to answer either of the said questions shall be permitted or qualified to vote until he has answered the same; and if any person wilfully make a false answer to either of the questions aforesaid he shall be deemed guilty of a misdemeanor, or in *Scotland* shall be deemed guilty of perjury.

* This section is repealed by the Ballot Act, schedule VI.
† The first part of this section is repealed by Polls Hours Act, 1885, and the Ballot Act, schedule VI.
‡ This portion of the section specifying the first question repealed by the Ballot Act.

*[XXIX. The presiding officer, at any place of voting, may close the voting or poll at any time before four of the clock, if one hour have elapsed during which no voting paper has been tendered at such place of voting.]

†XXX. After the close of the poll *   *   *   *
so many of such persons, being not more than the number of persons then to be chosen for the town or for each ward, as the case may be, and having the prescribed qualification, as shall have the greatest number of votes shall be deemed to be elected; and in case of an equality in the number of votes for any two or more such persons, the presiding officer shall, if necessary to prevent an excess in the number of Commissioners, decide by lot which of such persons shall be elected; and the presiding officer shall, not later than two of the clock in the afternoon of the day next but one following the day of such election, unless such day be *Sunday*, and then on the day following, publish a list of the names of the persons so elected, and he shall also send a notice to each person so elected, informing him of his being elected a Commissioner.

XXXII. If any person be elected a Commissioner in more than one ward, he shall, within three days after notice thereof, choose, or in default thereof the Commissioners at their next meeting shall declare, for which one of the wards such Commissioner shall serve, and he shall thereupon be held to be elected in that ward only which he shall so choose or which the Commissioners shall so declare, and shall cease to be a Commissioner for any other ward.

XXXIII. If from any cause, no election take place on the day appointed for the same either for the town or for any ward, the election shall stand adjourned until the same day of the following week, and the Returning Officer shall give not less than three days' previous notice thereof by advertisement, or by placards affixed in public places in the town; and in such case, the Commissioners who would on that day have retired from office by rotation shall continue in office until such adjourned election takes place.

XXXIV. No election of Commissioners shall be liable to be questioned by reason only of any defect in the title, or any want of title, of the person by or before whom such election shall have been held; provided that such person have been actually appointed to preside, or have been acting in the office giving the right to preside at such election.

XXXV. All expenses of or incident to any election incurred by the Returning Officer or presiding officer shall be repaid to them by the Commissioners out of the moneys arising from the rates

---

* Repealed by Polls Hours Act, 1885.
† First part of this section repealed by the Ballot Act, schedule VI.

authorized to be levied for the purposes of the special Act; and all overseers and other parochial officers or other persons shall be, in like manner paid a reasonable remuneration for attendance at the election with rate books, and for any other services performed in relation to such election; and any dispute respecting the amount of such remuneration shall be determined by a justice, or by the sheriff, who shall have power also to fix the costs attending such determination, and to order by whom the same shall be paid.

And *with respect to the meetings and other proceedings of the Commissioners, and their liabilities*, be it enacted as follows:—

XXXVII. At the first meeting of the Commissioners, they shall, by the majority of the votes of the Commissioners present, elect one of their body to be their Chairman until the next annual meeting of the Commissioners, when, and at every subsequent annual meeting, the Commissioners shall in like manner elect a Chairman for the ensuing year; and in case the Chairman die, or resign, or cease to be a Commissioner, or otherwise become disqualified to act as such, the Commissioners present at the meeting next after the occurrence of such vacancy shall choose some other of their body to fill such vacancy, and the Chairman so elected shall continue in office so long only as the person in whose place he was elected would have been entitled to continue Chairman; and if at any meeting of the Commissioners the Chairman be not present, one of the Commissioners present shall be elected Chairman of such meeting by the majority of the votes of the Commissioners present at such meeting.

XXXVIII. At all meetings of the Commissioners, the questions there considered shall be decided by the votes of the majority present, and if there be an equal division of votes upon any question, the Chairman or Commissioner acting as Chairman at such meeting shall, in addition to his own vote as a Commissioner, have a second or casting vote: Provided always, that if at any such meeting there be an equality of votes in the election of the Chairman, it shall be decided by lot which of the Commissioners having an equal number of votes shall be the Chairman: Provided also, that at every annual meeting the Chairman going out of office at that meeting shall, if present and willing to act, be the Chairman of such meeting.

TOWNS IMPROVEMENT CLAUSES ACT, 1847.
(10 & 11 Vict., c. 34.)

174. The Commissioners may from time to time amend any rate made by virtue of this or the special Act by inserting therein the name of any person claiming and entitled to have his name therein as owner or occupier, or by inserting therein the name of any person who ought to have been rated, or by striking out the name of any person who ought not to have been rated, or by raising or

reducing the sum at which any person has been rated if it appear to them that such person has been under-rated or over-rated, or by making such other amendments therein as will make such rate conformable to this and the special Act, and no such amendment shall be held to avoid the rate: Provided always, that every person aggrieved by any such alteration shall have the same right of appeal therefrom as he would have had if his name had been originally inserted in such rate, and no such alteration had been made; and as respects such person, the rates shall be considered to have been made at the time when he received notice of such alteration; and every person whose rates are altered shall be entitled to seven days' notice of such alteration before the rate shall be payable by him.

175. The annual value of all property rateable under this or the special Act shall be ascertained according to the next preceding assessment for the relief of the poor within the limits of the special Act, except in such cases as are hereinafter mentioned.

178. The Commissioners or any person by them authorized, may from time to time inspect any of the rates for the relief of the poor in any parish, township, or other district within the limits of the special Act, and the books in which are contained all the assessments by which the same are made, and may take copies thereof or extracts therefrom respectively; and any person having the custody of such rates or assessments who does not suffer the Commissioners, or any person authorized by them, to inspect the same at reasonable times, or to take copies thereof or extracts therefrom, shall be liable to a penalty not exceeding five pounds for every such offence.

181. The owners of all rateable property, of which the full net annual value does not exceed the prescribed sum, or (where no sum is prescribed) the sum of ten pounds, or which are let to weekly or monthly tenants, or in separate apartments, shall be rated to and pay the rates by this or the special Act directed to be made, instead of the occupiers thereof.

184. Provided also, that the occupiers of any rateable property, being tenants thereof from year to year, may demand to be assessed for the same, and to pay the rates in respect thereof made under the authority of this or the special Act; and the Commissioners shall assess every such occupier so long as he duly pays the said rates.

(13 & 14 Vict., c. 69.)

An Act to amend the laws which regulate the qualification and registration of Parliamentary Voters in *Ireland*, and to alter the law for rating immediate lessors of premises to the Poor rate in certain Boroughs. [14th August, 1850].

88. That in all elections whatever of a member or members to serve in Parliament for any county, or for any city, town, or

borough in Ireland, holden after the fifteenth day of March, one thousand eight hundred and fifty-one, no inquiry shall be permitted at the time of polling as to the right of any person to vote, nor any objection thereto made or received by any returning officer or his deputy, except only as follows ; (that is to say) that the returning officer or his respective deputy shall, if required on behalf of any candidate, put to any voter at the time of his tendering his vote, and not afterwards, the following questions, or either of them :—

1. " Are you the same person whose name appears as *A. B.* on the register of voters now in force for the county of [or for the city, or town, or borough of   as the case may be] ? "

2. " Have you already voted, either here or elsewhere, at this election for the county of   [or for the city, or town, or borough of   as the case may be] ? "

And if any person shall wilfully make a false answer to either of the questions aforesaid, he shall be deemed guilty of a misdemeanour, and shall and may be indicted and punished accordingly ; and the returning officer or his deputy, or a Commissioner or Commissioners (whom the returning officer is hereby authorized, if he shall think fit, to appoint for that purpose), shall, if required on behalf of any candidate at the time aforesaid, administer an oath, or (in the case of a Quaker, Moravian, or Separatist) an affirmation, to any voter in the following form :

" You do swear [or affirm, as the case may be] that you are the same person whose name appears as *A. B.* on the register of voters now in force for the county of   [or for the city, or town, or borough of   as the case may be], and that you have not before voted, either here or elsewhere, at the present election for the county of   [or for the city, or town, or borough of   as the case may be]. "So help you God."

89. That, save as aforesaid, it shall not be lawful to require any voter at any election whatever of a member or members to serve in Parliament [holden after the fifteenth day of March, one thousand eight hundred and fifty-one*], to take any note or affirmation, either in proof of his freehold, occupation, or of his residence, age, or other qualification or right to vote, or of his qualification continuing, or of his not owing any cesses, rates, or taxes whatsoever, any law or statute, local or general, to the contrary notwithstanding, nor to reject any vote tendered at such election by any person whose name shall be upon the register of voters in force for the time being, except by reason of its appearing to the returning officer or his deputy, upon putting such questions as aforesaid or either of them, that the person so claiming to vote is

*Repealed by Statute Law Revision Act, 1878.

not the same person whose name appears on such register as aforesaid, or that he had previously voted at the same election, or except by reason of such person refusing to answer the said questions or either of them, or to take the said oath or to make the said affirmation, or to take or make the oath or affirmation against bribery; and no scrutiny shall hereafter be allowed by or before any returning officer with regard to any vote given or tendered at any such election, any law, statute, or usage to the contrary notwithstanding.

90. That if at any election of a member or members to serve in Parliament for any county, city, town, or borough in Ireland, holden at any time after the fifteenth day of March, one thousand eight hundred and fifty-one, any person shall knowingly personate and falsely assume to vote in the name of any other person registered under the provisions of the said recited Act to amend the representation of the people of Ireland, or whose name appears on the register of voters then in force for any such county, city, town, or borough, whether such other person shall then be living or dead, or if the name of the said other person be the name of a fictitious person, every such person shall be guilty of a misdemeanour, and on being convicted thereof shall be punished by imprisonment for a term not exceeding two years, together with hard labour.

91. That every person who shall aid, abet, counsel, or procure the commission of any such last-mentioned misdemeanor shall be liable to be indicted and punished as a principal offender.

92. And for the more effectual detection of the personation of electors at elections, be it enacted, that it shall be lawful for any candidate at any election of a member or members to serve in Parliament for any county, city, town, or borough (holden after the fifteenth day of March, one thousand eight hundred and fifty-one), previous to the time fixed for taking the poll at such election, to nominate and appoint an agent or agents in his behalf, to attend at each or any of the booths appointed for taking the poll at such election, for the purpose of detecting personation; and such candidate shall give notice in writing to the returning officer or his respective deputy of the name and address of the person or persons so appointed by him to act as agents for such purpose, and thereupon it shall be lawful for every such agent to attend during the time of polling, at the booth or booths for which he shall have been so appointed.

93. That if at the time any person tenders his vote at such election, or after he has voted, and before he leaves the polling booth, any such agent so appointed as aforesaid shall declare to the returning officer or his respective deputy presiding therein, that he verily believes and undertakes to prove, that the said person so voting is not, in fact, the person in whose name he assumes to vote, or to the like effect, then, and in every such

case, it shall be lawful for the said returning officer or his said deputy, and he is hereby required immediately after such person shall have voted by word of mouth to order any constable or other peace officer to take the said person so voting into his custody, which said order shall be a sufficient warrant and authority to the said constable or peace officer for so doing : Provided always, that nothing herein contained shall be construed or taken to authorise any returning officer or his deputy to reject the vote of any person who shall answer in the affirmative the questions authorised by this Act to be put to him at the time of polling, and shall take the oaths or make the affirmations authorised and required of him, but the said returning officer or his deputy shall cause the words "protested against for personation" to be placed against the vote of the person so charged with personation when entered in the poll book.

94. That every such constable or peace officer shall take the person so in his custody, at the earliest convenient time, before some two justices of the peace acting in and for the county, city, town or borough within which the said person shall have so voted as aforesaid : Provided always, that in case the attendance of two such justices as aforesaid cannot be procured within the space of three hours after the close of the poll on the same day on which such person shall have been so taken into custody, it shall be lawful for the said constable or peace officer, and he is hereby required, at the request of such person so in his custody, to take him before any one Justice of the Peace acting as aforesaid ; and such Justice is hereby authorised and required to liberate such person, on his entering into a recognizance, with one sufficient surety, conditioned to appear before any two such justices as aforesaid, at a time and place to be specified in such recognizance, to answer the said charge ; and if no such justice shall be found within four hours after the closing of the said poll, then such person shall forthwith be discharged from custody : Provided also, that if, in consequence of the absence of such justices as aforesaid, or from any other cause, the said charge cannot be inquired into within the time aforesaid, it shall be lawful nevertheless for any two such justices as aforesaid to inquire into the same on the next, or on some other subsequent day, and, if necessary, to issue their warrant for the apprehension of the person so charged.

95. That if, on the hearing of the said charge, the said two justices shall be satisfied, upon the evidence on oath of not less than two credible witnesses, that the said person so brought before them has knowingly personated and falsely assumed to vote in the name of some other person within the meaning of this Act, and is not in fact the person in whose name he voted, then it shall be lawful for the said two justices to commit the said offender to the gaol of the county, city, town, or borough within which the

offence was committed, to take his trial according to law, and to bind over the witnesses in their respective recognizances to appear and give evidence on such trial, as in the case of other misdemeanors.

96. That if the said justices shall, on the hearing of the said charge, be satisfied that the said person so charged with personation, is really and in truth the person in whose name he voted, and that the charge of personation has been made against him without reasonable or just cause, or if the agent so declaring as aforesaid, or some one on his behalf, shall not appear to support such charge before the said justices, then it shall be lawful for the said justices, and they are hereby required to make an order in writing under their hands on the said agent so declaring as aforesaid to pay to the said person so falsely charged, if he shall consent to accept the same, any sum not exceeding the sum of ten pounds nor less than five pounds by way of damages and costs; and if the said sum shall not be paid within twenty-four hours after such order shall have been made, then the same shall be levied, by warrant under the hand and seal of any justice of the peace acting as aforesaid by distress and sale of the goods and chattels of the said agent; and in case no sufficient goods or chattels of the said agent can be found on which such levy can be made, then the same shall be levied in like manner on the goods and chattels of the candidate by whom such agent was so appointed to act; and in case the said sum shall not be paid or levied in the manner aforesaid, then it shall be lawful for the said person to whom the said sum of money was so ordered to be paid to recover the same from the said agent or candidate, by civil bill, or, with full costs of suit, in an action of debt to be brought in any one of Her Majesty's superior courts of Record at Dublin: Provided always, that if the person so falsely charged shall have declared to the said justices his consent to accept such sum as aforesaid by way of damages and costs, and if the whole amount of the sum so ordered to be paid shall have been paid or tendered to such person, in every such case, but not otherwise, the said agent, candidate, and every other person shall be released from all actions or other proceedings, civil or criminal, for or in respect of the said charge and apprehension.

97. That it shall and may be lawful for the high sheriff of any county, and for the mayor or returning officer of any city, town, or borough, and he and they are hereby required, for the purposes aforesaid, to provide a sufficient attendance of constables or peace officers in each booth at the different polling places within their respective counties, cities, towns, or boroughs.

THE CORRUPT PRACTICES PREVENTION ACT, 1854.
(17 & 18 Vict., c. 102.)

II. The following persons shall be deemed guilty of bribery, and shall be punished accordingly :

1. Every person who shall, directly or indirectly, by himself, or by any other person on his behalf, give, lend, or agree to give or lend, or shall offer, promise, or promise to procure or to endeavour to procure, any money, or valuable consideration, to or for any voter, or to or for any person on behalf of any voter, or to or for any other person in order to induce any voter to vote, or refrain from voting, or shall corruptly do any such act as aforesaid, on account of such voter having voted or refrained from voting at any election :

2. Every person who shall, directly or indirectly, by himself or by any other person on his behalf, give or procure, or agree to give or procure, or offer, promise, or promise to procure or to endeavour to procure, any office, place, or employment to or for any voter, or to or for any person on behalf of any voter, or to or for any other person, in order to induce such voter to vote, or refrain from voting, or shall corruptly do any such act as aforesaid, on account of any voter having voted or refrained from voting at any election :

3. Every person who shall, directly or indirectly, by himself, or by any other person on his behalf, make any such gift, loan, offer, promise, procurement, or agreement as aforesaid, to or for any person, in order to induce such person to procure, or endeavour to procure, the return of any person to serve in Parliament, or the vote of any voter at any election :

4. Every person who shall, upon or in consequence of any such gift, loan, offer, promise, procurement, or agreement, procure or engage, promise, or endeavour to procure the return of any person to serve in Parliament, or the vote of any voter at any election :

5. Every person who shall advance or pay, or cause to be paid, any money to or to the use of any other person with the intent that such money or any part thereof shall be expended in bribery at any election, or who shall knowingly pay or cause to be paid any money to any person in discharge or repayment of any money wholly or in part expended in bribery at any election :

And any person so offending shall be guilty of a misdemeanor, and in *Scotland* of an offence punishable by fine and imprisonment, and shall also be liable to forfeit the sum of one hundred pounds to any person who shall sue for the same, together with full costs of suit: Provided always, that the aforesaid enactment shall not extend or be construed to extend to any money paid or agreed to be paid for or on account of any legal expenses *bonâ fide* incurred at or concerning any election.

III. The following persons shall also be deemed guilty of bribery, and shall be punishable accordingly:

1. Every voter who shall, before or during any election, directly or indirectly, by himself or by any other person on his behalf, receive, agree, or contract for any money, gift, loan, or valuable consideration, office, place, or employment, for himself or for any other person, for voting or agreeing to vote, or for refraining or agreeing to refrain from voting, at any election :
2. Every person who shall, after any election, directly or indirectly, by himself or by any other person on his behalf, receive any money or valuable consideration on account of any person having voted or refrained from voting, or having induced any other person to vote or to refrain from voting, at any election :

And any person so offending shall be guilty of a misdemeanor and in *Scotland* of an offence punishable by fine and imprisonment, and shall also be liable to forfeit the sum of ten pounds to any person who shall sue for the same, together with full costs of suit.

IV. Every candidate at an election, who shall corruptly by himself, or by or with any person, or by any other ways or means on his behalf, at any time, either before, during, or after any election, directly or indirectly give or provide, or cause to be given or provided, or shall be accessory to the giving or providing, or shall pay, wholly or in part, any expenses incurred for any meat, drink, entertainment, or provision to or for any person, in order to be elected, or for being elected, or for the purpose of corruptly influencing such person or any other person to give or refrain from giving his vote at such election, or on account of such person having voted or refrained from voting, or being about to vote or refrain from voting, at such election, shall be deemed guilty of the offence of treating, and shall forfeit the sum of fifty pounds to any person who shall sue for the same, with full costs of suit; and every voter who shall corruptly accept or take any such meat, drink, entertainment, or provision, shall be incapable of voting at such election, and his vote, if given, shall be utterly void and of none effect.

V. Every person who shall, directly or indirectly, by himself, or by any other person on his behalf, make use of, or threaten to make use of, any force, violence, or restraint, or inflict or threaten the infliction, by himself or by or through any other person, of any injury, damage, harm, or loss, or in any other manner practice intimidation upon or against any person in order to induce or compel such person to vote or refrain from voting, or on account of such person having voted or refrained from voting, at any election, or who shall, by abduction, duress, or any fraudulent device or contrivance, impede, prevent, or otherwise interfere with the free exercise of the franchise of any voter, or shall thereby compel, induce, or prevail upon any voter, either to give or to refrain from giving his vote at any election, shall be deemed to have committed the offence of undue influence, and shall be guilty of a misdemeanor, and in *Scotland* of an offence punishable by fine or imprisonment, and shall also be liable to forfeit the sum of fifty pounds to any person who shall sue for the same, together with full costs of suit.

VI. Whenever it shall be proved before the revising barrister that any person who is or claims to be placed on the list or register of voters for any county, city, or borough has been convicted of bribery or undue influence at an election, or that judgment has been obtained against any such person for any penal sum hereby made recoverable in respect of the offences of bribery, treating, or undue influence, or either of them, then and in that case such revising barrister shall, in case the name of such person is in the list of voters, expunge the same therefrom, or shall, in case such person is claiming to have his name inserted therein, disallow such claim; and the names of all persons whose names shall be so expunged from the list of voters, and whose claims shall be so disallowed, shall be thereupon inserted in a separate list, to be entitled "the list of persons disqualified for bribery, treating, or undue influence," which last-mentioned list shall be appended to the list or register of voters, and shall be printed and published therewith, wherever the same shall be or is required to be printed or published.

VII. No candidate before, during, or after any election shall in regard to such election, by himself or agent, directly or indirectly, give or provide to or for any person having a vote at such election, or to or for any inhabitant of the county, city, borough, or place for which such election is had, any cockade, ribbon, or other mark of distinction; and every person so giving or providing shall for every such offence forfeit the sum of two pounds to such person as shall sue for the same, together with full costs of suit; and all payments made for or on account of any chairing, or any such cockade, ribbon, or mark of distinction as aforesaid, or of any bands of music or flags or banners, shall be deemed illegal payments within this Act.

VIII. No person having a right to vote at the election for any county, city, borough, or other place shall be liable or compelled to serve as a special constable at or during any election for a member or members to serve in Parliament for such county, city, borough, or other place, unless he shall consent so to act; and he

B

shall not be liable to any fine, penalty, or punishment whatever for refusing so to act, any statute, law, or usage to the contrary notwithstanding.

IX. The pecuniary penalties hereby imposed for the offences of bribery, treating, or undue influence respectively shall be recoverable by action or suit by any person who shall sue for the same in any of Her Majesty's superior courts at *Westminster*, if the offence be committed in *England* or *Wales*, and in any of Her Majesty's superior courts in *Dublin* if the offence be committed in *Ireland*, and in or before the Court of Session if the offence be committed in *Scotland*, and not otherwise.

X. It shall be lawful for any criminal court, before which any prosecution shall be instituted for any offence against the provisions of this Act, to order payment to the prosecutor of such costs and expenses as to the said court shall appear to have been reasonably incurred in and about the conduct of such prosecution: Provided always, that no indictment for bribery or undue influence shall be triable before any Court of Quarter Sessions.

[Section XI. repealed by Ballot Act].

XII. In case of any indictment or information by a private prosecutor for any offence against the provisions of this Act, if judgment shall be given for the defendant, he shall be entitled to recover from the prosecutor the costs sustained by the defendant by reason of such indictment or information, such costs to be taxed by the proper officer of the court in which such judgment shall be given.

XIII. It shall not be lawful for any court to order payment of the costs of a prosecution for any offence against the provisions of this Act, unless the prosecutor shall, before or upon the finding of the indictment or the granting of the information, enter into a recognizance, with two sufficient sureties in the sum of two hundred pounds (to be acknowledged in like manner as is now required in cases of writs of certiorari awarded at the instance of a defendant in an indictment), with the conditions following; that is to say, that the prosecutor shall conduct the prosecution with effect, and shall pay to the defendant or defendants, in case he or they shall be acquitted, his or their costs.

XIV. No person shall be liable to any penalty or forfeiture hereby enacted or imposed, unless some prosecution, action, or suit for the offence committed shall be commenced against such person within the space of one year next after such offence against this Act shall be committed, and unless such person shall be summoned or otherwise served with writ or process within the same space of time, so as such summons or service of writ or process shall not be prevented by such person absconding or withdrawing out of the jurisdiction of the court out of which such writ or other process shall have issued ; and in case of any such prosecution, suit, or process as aforesaid, the same shall be proceeded with and carried on without any wilful delay.

XXIII. And whereas doubts have also arisen as to whether the giving of refreshment to voters on the day of nomination or day of polling be or be not according to law, and it is expedient that such doubts should be removed: Be it declared and enacted, that the giving or causing to be given to any voter on the day of nomination or day of polling, on account of such voter having polled or being about to poll, any meat, drink, or entertainment by way of refreshment, or any money or ticket to enable such voter to obtain refreshment, shall be deemed an illegal act, and the person so offending shall forfeit the sum of forty shillings for each offence, to any person who shall sue for the same, together with full costs of suit.

XXXV. On the trial of any action for recovery of any pecuniary penalty under this Act, the parties to such action, and the husbands and wives of such parties respectively, shall be competent and compellable to give evidence in the same manner as parties, and their husbands and wives, are competent and compellable to give evidence in actions and suits under the Act of the fourteenth and fifteenth *Victoria*, chapter ninety-nine, and "The Evidence Amendment Act, 1853," but subject to and with the exceptions contained in such several Acts: Provided always, that any such evidence shall not thereafter be used in any indictment or criminal proceeding under this Act against the party giving it.

XXXVI. If any candidate at an election for any county, city, or borough shall be declared by any election committee guilty, by himself or his agents, of bribery, treating, or undue influence at such election, such candidate shall be incapable of being elected or sitting in Parliament for such county, city, or borough during the Parliament then in existence.

XXXVII. In citing this Act in any instrument, document, or proceeding, or for any purpose whatsoever, it shall be sufficient to use the expression "The Corrupt Practices Prevention Act, 1854."

XXXVIII. Throughout this Act, in the construction thereof, except there be something in the subject or context repugnant to such construction, the word "county" shall extend to and mean any county, riding, parts, or division of a county, stewartry, or combined counties respectively returning a member or members to serve in Parliament; and the words "city or borough" shall mean any university, city, borough, town corporate, county of a city, county of a town, Cinque Port, district of burghs, or other place or combination of places (not being a county as herein-before defined) returning a member or members to serve in Parliament; and the word "election" shall mean the election of any member or members to serve in Parliament; and the words "returning officer" shall apply to any person or persons to whom, by virtue of his or their office, under any law, custom, or statute, the execution of any writ or precept doth or shall belong for the election of a member or members to serve in Parliament, by whatever name or title such person or persons may be called; and the words "revising barrister" shall extend to and include an assistant barrister and chairman presiding in any court held for the revision of the list of voters, or his deputy in *Ireland*, and a sheriff or sheriff's court of appeal in *Scotland*, and every other person whose duty it may be to hold a court for the revision and correction of the lists or registers of voters in any part of the United Kingdom; and the word "voter" shall mean any person who has or claims to have a right to vote in the election of a member or members to serve in Parliament; and the words "candidate at an election" shall include all persons elected as members to serve in Parliament at such election, and all persons nominated as candidates, or who shall have declared themselves candidates at or before such election; and the words "personal expenses," as used herein with respect to the expenditure of any candidate in relation to any election, shall include the reasonable travelling expenses of such candidate, and the reasonable expenses of his living at hotels or elsewhere for the purposes of and in relation to such election.

TOWNS IMPROVEMENT (IRELAND) ACT, 1854.

17 & 18 VICT., c. 103.

I. The following words and expressions in this Act shall have the meanings hereby assigned to them, unless there be something in the subject or context repugnant to such construction; (that is to say,) the word "town" shall mean and include a city, town corporate, borough, market town, or other town in *Ireland*, containing a population of one thousand five hundred inhabitants or upwards, as ascertained by their last population returns made pursuant to Act of Parliament;   *   *   *   *   *   the word "person," and words applying to any person or individual, shall apply to and include corporations; the word "householder" shall mean a male occupier of a dwelling-house, or of any lands, tenements, or hereditaments within the prescribed boundaries of the town rated to the relief of the poor in respect thereof; the word "occupier" shall extend to and include an immediate lessor made liable under this Act to assessments in cases of premises of such small annual value as herein-after mentioned respectively in that behalf, and such word "occupier" shall not include a lodger or a party in the occupation as tenant of a furnished house let for a less period than one year, but shall include the party by whom such furnished house is so let; the expression "lodging-house" shall mean a house in which lodgers are housed for a less period than one week at a time, at an amount not exceeding four pence *per* head *per* night; the word "county" shall include a county of a city or county of a town; the expression "the Commissioners" shall mean a majority of the Commissioners for the purposes of this Act acting in and for a town by which this Act has been in whole or in part adopted; . . . . . . the word "lands" and the word "premises" shall include all lands, springs, dwelling-houses, shops, warehouses, vaults, cellars, stables, breweries, manufactories, mills, and other houses and buildings, and yards and places; the word "street" shall extend to and include any road, bridge, lane, square, court, alley, and thoroughfare or public passage; the word "oath" shall include affirmation in the case of Quakers, and declaration in the case of persons allowed by law to make a declaration in lieu of an oath; the word "owner" used with reference to any lands or premises in respect of which any work is required to be done, or any assessment paid under this Act, shall mean the person for the time entitled to receive, or who, if such lands or premises were let to a tenant at a rackrent, would be entitled to receive the rackrent from the occupier thereof; . . . . . . the expression "rackrent" shall mean rent which is not less than two-thirds of the full net annual value of the property out of which the rent arises, and the full net annual value shall (save as regards any valuation for poor rates or valuation for assessments under this Act) be taken to be the rent at which the property ought reasonably to be expected to let from year to year, free from all quit rent, head rent, ground rent, and usual tenants' rates and taxes, and deducting therefrom the probable annual cost of the repairs, insurance, and other expenses (if any) necessary to maintain the same in a state to command such rent; . . . . . . the expression "lawful day" shall mean a day not being *Sunday*, *Christmas Day*, or *Good Friday*, and when any number of days is appointed by this Act the same shall be construed to mean such lawful days, and be computed inclusive of the first and exclusive of the last of such days; words importing the singular number shall include the plural number, and words importing the plural number shall include the singular number; and words importing the masculine gender (except only the word "male") shall include females.

XVI. The Commissioners for the purpose of executing this Act, to be elected as herein provided, shall be in number not less than nine nor more than twenty-one, as may be determined as aforesaid, such number to be divisible by three; and where the town shall be divided into wards as aforesaid, the number thereof, and the number of Commissioners to be elected, shall be so settled and adjusted that there shall be not less than three such Commissioners for each such ward.

XVII. In any town where the Act of the ninth year of King George the Fourth, chapter eighty-two, shall be in force, and by which town application shall be made and proceedings had in manner aforesaid under this Act, then, from and after the first election of Commissioners under this Act for such town, the said Act of the ninth year of King *George* the Fourth shall be no longer in force therein, save and except as to matters or things theretofore done. . . . . .

XIX. From and after the commencement of this Act it shall not be lawful for the Lord Lieutenant of Ireland to order or direct any meeting to be called or convened for the purpose of carrying the said Act of the ninth year of King *George* the Fourth, chapter eighty-two, into execution.

XXII. At such first and every other meeting for the election of Commissioners in said town as hereinafter prescribed such persons as next hereinafter mentioned shall be admitted and entitled to vote, and no other person whatsoever; that is to say, every person of full age who is the immediate lessor of lands, tenements, and hereditaments within such town, or within such boundaries of the same respectively as aforesaid, of the value of fifty pounds or upwards according to the last poor law valuation, and who shall reside within five miles of the boundary of such town, also every person of full age who shall have occupied as tenant or owner or joint occupier, or shall have been the immediate lessor (rated for such premises to the relief of the poor to the net annual value of four pounds or upwards, and in the case of joint occupiers rated in respect of premises of the net annual value of four pounds or upwards for each of such joint occupiers) of any lands, tenements, or hereditaments within such town, or within such boundaries of the same respectively as aforesaid, and shall have been rated in respect of such premises for the period of twelve months preceding the first day of January in the year in which any such election shall be held, under the Acts for the relief of the destitute poor in Ireland, and shall have paid all such poor rates as aforesaid as shall have become payable by him in respect of such premises and all Grand Jury Rates, and all such rates as shall have become payable by him under any Local Act in force in the city or town or under this Act, except such as shall have become payable within six months next preceding such election; and of the payment or nonpayment of such rate, a receipt, certificate, or certified list, under the hand of the collector of poor rate, the barony collector, and the collector under any Local Act in force in the city or town, shall for such purpose be deemed sufficient evidence, and which certificate or certified list such collectors and barony constables are hereby required to furnish to the person or persons presiding at such election; and if any controversy shall arise at such meeting as to the qualification or right to vote of any person claiming to vote or to be qualified, such controversy shall be determined by the person or persons presiding at such meeting upon reference to the rate book, which the Clerk of the Union is hereby required to produce at such meeting.

XXIII. The day upon which one-third of the Commissioners elected under this Act shall annually go out of office, as hereinafter provided, shall be the fifteenth day of October in each year, or the next lawful day thereto, and on the same day annually the places of Commissioners going out of office shall be supplied by an equal number of newly elected Commissioners, to be chosen from among the householders or occupiers of the town, qualified to be Commissioners, as hereinafter prescribed; and where the town is divided into wards, the place of each Commissioner going out of office shall in all cases under this Act be filled up by the ward which returned him: provided always, that if such first election of Commissioners under this Act shall take place before the fifteenth day of October in the year of such election, the Commissioners then first elected shall all continue in office until the fifteenth day of October in the year next ensuing that in which such election shall have been held, or the next lawful day afterwards.

XXIV. Save as hereinbefore in that behalf provided, so much of " The Commissioners Clauses Act, 1847," as relates to the election and rotation of the Commissioners, save so much thereof as relates to the scale of votes of owners and occupiers, shall be incorporated with and read as part of this Act; and that wherever in the portions of said Act so incorporated, or in any other portions of said Act, or of "The Towns Improvement Clauses Act, 1847," hereinafter incorporated with this Act, the expression "Special Act" occurs, same shall be construed, but so far only as relates to towns which shall adopt the provisions of this Act, to mean this Act, and shall be read as if, instead of such expression, there were inserted in such provisions the words "The Towns Improvement (Ireland) Act, 1854," as applied to any particular town adopting the provisions of this Act and of the Acts incorporated herewith.

And with respect to the qualification of Commissioners, be it enacted as follows:

XXV. Every person who shall have been for twelve months preceding the first day of January in the year in which such election is held the immediate lessor of lands, tenements, and hereditaments within such town, or within such boundaries of the same respectively as aforesaid, of the value of fifty pounds or upwards, according to the last poor law valuation, and who shall reside within five miles of the boundary of such town, and also any householder or occupier of full age rated to the relief of the poor in respect of a dwelling-house in the town at the net annual value of twelve pounds or upwards, not being an ecclesiastic of any religious denomination, shall be eligible to be elected a Commissioner for the purposes of this Act, and may be proposed at such meeting by any householder or occupier qualified to vote under the provision hereinbefore contained, and may be seconded by any other householder or occupier qualified to vote as aforesaid.

XXVI. So much of "The Commissioners Clauses Act, 1847," as relates to the qualification of the Commissioners shall be incorporated with and read as part of this Act.

XXVIII. Save as herein in that behalf provided, so much of "The Commissioners Clauses Act, 1847," as relates to the meetings and other proceedings of the Commissioners, and their liabilities, shall be incorporated with and read as part of this Act.

And with respect to general assessments under this Act, be it enacted as follows:

LX. Once in each year the Commissioners shall assess all occupiers of premises within the town, and the boundaries thereof as before determined on and declared and settled, rated in respect of such premises under the Acts for the relief of the destitute poor in the sums necessary to be levied for the purposes of this Act, other than by way of private or district assessments, and shall fix a day, not being less than one month from the date of laying on such assessment, on which the same shall be payable; and the rate of assessment, and day so fixed by the Commissioners, shall be published by handbills posted in the town, and by advertisement in any newspaper or newspapers published therein (if any), or otherwise in some newspaper or newspapers published nearest to such city or town: provided that such assessment other than private and district assessments shall not in any year exceed the rate of one shilling and sixpence in the pound where the enactments of this Act with respect to water have been adopted, or the rate of one shilling in the pound where such enactments with respect to water have not been adopted; provided that all unoccupied houses, tenements, or premises, being at the time of such assessment unproductive to the lessors or landlords thereof, shall be exempt from taxation under this Act during the period that such premises are so unoccupied and unproductive, and no longer.

LXI. The clerk of the union shall, on the requisition of the Commissioners, produce the rate book of the union, and the said Commissioners shall annually cause to be made up a book of assessment, to be signed by the chairman and two others of the Commissioners, showing the net annual value of the whole premises in the town under the poor law valuation liable to be assessed under this Act, and according to which the assessments under this Act are intended to be levied; and such book of assessment shall be open to inspection by all ratepayers, in the hands of the clerk; and the Commissioners shall have power to rectify any mistake or error, upon the ground of any variance from the last assessment for poor rates, or on the ground of any change of occupation of premises since such last assessment for poor rates; and in each year a copy of the said book of assessment, as finally adjusted by the Commissioners, signed by the chairman and two Commissioners, and countersigned by the clerk, shall be delivered over to the collector, as the rule for levying and collecting the annual assessment under this Act, and shall be deemed to be evidence of each and every separate assessment for the purposes of this Act.

LXIV. Whenever the net annual value of the rateable hereditaments in any such town actually occupied by any person or persons shall not exceed four pounds the assessment under this Act in respect of such property shall be made on the immediate lessor or lessors of such person or persons ; and if at the time of making any such assessment the name of the immediate lessor be not accurately known to the persons making the assessment, it shall be sufficient to describe him therein as " the immediate lessor," with or without any name or further addition, and such assessment shall be held to be duly made on him by such description, and shall be recoverable from him accordingly, notwithstanding any error or defect in his name or description, or the entire omission of his name therein : provided, that wherever any occupier shall claim to be and shall be accordingly rated to the relief of the poor although the net annual value of the rateable hereditaments occupied in any town by such person shall not exceed four pounds, the assessment under this Act shall be made upon the person so claiming to be rated to the relief of the poor.

LXV. . . . . . and so much of the " Towns Improvement Clauses Act, 1847," as relates to the manner of making rates, shall be incorporated with and form part of this Act.

MUNICIPAL ELECTIONS ACT, 1859.
(22 VICT., c. 35.)
Notice of Election.

V. Seven days at least before the day fixed for the election of any councillor or councillors, the Town Clerk shall prepare, sign, and publish a notice in the form contained in Schedule (B.) to this Act annexed, or to the like effect, by causing the same to be placed on the door of the Town Hall and in some other conspicuous parts of the borough or ward for which any such election is to be held.

Election of Councillors.

VI. At any election of councillors to be held for any borough or ward any person entitled to vote may nominate for the office of councillor himself (if duly qualified), or any other person or persons so qualified (not exceeding the number of persons to be elected for the borough or ward, as the case may be), and every such nomination shall be in writing, and shall state the Christian names and surnames of the persons nominated, with their respective places of abode and descriptions, and shall be signed by the party nominating, and sent to the Town Clerk at least two whole days (Sunday excluded) before the day of election; and the Town Clerk shall at least one whole day (Sunday excluded) before the said day of election cause the Christian names and surnames of the persons so nominated, with such statement of their respective places of abode and descriptions, and with the names of the party nominating them, respectively to be printed and placed on the door of the Town Hall, and in some other conspicuous parts of the borough or ward for which such election is to be held.

VII. Any nomination paper may be in the form contained in the schedule to this Act annexed, or to the like effect; and the Town Clerk shall provide so many nomination papers as may be required, and at the request of any person entitled to nominate, shall fill up a nomination paper in due form; provided, nevertheless, that such paper shall be signed by the person nominating.

VIII. At any election of councillors to be held for any borough or ward :

1. If the number of persons so nominated shall exceed the number to be elected,

    The councillors to be elected shall be elected from the persons so nominated, and from them only:

2. If the number of persons so nominated shall be the same as the number to be elected,

    Such persons shall be deemed to be elected; and the mayor or aldermen and two assessors, as the case may be, shall publish a list of the names of the persons so elected, not later than eleven of the clock in the morning of the said day of election:

3. If the number of persons so nominated shall be less than the number to be elected,

    Such persons shall be deemed to be elected: such of the retiring councillors highest on the poll at their election, or, if the poll were equal, or there were no poll, such as shall be nominated by the mayor, shall be deemed to be re-elected to make up the number required to be elected: and the mayor or alderman and two assessors, as the case may be, shall publish a list of the names of all the persons so elected respectively, not later than eleven of the clock in the morning of the said day of election:

4. If no persons be so nominated,
   The retiring councillors shall be deemed to be re-elected, and the mayor or alderman and two assessors, as the case may be, shall publish a list of the names of all the persons so elected, not later than eleven of the clock in the morning of the said day of election.

SCHEDULES.

Schedule A.

Election of Councillors for the [Ward of   in the]
Borough of   to be held on the   day of
                A.D.

Nomination Paper.

Christian Name and Surname of Person nominated.	Place of Abode of Person nominated.	Description of Person nominated.	Christian Name and Surname of Nominator.	Address of Nominator.

Dated the   day of
A.D.

(Signed)

Schedule B.

Borough of   }
in the County of   } to wit.
Election of Councillors for the [Ward of   in the]
Borough of   in the County of

Take notice

1. That an election of [*three*] councillors will be held for the said ward [*or* borough] on   the   day of
           A.D.   in the said ward [*or* borough.]

2. That any person entitled to vote may nominate for the said office himself (if duly qualified), or any other person or persons so qualified, not exceeding [*three*] in number.

3. That every such nomination must be in writing, and must state the Christian names and surnames of the persons nominated, with their respective places of abode and descriptions.

4. That any nomination paper must be signed by the party nominating, and may be in the following form or to the like effect [*set out Form as given in Schedule*].

5. That all nomination papers must be delivered to the Town Clerk on or before the   day of   next.

Dated this   day of   , A.D.

(Signed)   A.B., Town Clerk.

LOCAL GOVERNMENT (IRELAND) ACT, 1871.

34 and 35 Vict., c. 109.

* 3. In the construction of this Act—

The term "Lord Lieutenant" shall mean the Lord Lieutenant of Ireland for the time being, and shall include the Lords Justices or other Chief Governors or Governor of Ireland for the time being;

The term "Chief Secretary" shall mean the Chief Secretary to the Lord Lieutenant;

The term "governing body," in the several places mentioned in the first column of the schedule annexed to this Act, shall mean the persons or bodies of persons in that behalf described in the second column of the said schedule;

The term "town," in relation to any governing body, shall mean the area within which such governing body has jurisdiction;

The term "special Act" in relation to any governing body shall mean and include any and every Act of Parliament under the provisions of which such governing body is constituted or in the execution of which such governing body is acting;

The term "principal Act" shall mean the "The Towns Improvement (Ireland) Act, 1854;"

The term "Court" shall mean the Court of Common Pleas at Dublin;

The term "Rules of Court" shall mean rules to be made by the Court under the authority of Part I. of this Act; and the term "prescribed" shall mean prescribed by the rules of Court.

* Repealed by Public Health (Ireland) Act, 1878.

Audit of Accounts.

11. The accounts of the receipts and expenditure of the governing body of every town in Ireland, except the boroughs or municipalities of Cork, Kilkenny, and Waterford, shall be audited and examined once in every year by the auditor of accounts relating to the relief of the poor for the union in which such town or the greater part thereof is situate, unless such auditor be a contractor for any articles or things supplied to, or be a member of the governing body of, such town, or unless such auditor is unable to undertake the duties incident to such audit, in any of which cases such accounts shall be audited by such auditor of accounts relating to the relief of the poor for any other union, or by such other person as may, from time to time, be appointed by the Chief Secretary for that purpose.

Controverted Elections.

20. Where any person who voted or who was qualified to vote at any election of members of the governing body of any town thinks that there was, in respect of the election of any member of such governing body, any undue or unlawful proceeding, or that such member was not at the time of such election duly qualified to act as such, it shall be lawful for such person, within one month after such election, to present a petition to the court complaining of such undue or unlawful proceeding, or that such member was not duly qualified as aforesaid.

Every such petition shall be in the prescribed form, and shall be delivered to the prescribed officer of the court.

Every person so petitioning shall within three days after lodging such petition deliver a copy of such petition to the clerk of the governing body, and to any member of such governing body in respect of whose election such petition has been presented.

At the time of the delivery of the petition to the prescribed officer, or within three days afterwards, security for the payment of all costs, charges, and expenses that may become payable by the petitioner—

(*a.*) To any person summoned as a witness on his behalf, or

(*b.*) To the member whose election or return is complained of,

shall be given on behalf of the person presenting the petition.

The security shall be to an amount of one hundred pounds; it shall be given either by recognizance to be entered into by any number of sureties not exceeding four, or by a deposit of money in manner prescribed, or partly in one way and partly in the other.

As soon as conveniently may be after the presenting of such petition and the giving of such security, but not sooner than ten days thereafter, the court or one of the judges thereof shall proceed to inquire into and decide upon the matters and allegations contained in such petition, and shall have power to take evidence upon oath, and to compel the attendance of witnesses, and shall have all and the same powers, jurisdiction, and authority as in other cases coming within the jurisdiction of the court, and shall either confirm the election, or order a new election, or make such order and give such relief in the premises as to them or him may seem right, and such decision and orders shall in all respects be final and conclusive upon all parties.

Where the court or judge has declared that the election of any member of the governing body of any town was void, such member shall cease to act as such, and there shall be a vacancy in such governing body, which vacancy shall be filled by the election of a new member by the persons qualified to vote at such election, according to the provisions of the special Act in respect of the election of members.

21. The court may from time to time make, and may from time to time revoke and alter, general rules and orders for the regulation of the practice, procedure, and costs of petitions under the authority of this part of this Act, and the trial thereof.

Any general rules and orders made as aforesaid shall be deemed to be within the powers conferred by this part of this Act, and shall be of the same force as if they were enacted in the body of this part of this Act.

Any general rules and orders made in pursuance of this section shall be laid before Parliament within three weeks after they are made, if Parliament be then sitting, and if Parliament be not then sitting, within three weeks after the beginning of the then next Session of Parliament.

PART II.

Additional and Special Provisions,

Relating to the Local Government of Towns under the Principal Act or under special Acts incorporating said Act, in whole or in part.

24. The Principal Act, so far as not inconsistent with this part of this Act, and this Act shall be construed together as one Act.

26. So much of section twenty-two of the principal Act as enacts that the payment of poor rates and grand jury rates by any person shall be necessary for the purpose of qualifying such person to vote at the election of commissioners shall be and the same is hereby repealed.

27. The clerk to the commissioners, at least fifteen days before the day appointed for the annual election of commissioners in each

year, shall make out an alphabetical list of the names of all persons, with their respective residences, entitled to vote at such election in respect of premises within the town as they appear in the rates made for the purposes of the principal Act, and also of all persons entitled to vote at such election in respect of property within the town.

Such list shall be evidence that the persons therein named are entitled to vote at the next annual election for commissioners, and also at any other election for one or more commissioners which may be held before the next annual list is made out.

The clerk to the commissioners shall forthwith cause to be printed copies of the list to be made out by him in every year as aforesaid, and shall deliver a copy of such list to all persons requiring the same, on the payment of the sum of one shilling for each copy, and shall cause a copy of such list to be fixed on or near the outer door of the office of the commissioners, and in some other public and conspicuous situation within the town, on every day during the ten days next preceding the day appointed for the election of the commissioners in each year.

SCHEDULE.

Description of Places.	Description of Governing Body.
The City of Dublin,	The Right Honorable the Lord Mayor, Aldermen, and Burgesses acting by the Town Council.
Towns corporate, with exception of Dublin.	The Mayor, Aldermen, and Burgesses acting by the Town Council.
Towns having Commissioners appointed by virtue of an Act made in the 9th year of the reign of George the Fourth, intituled "An Act to make provision "for the Lighting, Cleansing, and "Watching of Cities and Towns Cor- "porate and Market Towns in Ireland "in certain cases."	The Commissioners.
Towns having municipal commissioners under 3 & 4 Vict., c. 108.	The Municipal Commissioners.
Towns having town commissioners under the Towns Improvement (Ireland) Act, 1854 (17 & 18 Vict., c. 103), or under any Local Act.	The Town Commissioners.
Townships having commissioners under Local Acts.	The Township Commissioners.

BALLOT ACT, 1872.

35 & 36 Vict., c. 33.

An Act to amend the law relating to procedure at Parliamentary and Municipal elections. [18th July, 1872.]

*2. In the case of a poll at an election the votes shall be given by ballot. The ballot of each voter shall consist of a paper (in this Act called a ballot paper) showing the names and description of the candidates. Each ballot paper shall have a number printed on the back, and shall have attached a counterfoil with the same number printed on the face. At the time of voting, the ballot paper shall be marked on both sides with an official mark, and delivered to the voter within the polling station, and the number of such voter on the register of voters shall be marked on the counterfoil, and the voter having secretly marked his vote on the paper, and folded it up so as to conceal his vote, shall place it in a closed box in the presence of the officer presiding at the polling station (in this Act called "the presiding officer") after having shown to him the official mark at the back.

Any ballot paper which has not on its back the official mark, or on which votes are given to more candidates than the voter is entitled to vote for, or on which anything, except the said number on the back, is written or marked by which the voter can be identified, shall be void and not counted.

After the close of the poll the ballot boxes shall be sealed up, so as to prevent the introduction of additional ballot papers, and shall be taken charge of by the returning officer, and that officer shall, in the presence of such agents, if any, of the candidates as may be in attendance, open the ballot boxes, and ascertain the result of the poll by counting the votes given to each candidate, and shall forthwith declare to be elected the candidates or candidate to whom the majority of votes have been given, and return their names to the Clerk of the Crown in Chancery. The decision of the returning officer as to any question arising in respect of any ballot paper shall be final, subject to reversal on petition questioning the election or return.

Where an equality of votes is found to exist between any candidates at an election for a county or borough, and the addition of a vote would entitle any of such candidates to be declared elected, the returning officer, if a registered elector of such county or borough, may give such additional vote, but shall not in any other case be entitled to vote at an election for which he is returning officer.

* [Section 1 deals with the nomination of candidates for Parliamentary elections only.]

Offences at Elections.

3. Every person who,—
   (1.) Forges or fraudulently defaces or fraudulently destroys any nomination paper, or delivers to the returning officer any nomination paper, knowing the same to be forged ; or
   (2.) Forges or counterfeits or fraudulently defaces or fraudulently destroys any ballot paper or the official mark on any ballot paper; or
   (3.) Without due authority supplies any ballot paper to any person ; or
   (4.) Fraudulently puts into any ballot box any paper other than the ballot paper which he is authorised by law to put in ; or
   (5.) Fraudulently takes out of the polling station any ballot paper ; or
   (6.) Without due authority destroys, takes, opens, or otherwise interferes with any ballot box or packet of ballot papers then in use for the purposes of the election ;

shall be guilty of a misdemeanor, and be liable, if he is a returning officer or an officer or clerk in attendance at a polling station, to imprisonment for any term not exceeding two years, with or without hard labour, and if he is any other person, to imprisonment for any term not exceeding six months, with or without hard labour.

Any attempt to commit any offence specified in this section shall be punishable in the manner in which the offence itself is punishable.

In any indictment or other prosecution for an offence in relation to the nomination papers, ballot boxes, ballot papers, and marking instruments at an election, the property in such papers, boxes, and instruments may be stated to be in the returning officer at such election, as well as the property in the counterfoils.

4. Every officer, clerk, and agent in attendance at a polling station shall maintain, and aid in maintaining the secrecy of the voting in such station, and shall not communicate, except for some purpose authorised by law, before the poll is closed, to any person any information as to the name or number on the register of voters of any elector who has or has not applied for a ballot paper or voted at that station, or as to the official mark, and no such officer, clerk, or agent, and no person whosoever, shall interfere with or attempt to interfere with a voter when marking his vote, or otherwise attempt to obtain in the polling station information as to the candidate for whom any voter in such station is about to vote or has voted, or communicate at any time to any person any information obtained in a polling station as to the candidate for whom any voter in such station is about to vote or has voted, or as to the number on the back of the ballot paper given to any voter at

such station. Every officer, clerk, and agent in attendance at the counting of the votes shall maintain and aid in maintaining the secrecy of the voting, and shall not attempt to ascertain at such counting the number on the back of any ballot paper, or communicate any information obtained at such counting as to the candidate for whom any vote is given in any particular ballot paper. No person shall directly or indirectly induce any voter to display his ballot paper after he shall have marked the same, so as to make known to any person the name of the candidate for or against whom he has so marked his vote.

Every person who acts in contravention of the provisions of this section shall be liable, on summary conviction before two justices of the peace, to imprisonment for any term not exceeding six months, with or without hard labour.

(Sec. 5 deals with the division of counties and boroughs into polling districts for Parliamentary elections in England.)

*6. The returning officer at a parliamentary election may use, free of charge, for the purpose of taking the poll at such election, any room in a school receiving a grant out of moneys provided by Parliament, and any room the expense of maintaining which is payable out of any local rate, but he shall make good any damage done to such room, and defray any expense incurred by the person or body of persons, corporate or unincorporate, having control over the same on account of its being used for the purpose of taking the poll as aforesaid.

The use of any room in an unoccupied house for the purpose of taking the poll shall not render any person liable to be rated or to pay any rate for such house.

*7. At any election for a county or borough, a person shall not be entitled to vote unless his name is on the register of voters for the time being in force for such county or borough, and every person whose name is on such register shall be entitled to demand and receive a ballot paper and to vote : Provided that nothing in this section shall entitle any person to vote who is prohibited from voting by any statute, or by the common law of Parliament, or relieve such person from any penalties to which he may be liable for voting.

Duties of Returning and Election Officers.

8. Subject to the provisions of this Act, every returning officer shall provide such nomination papers, polling stations, ballot boxes, ballot papers, stamping instruments, copies of register of voters, and other things, appoint and pay such officers, and do such other acts and things as may be necessary for effectually conducting an election in manner provided by this Act.

All expenses properly incurred by any returning officer in carry-

---

* Sections 6 and 7 apply to Parliamentary elections only.

ing into effect the provisions of this Act, in the case of any parliamentary election, shall be payable in the same manner as expenses incurred in the erection of polling booths at such election are by law payable.

[* Where the sheriff is returning officer for more than one county as defined for the purposes of parliamentary elections, he may, without prejudice to any other power, by writing under his hand, appoint a fit person to be his deputy for all or any of the purposes relating to an election in any such county, and may, by himself or such deputy, exercise any powers and do any things which the returning officer is authorised or required to exercise or do in relation to such election. Every such deputy, and also any under sheriff, shall, in so far as he acts as returning officer, be deemed to be included in the term returning officer in the provisions of this Act relating to parliamentary elections, and the enactments with which this part of this Act is to be construed as one.]

9. If any person misconducts himself in the polling station, or fails to obey the lawful orders of the presiding officer, he may immediately, by order of the presiding officer, be removed from the polling station by any constable in or near that station, or any other person authorized in writing by the returning officer to remove him ; and the person so removed shall not, unless with the permission of the presiding officer, again be allowed to enter the polling station during the day.

Any person so removed as aforesaid, if charged with the commission in such station of any offence, may be kept in custody until he can be brought before a justice of the peace.

Provided that the powers conferred by this section shall not be exercised so as to prevent any elector who is otherwise entitled to vote at any polling station from having an opportunity of voting at such station.

10. For the purpose of the adjournment of the poll, and of every other enactment relating to the poll, a presiding officer shall have the power by law belonging to a deputy returning officer ; and any presiding officer and any clerk appointed by the returning officer to attend at a polling station shall have the power of asking the questions and administering the oath authorised by law to be asked of and administered to voters, and any justice of the peace and any returning officer may take and receive any declaration authorised by this Act to be taken before him.

11. Every returning officer, presiding officer, and clerk who is guilty of any wilful misfeasance or any wilful act or omission in contravention of this Act shall, in addition to any other penalty or liability to which he may be subject, forfeit to any person aggrieved by such misfeasance, act, or omission a penal sum not exceeding one hundred pounds.

* The remainder of this section applies only to Parliamentary elections.

Section fifty of the Representation of the People Act, 1867, (which relates to the acting of any returning officer, or his partner or clerk, as agent for a candidate,) shall apply to any returning officer or officer appointed by him in pursuance of this Act, and to his partner or clerk.

Miscellaneous.

12. No person who has voted at an election shall, in any legal proceeding to question the election or return, be required to state for whom he has voted.

13. No election shall be declared invalid by reason of a non-compliance with the rules contained in the First Schedule to this Act, or any mistake in the use of the forms in the Second Schedule to this Act, if it appears to the tribunal having cognizance of the question that the election was conducted in accordance with the principles laid down in the body of this Act, and that such non-compliance or mistake did not affect the result of the election.

14. Where a parliamentary borough and municipal borough occupy the whole or any part of the same area, any ballot boxes or fittings for polling stations and compartments provided for such parliamentary borough or such municipal borough may be used in any municipal or parliamentary election in such borough free of charge, and any damage other than reasonable wear and tear caused to the same shall be paid as part of the expenses of the election at which they are so used.

15. This part of this Act shall, so far as is consistent with the tenor thereof, be construed as one with the enactments for the time being in force relating to the representation of the people, and to the registration of persons entitled to vote at the election of members to serve in Parliament, and with any enactments otherwise relating to the subject matter of this part of this Act, and terms used in this part of this Act shall have the same meaning as in the said enactments; and in construing the said enactments relating to an election or to the poll or taking the votes by poll, the mode of election and of taking the poll established by this Act shall for the purposes of the said enactments be deemed to be substituted for the mode of election or poll, or taking the votes by poll, referred to in the said enactments; and any person applying for a ballot paper under this Act shall be deemed "to tender his vote," or "to assume to vote," within the meaning of the said enactments; and any application for a ballot paper under this Act, or expressions relative thereto, shall be equivalent to "voting" in the said enactments and any expressions relative thereto; and the term "polling booth" as used in the said enactments shall be deemed to include a polling station; and the term "proclamation" as used in the said enactments shall be deemed to include a public notice given in pursuance of this Act.

(Section 16 deals with Application of part of Act to Scotland.)

Application of Part of Act to Ireland.

[17. † This part of this Act shall apply to Ireland, subject to the following modifications :—

(1.) The expression "Clerk of the Crown in Chancery" shall mean the Clerk of the Crown and Hanaper in Ireland:

(2.) The preceding provisions of this part of this Act with respect to the division of counties and boroughs into polling districts shall not extend to Ireland :]

(3.) In the construction of the preceding provisions of this part of this Act as applying to Ireland, section thirteen of "The Representation of the People (Ireland) Act, 1868," shall be substituted for section fifty of "The Representation of the People Act, 1867," wherever in such provisions the said last-mentioned section occurs. [The provision contained in the sixth section of this Act providing for the use of school rooms free of charge, for the purpose of taking the poll at elections, shall not apply to any school adjoining or adjacent to any church or other place of worship, nor to any school connected with a nunnery or other religious establishment :

(4.) No returning officer shall be entitled to claim, or be paid, any sum or sums of money for the erection of polling booths or stations and compartments other than the sum or sums actually and necessarily incurred and paid by him in reference to the same, any statute or statutes to the contrary now in force notwithstanding, nor shall the expenses of providing sufficient polling stations or booths and compartments at every polling place exceed the sum or sums now given and allowed by statute in Ireland.]

(Section 18 enacts provisions as to polling districts and polling places in Ireland, which refer only to parliamentary election.)

Part II.

Municipal Elections.

20. The poll at every contested municipal election shall, so far as circumstances admit, be conducted in the manner in which the poll is by this Act directed to be conducted at a contested parliamentary election, and, subject to the modifications expressed in the schedules annexed hereto, such provisions of this Act and of

* Section 17 (with the exception of a portion of subsection 3), only applies to parliamentary elections).

the said schedules as relate to or are concerned with a poll at a parliamentary election shall apply to a poll at a contested municipal election: Provided as follows:

(1.) The term "returning officer" shall mean the mayor or other officer who, under the law relating to municipal elections, presides at such elections:

(2.) The term "petition questioning the election or return" shall mean any proceeding in which a municipal election can be questioned:

(3.) The mayor shall provide everything which in the case of a parliamentary election is required to be provided by the returning officer for the purpose of a poll:

(4.) All expenses shall be defrayed in manner provided by law with respect to the expenses of a municipal election:

(5.) No return shall be made to the Clerk of the Crown in Chancery:

(6.) Nothing in this Act shall be deemed to authorize the appointment of any agents of a candidate in a municipal election, but if in the case of a municipal election any agent of a candidate is appointed, and a notice in writing of such appointment is given to the returning officer, the provisions of this Act, with respect to agents of candidates shall, so far as respects such agent, apply in the case of that election:

(7.) The provisions of this Act with respect to—
   (a.) The voting of a returning officer; and
   (b.) The use of a room for taking a poll; and
   (c.) The right to vote of persons whose names are on the register of voters;
shall not apply in the case of a municipal election.

A municipal election shall, except in so far as relates to the taking of the poll in the event of its being contested, be conducted in the manner in which it would have been conducted if this Act had not passed.

21. Assessors shall not be elected in any ward of any municipal borough, and a municipal election need not be held before the assessors or their deputies, but may be held before the mayor, alderman, or other returning officer only.

(Sec. 22 deals with the application of this part of Act to Scotland.)

Application of Part of Act to Ireland.

23. This part of this Act shall apply to Ireland, with the following modifications:—

   (1.) The term "mayor" shall include the chairman of commissioners, chairman of municipal commissioners, chairman of town commissioners, and chairman of township commissioners:

(2.) The provisions of "The Municipal Corporation Act, 1859," following; that is to say, section five and section six, and section seven except so much thereof as relates to the form of nomination papers, and section eight except so much thereof as relates to assessors, shall extend and apply to every municipal borough in Ireland, and shall be substituted for any provisions in force in relation to the nomination at municipal elections : Provided always, that the term "councillor" in these sections shall for the purposes of this section include alderman, commissioner, municipal commissioner, town commissioner, township commissioner, or assessor of any municipal borough.

PART III.

PERSONATION.

24. The following enactments shall be made with respect to personation at parliamentary and municipal elections :

A person shall for all purposes of the laws relating to parliamentary and municipal elections be deemed to be guilty of the offence of personation who at an election for a county or borough, or at a municipal election, applies for a ballot paper in the name of some other person, whether that name be that of a person living or dead or of a fictitious person, or who having voted once at any such election applies at the same election for a ballot paper in his own name.

The offence of personation, or of aiding, abetting, counselling, or procuring the commission of the offence of personation by any person, shall be a felony, and any person convicted thereof shall be punished by imprisonment for a term not exceeding two years together with hard labour. It shall be the duty of the returning officer to institute a prosecution against any person whom he may believe to have been guilty of personation, or of aiding, abetting, counselling, or procuring the commission of the offence of personation by any person, at the election for which he is returning officer, and the costs and expenses of the prosecutor and the witnesses in such case, together with compensation for their trouble and loss of time, shall be allowed by the court in the same manner in which courts are empowered to allow the same in cases of felony.

The provisions of the Registration Acts, specified in the third schedule to this Act, shall in England and Ireland respectively apply to personation under this Act in the same manner as they apply to a person who knowingly personates and falsely assumes to vote in the name of another person as mentioned in the said Acts.

The offence of personation shall be deemed to be a corrupt practice within the meaning of the Parliamentary Elections Act, 1868.

If, on the trial of any election petition questioning the election or return for any county or borough, any candidate is found by the report of the judge by himself or his agents to have been guilty of personation, or by himself or his agents to have aided, abetted, counselled, or procured the commission at such election of the offence of personation by any person, such candidate shall be incapable of being elected or sitting in Parliament for such county or borough during the Parliament then in existence.

25. Where a candidate, on the trial of an election petition claiming the seat for any person, is proved to have been guilty, by himself or by any person on his behalf, of bribery, treating, or undue influence in respect of any person who voted at such election, or where any person retained or employed for reward by or on behalf of such candidate for all or any of the purposes of such election, as agent, clerk, messenger, or in any other employment, is proved on such trial to have voted at such election, there shall, on a scrutiny, be struck off from the number of votes appearing to have been given to such candidate one vote for every person who voted at such election and is proved to have been so bribed, treated, or unduly influenced, or so retained or employed for reward as aforesaid.

(Sec. 26—refers to alterations in this part of the Act as applying to Scotland.)

(Sec. 27—to construction of this part of the Act as regards Parliamentary elections.)

Part IV.

Miscellaneous.

28. The schedules to this Act, and the notes thereto, and directions therein, shall be construed and have effect as part of this Act.

29. In this Act—

The expression " municipal borough " means any place for the time being subject to the Municipal Corporation Acts, or any of them :

The expression " Municipal Corporation Acts " means—*

(c.) As regards Ireland, the Act of the session of the third and fourth years of the reign of Her present Majesty, chapter one hundred and eight, intituled "An Act for the Regulation of Municipal Corporations in Ireland," the Act of the ninth year of George the Fourth, chapter eighty-two, The Towns Improvement(Ireland) Act, 1854, and every local and personal Act providing for the election of Commissioners in any towns or places for purposes similiar to the purposes of the said Acts.

* Sub-sections (*a*) and (*b*) refer to England and Scotland.

The expression "municipal election" means—

(c.) As regards Ireland, an election of any person to serve the office of alderman, councillor, commissioner, municipal commissioner, town commissioner, township commissioner, or assessor of any municipal borough.

30. This Act shall apply to any parliamentary or municipal election which may be held after the passing thereof.

Repeal.

32. The Acts specified in the fourth, fifth, and sixth schedules to this Act, to the extent specified in the third column of those schedules, and all other enactments inconsistent with this Act, are hereby repealed.

Provided that this repeal shall not affect—

(a.) Anything duly done or suffered under any enactment hereby repealed; or

(b.) Any right or liability acquired, accrued, or incurred under any enactment hereby repealed; or

(c.) Any penalty, forfeiture, or punishment incurred in respect of any offence committed against any enactment hereby repealed; or

(d.) Any investigation, legal proceeding, or remedy in respect of any such right, liability, penalty, forfeiture, or punishment as aforesaid; and any such investigation, legal proceeding, and remedy may be carried on as if this Act had not passed.

33. This Act may be cited as The Ballot Act, 1872, and shall continue in force till the thirty-first day of December, one thousand eight hundred and eighty, and no longer, unless Parliament shall otherwise determine; and on the said day the Acts in the fourth, fifth, and sixth schedules shall be thereupon revived; provided that such revival shall not affect any act done, any rights acquired, any liability or penalty incurred, or any proceeding pending under this Act, but such proceeding shall be carried on as if this Act had continued in force.

FIRST SCHEDULE.
Part I.
Rules for Parliamentary Elections.
Election.

(Sections 1 to 13, both inclusive, refer to nominations in Parliamentary elections).

The Poll.

14. The poll shall take place on such day as the returning officer may appoint, not being in the case of an election for a

county or a district borough less than two nor more than six clear days, and not being in the case of an election for a borough other than a district borough more than three clear days after the day fixed for the election.

15. At every polling place the returning officer shall provide a sufficient number of polling stations for the accommodation of the electors entitled to vote at such polling place, and shall distribute the polling stations amongst those electors in such manner as he thinks most convenient, provided that in a district borough there shall be at least one polling station at each contributory place of such borough.

16. Each polling station shall be furnished with such number of compartments, in which the voters can mark their votes screened from observation, as the returning officer thinks necessary, so that at least one compartment be provided for every one hundred and fifty electors entitled to vote at such polling station.

17. A separate room or separate booth may contain a separate polling station, or several polling stations may be constructed in the same room or booth.

18. No person shall be admitted to vote at any polling station except the one allotted to him.

19. The returning officer shall give public notice of the situation of polling stations and the decription of voters entitled to vote at each station, and of the mode in which electors are to vote.

20. The returning officer shall provide each polling station with materials for voters to mark the ballot papers, with instruments for stamping thereon the official mark, and with copies of the register of voters, or such part thereof as contains the names of the voters allotted to vote at such station. He shall keep the official mark secret, and an interval of not less than seven years shall intervene between the use of the same official mark at elections for the same county or borough.

21. The returning officer shall appoint a presiding officer to preside at each station, and the officer so appointed shall keep order at his station, shall regulate the number of electors to be admitted at a time, and shall exclude all other persons except the clerks, the agents of the candidates, and the constables on duty.

22. Every ballot paper shall contain a list of the candidates described as in their respective nomination papers, and arranged alphabetically in the order of their surnames, and (if there are two or more candidates with the same surname) of their other names: it shall be in the form set forth in the Second Schedule to this Act or as near thereto as circumstances admit, and shall be capable of being folded up.

23. Every ballot box shall be so constructed that the ballot papers can be introduced therein, but cannot be withdrawn therefrom, without the box being unlocked. The presiding officer at any

polling station, just before the commencement of the poll, shall show the ballot box empty to such persons, if any, as may be present in such station, so that they may see that it is empty, and shall then lock it up, and place his seal upon it in such manner as to prevent its being opened without breaking such seal, and shall place it in his view for the receipt of ballot papers, and keep it so locked and sealed.

24. Immediately before a ballot paper is delivered to an elector, it shall be marked on both sides with the official mark, either stamped or perforated, and the number, name, and description of the elector as stated in the copy of the register shall be called out, and the number of such elector shall be marked on the counterfoil, and a mark shall be placed in the register against the number of the elector, to denote that he has received a ballot paper, but without showing the particular ballot paper which he has received.

25. The elector, on receiving the ballot paper, shall forthwith proceed into one of the compartments in the polling station, and there mark his paper, and fold it up so as to conceal his vote, and shall then put his ballot paper, so folded up, into the ballot box; he shall vote without undue delay, and shall quit the polling station as soon as he has put his ballot paper into the ballot box.

26. The presiding officer, on the application of any voter who is incapacitated by blindness or other physical cause from voting in manner prescribed by this Act, or (if the poll be taken on Saturday, of any voter who declares that he is of the Jewish persuasion, and objects on religious grounds to vote in manner prescribed by this Act, or of any voter who makes such a declaration as hereinafter mentioned that he is unable to read, shall, in the presence of the agents of the candidates, cause the vote of such voter to be marked on a ballot paper in manner directed by such voter, and the ballot paper to be placed in the ballot box, and the name and number on the register of voters of every voter whose vote is marked in pursuance of this rule, and the reason why it is so marked, shall be entered on a list, in this Act called "the list of votes marked by the presiding officer."

The said declaration, in this Act referred to as "the declaration of inability to read," shall be made by the voter at the time of polling, before the presiding officer, who shall attest it in the form hereinafter mentioned, an d no fee, stamp, or other payment shall be charged in respect of such declaration, and the said declaration shall be given to the presiding officer at the time of voting.

27. If a person, representing himself to be a particular elector named on the register, applies for a ballot paper after another person has voted as such elector, the applicant shall, upon duly answering the questions and taking the oath permitted by law to be asked of and to be administered to voters at the time of

polling, be entitled to mark a ballot paper in the same manner as any other voter, but the ballot paper (in this Act called a tendered ballot paper) shall be of a colour differing from the other ballot papers, and, instead of being put into the ballot box, shall be given to the presiding officer and endorsed by him with the name of the voter and his number in the register of voters, and set aside in a separate packet, and shall not be counted by the returning officer. And the name of the voter and his number on the register shall be entered on a list, in this Act called the tendered votes list.

28. A voter who has inadvertently dealt with his ballot paper in such manner that it cannot be conveniently used as a ballot paper, may, on delivering to the presiding officer the ballot paper so inadvertently dealt with, and proving the fact of the inadvertence to the satisfaction of the presiding officer, obtain another ballot paper in the place of the ballot paper so delivered up (in this Act called a spoilt ballot paper), and the spoilt ballot paper shall be immediately cancelled.

29. The presiding officer of each station, as soon as practicable after the close of the poll, shall, in the presence of the agents of the candidates, make up into separate packets sealed with his own seal and the seals of such agents of the candidates as desire to affix their seals,—

(1.) Each ballot box in use at his station, unopened but with the key attached ; and

(2.) The unused and spoilt ballot papers, placed together ; and

(3.) The tendered ballot papers ; and

(4.) The marked copies of the register of voters, and the counterfoils of the ballot papers ; and

(5.) The tendered votes list, and the list of votes marked by the presiding officer, and a statement of the number of the voters whose votes are so marked by the presiding officer under the heads "physical incapacity," "Jews," and "unable to read," and the declarations of inability to read ;

and shall deliver such packets to the returning officer.

30. The packets shall be accompanied by a statement made by such presiding officer, showing the number of ballot papers entrusted to him, and accounting for them under the heads of ballot papers in the ballot box, unused, spoilt, and tendered ballot papers, which statement is in this Act referred to as the ballot paper account.

Counting Votes.

31. The candidates may respectively appoint agents to attend the counting of the votes.

32. The returning officer shall make arrangements for counting the votes in the presence of the agents of the candidates as soon

as practicable after the close of the poll, and shall give to the agents of the candidates appointed to attend at the counting of the votes notice in writing of the time and place at which he will begin to count the same.

33. The returning officer, his assistants and clerks, and the agents of the candidates, and no other person, except with the sanction of the returning officer, may be present at the counting of the votes.

34. Before the returning officer proceeds to count the votes, he shall, in the presence of the agents of the candidates, open each ballot box, and, taking out the papers therein, shall count and record the number thereof, and then mix together the whole of the ballot papers contained in the ballot boxes. The returning officer, while counting and recording the number of ballot papers and counting the votes, shall keep the ballot papers with their faces upwards, and take all proper precautions for preventing any person from seeing the numbers printed on the backs of such papers.

35. The returning officer shall, so far as practicable, proceed continuously with counting the votes, allowing only time for refreshment, and excluding (except so far as he and the agents otherwise agree) the hours between seven o'clock at night and nine o'clock on the succeeding morning. During the excluded time the returning officer shall place the ballot papers and other documents relating to the election under his own seal and the seals of such of the agents of the candidates as desire to affix their seals, and shall otherwise take proper precautions for the security of such papers and documents.

36. The returning officer shall endorse "rejected" on any ballot paper which he may reject as invalid, and shall add to the endorsement "rejection objected to," if an objection be in fact made by any agent to his decision. The returning officer shall report to the Clerk of the Crown in Chancery, the number of ballot papers rejected and not counted by him under the several heads of—

1. Want of official mark;
2. Voting for more candidates than entitled to;
3. Writing or mark by which voter could be identified;
4. Unmarked or void for uncertainty;

and shall on request allow any agents of the candidates, before such report is sent, to copy it.

37. Upon the completion of the counting, the returning officer shall seal up in separate packets the counted and rejected ballot papers. He shall not open the sealed packet of tendered ballot papers or marked copy of the register of voters and counterfoils, but shall proceed, in the presence of the agents of the candidates, to verify the ballot paper account given by each presiding officer

by comparing it with the number of ballot papers recorded by him as aforesaid, and the unused and spoilt ballot papers in his possession and the tendered votes list, and shall reseal each sealed packet after examination. The returning officer shall report to the Clerk of the Crown in Chancery the result of such verification, and shall, on request, allow any agents of the candidates, before such report is sent, to copy it.

38. Lastly, the returning officer shall forward to the Clerk of the Crown in Chancery (in manner in which the poll books are by any existing enactment required to be forwarded to such clerk, or as near thereto as circumstances admit) all the packets of ballot papers in his possession, together with the said reports, the ballot paper accounts, tendered votes lists, lists of votes marked by the presiding officer, statements relating thereto, declarations of inability to read, and packets of counterfoils, and marked copies of registers, sent by each presiding officer, endorsing on each packet a description of its contents and the date of the election to which they relate, and the name of the county or borough for which such election was held; and the term poll book in any such enactment shall be construed to include any document forwarded in pursuance of this rule.

39. The Clerk of the Crown shall retain for a year all documents relating to an election forwarded to him in pursuance of this Act by a returning officer, and then, unless otherwise directed by an order of the House of Commons, or of one of Her Majesty's Superior Courts, shall cause them to be destroyed.

40. No person shall be allowed to inspect any rejected ballot papers in the custody of the Clerk of the Crown in Chancery, except under the order of the House of Commons or under the order of one of Her Majesty's Superior Courts, to be granted by such court on being satisfied by evidence on oath that the inspection or production of such ballot papers is required for the purpose of instituting or maintaining a prosecution for an offence in relation to ballot papers, or for the purpose of a petition questioning an election or return; and any such order for the inspection or production of ballot papers may be made subject to such conditions as to persons, time, place, and mode of inspection or production as the House or court making the same may think expedient, and shall be obeyed by the Clerk of the Crown in Chancery. Any power given to a court by this rule may be exercised by any judge of such court at chambers.

41. No person shall, except by order of the House of Commons or any tribunal having cognizance of petitions complaining of undue returns or undue elections, open the sealed packet of counterfoils after the same has been once sealed up, or be allowed to inspect any counted ballot papers in the custody of the Clerk of the Crown in Chancery; such order may be made subject to such conditions as to persons, time, place, and mode of opening or

inspection as the House or tribunal making the order may think expedient; provided that on making and carrying into effect any such order, care shall be be taken that the mode in which any particular elector has voted shall not be discovered until he has been proved to have voted, and his vote has been declared by a competent court to be invalid.

42. All documents forwarded by a returning officer in pursuance of this Act to the Clerk of the Crown in Chancery, other than ballot papers and counterfoils, shall be open to public inspection at such time and under such regulations as may be prescribed by the Clerk of the Crown in Chancery, with the consent of the Speaker of the House of Commons, and the Clerk of the Crown shall supply copies of or extracts from the said documents to any person demanding the same, on payment of such fees and subject to such regulations as may be sanctioned by the Treasury.

43. Where an order is made for the production by the Clerk of the Crown in Chancery of any document in his possession relating to any specified election, the production by such clerk or his agent of the document ordered, in such manner as may be directed by such order, or by a rule of the court having power to make such order, shall be conclusive evidence that such document relates to the specified election; and any endorsement appearing on any packet of ballot papers produced by such Clerk of the Crown or his agent shall be evidence of such papers being what they are stated to be by the endorsement. The production from proper custody of a ballot paper purporting to have been used at any election, and of a counterfoil marked with the same printed number and having a number marked thereon in writing, shall be primâ facie evidence that the person who voted by such ballot paper was the person who at the time of such election had affixed to his name in the register of voters at such election the same number as the number written on such counterfoil.

[Sec. 44 refers to the return made by the returning officer in Parliamentary elections.]

General Provisions.

45. The returning officer shall, as soon as possible, give public notice of the names of the candidates elected, and, in the case of a contested election, of the total number of votes given for each candidate, whether elected or not.

46. Where the returning officer is required or authorised by this Act to give any public notice, he shall carry such requirement into effect by advertisements, placards, handbills, or such other means as he thinks best calculated to afford information to the electors.

47. The returning officer may, if he think fit, preside at any polling station, and the provisions of this Act relating to a presiding

officer shall apply to such returning officer with the necessary modifications as to things to be done by the returning officer to the presiding officer, or the presiding officer to the returning officer.

48. In the case of a contested election for any county or borough, the returning officer may, in addition to any clerks, appoint competent persons to assist him in counting the votes.

49. No person shall be appointed by a returning officer for the purposes of an election who has been employed by any other person in or about the election.

50. The presiding officer may do, by the clerks appointed to assist him, any act which he is required or authorised to do by this Act at a polling station except ordering the arrest, exclusion, or ejection from the polling station of any person.

51. A candidate may himself undertake the duties which any agent of his if appointed might have undertaken, or may assist his agent in the performance of such duties, and may be present at any place at which his agent may, in pursuance of this Act, attend.

52. The name and address of every agent of a candidate appointed to attend the counting of the votes shall be transmitted to the returning officer one clear day at the least before the opening of the poll; and the returning officer may refuse to admit to the place where the votes are counted any agent whose name and address has not been so transmitted, notwithstanding that his appointment may be otherwise valid, and any notice required to be given to an agent by the returning officer may be delivered at or sent by post to such address.

53. If any person appointed an agent by a candidate for the purposes of attending at the polling station or at the counting of the votes dies, or becomes incapable of acting during the time of the election, the candidate may appoint another agent in his place, and shall forthwith give to the returning officer notice in writing of the name and address of the agent so appointed.

54. Every returning officer, and every officer, clerk, or agent authorised to attend at a polling station, or at the counting of the votes, shall, before the opening of the poll, make a statutory declaration of secrecy, in the presence, if he is the returning officer, of a justice of the peace, and if he is any other officer or an agent, of a justice of the peace or of the returning officer ; but no such returning officer, officer, clerk, or agent as aforesaid shall, save as aforesaid, be required, as such, to make any declaration or take any oath on the occasion of any election.

55. Where in this Act any expressions are used requiring or authorising or inferring that any act or thing is to be done in the presence of the agents of the candidates, such expressions shall be deemed to refer to the presence of such agents of the candidates as may be authorised to attend, and as have in fact attended, at the time and place where such act or thing is being done, and the non-attendance of any agents or agent at such time and place

shall not, if such act or thing be otherwise duly done, in anywise invalidate the act or thing done.

56. In reckoning time for the purposes of this Act, Sunday, Christmas Day, Good Friday, and any day set apart for a public fast or public thanksgiving, shall be excluded; and where anything is required by this Act to be done on any day which falls on the above-mentioned days such thing may be done on the next day, unless it is one of the days excluded as above mentioned.

57. In this Act—

> The expression "polling place" means, in the case of a borough, such borough or any part thereof in which a separate booth is required or authorised by law to be provided; and
>
> The expression "agents of the candidates," used in relation to a polling station, means agents appointed in pursuance of section eighty-five of the Act of the session of the sixth and seventh years of the reign of Her present Majesty, chapter eighteen.

[Sections 58, 59, 60 and 61 apply to modifications of Part One of Schedule to Scotland].

Modifications in Application of Part One of Schedule to Ireland.

62. The expression "Clerk of the Crown in Chancery" in this schedule shall mean, as regards Ireland, "the Clerk of the Crown and Hanaper in Ireland."

[63. A presiding officer at a polling station in a county in Ireland need not be a freeholder of the county.]

Part II.

Rules for Municipal Elections.

64. In the application of the provisions of this schedule to municipal elections the following modifications shall be made:—

> (*a*.) The expression "register of voters" means the burgess roll of the burgesses of the borough, or, in the case of an election for the ward of a borough, the ward list; and the mayor shall provide true copies of such register for each polling station:
>
> (*b*.) All ballot papers and other documents which, in the case of a parliamentary election, are forwarded to the Clerk of the Crown in Chancery shall be delivered to the town clerk of the municipal borough in which the election is held, and shall be kept by him among the records of the borough; and the provisions of part one of this schedule with respect to the inspection, production, and destruction of such ballot papers

and documents, and to the copies of such documents, shall apply respectively to the ballot papers and documents so in the custody of the town clerk, with these modifications; namely,

(*a*.) An order of the county court having jurisdiction in the borough, or any part thereof, or of any tribunal in which a municipal election is questioned, shall be substituted for an order of the House of Commons, or of one of Her Majesty's Superior Courts; but an appeal from such county court may be had in like manner as in other cases in such county court;

(*b*.) The regulations for the inspection of documents and the fees for the supply of copies of documents of which copies are directed to be supplied, shall be prescribed by the council of the borough with the consent of one of Her Majesty's Principal Secretaries of State; and, subject as aforesaid, the town clerk, in respect of the custody and destruction of the ballot papers and other documents coming into his possession in pursuance of this Act, shall be subject to the directions of the council of the borough:

(*c*.) Nothing in this schedule with respect to the day of the poll shall apply to a municipal election.

Modifications in Application of Part II. of Schedule to Ireland.

66. In part two of this schedule as applying to Ireland—

The expression "register of voters," in addition to the meaning specified in such part, means, in relation to any municipal borough subject to the provisions of a Local Act (requiring an annual revision of the lists of voters at municipal elections), the register of voters made in conformity with the said provisions of such Local Act, and in relation to municipal boroughs to which Part II. of the Local Government (Ireland) Act, 1871, applies, the list to be made under the provisions of section twenty-seven of the said Act, and in relation to other municipal boroughs a list which the town clerk of every municipal borough is hereby authorised and directed to make, in like manner in every respect as if the provisions of the said section were applicable to and in force within such municipal borough.

The expression "county court" means the Civil Bill Court.

The expression "town clerk" includes clerk to the commissioners, municipal commissioners, town commissioners, or township commissioners of any municipal borough, and any person executing the duties of such town clerk.

The expression "council of the borough" includes commissioners, municipal commissioners, and town commissioners of the town, and township commissioners of the township.

The expression "one of Her Majesty's Principal Secretaries of State" means the Chief Secretary of the Lord Lieutenant of Ireland.

SECOND SCHEDULE.

Note.—The forms contained in this schedule, or forms as nearly resembling the same as circumstances will admit, shall be used in all cases to which they refer and are applicable, and when so used shall be sufficient in law.

Form of Notice of Parliamentary Election.

* * * * * *

Form of Nomination Paper in Parliamentary Election.

We, the undersigned *A.B.* of   in the of   and *C.D.* of   in the   of   , being electors for the   of   , do hereby nominate the following person as a proper person to serve as member for the said   in Parliament:

Surname.	Other Names.	Abode.	Rank, Profession, or Occupation.
BROWN,	JOHN,	52, George St., Bristol,	Merchant.
JONES,	*or* WILLIAM DAVID,	High Elms, Wilts	Esquire.
MERTON,	*or* Hon. GEORGE TRAVIS, commonly called Viscount.	Swanworth, Berks	Viscount.
SMITH,	*or* HENRY SYDNEY,	72, High St., Bath	Attorney.

(Signed)   *A.B.*
                  C.D.

We, the undersigned, being registered electors of the do hereby assent to the nomination of the above-mentioned *John Brown* as a proper person to serve as member for the said in Parliament.

      (Signed)   *E.F.* of
            G.H. of
            I.J. of
            K.L. of
            M.N. of
            O.P. of
            Q.R. of
            S.T. of

Note.—Where a candidate is an Irish peer, or is commonly known by some title, he may be described by his title as if it were his surname.

Form of Nomination Paper in Municipal Election.

Note.—The form of nomination paper in a municipal election shall as nearly as circumstances admit be the same as in the case of a parliamentary election.

Form of Ballot Paper.

Form of front of Ballot Paper.

Counterfoil No.

NOTE: The counterfoil is to have a number to correspond with that on the back of the Ballot Paper.

1	**BROWN** (John Brown, of 52, George St., Bristol, merchant.)	
2	**JONES** (William David Jones, of High Elms, Wilts, Esq.)	
3	**MERTON** (Hon. George Travis, commonly called Viscount Merton, of Swanworth, Berks.)	
4	**SMITH** (Henry Sydney Smith, of 72, High Street, Bath, attorney.)	

Form of back of Ballot Paper.

No.
  Election for   county [or borough, or ward].
    18 .

Note.—The number on the ballot paper is to correspond with that in the counterfoil.

Directions as to printing Ballot Paper.

Nothing is to be printed on the ballot paper except in accordance with this schedule.

The surname of each candidate, and if there are two or more candidates of the same surname, also the other names of such candidates, shall be printed in large characters, as shown in the form, and the names, addresses, and descriptions, and the number on the back of the paper, shall be printed in small characters.

Form of Directions for the Guidance of the Voter in voting, which shall be printed in conspicuous Characters, and placarded outside every Polling Station and in every Compartment of every Polling Station.

  The voter may vote for   candidate .

The voter will go into one of the compartments, and, with the pencil provided in the compartment, place a cross on the right-hand side, opposite the name of each candidate for whom he votes, thus ✗

The voter will then fold up the ballot paper so as to show the official mark on the back, and leaving the compartment will, without showing the front of the paper to any person, show the official mark on the back to the presiding officer, and then, in the presence of the presiding officer, put the paper into the ballot box, and forthwith quit the polling station.

If the voter inadvertently spoils a ballot paper, he can return it to the officer, who will, if satisfied of such inadvertence, give him another paper.

If the voter votes for more than———candidate , or places any mark on the paper by which he may be afterwards identified, his ballot paper will be void, and will not be counted.

If the voter takes a ballot paper out of the polling station, or deposits in the ballot box any other paper than the one given him by the officer, he will be guilty of a misdemeanor, and be subject to imprisonment for any term not exceeding six months, with or without hard labour.

Note.—These directions shall be illustrated by examples of the ballot paper.

Form of Statutory Declaration of Secrecy.

I solemnly promise and declare, that I will not at this election for   do anything forbidden by section four of the Ballot Act, 1872, which has been read to me.

Note.—The section must be read to the declarant by the person taking the declaration.

Form of Declaration of inability to read.

I, *A.B.*, of   , being numbered   on the Register of Voters for the county [*or* borough] of   , do hereby declare that I am unable to read.

A.B.,   his mark.

day of   .

I, the undersigned, being the presiding officer for the   polling station for the county [*or* borough] of   , do hereby certify, that the above declaration, having been first read to the above-named *A.B.*, was signed by him in my presence with his mark.

Signed, *C.D.*,

Presiding officer for   polling station for the county [*or* borough] of   .

day of   .

Third Schedule.

Provisions of Registration Acts referred to in Part III. of the foregoing Act.

Session and Chapter.	Title.	Part applied.
13 & 14 Vict., c. 69,	*As to Ireland.* An Act to amend the laws which regulate the qualification and registration of parliamentary voters in Ireland, and to alter the law for rating immediate lessors of premises to the poor rate in certain boroughs.	Sections ninety-two to ninety-six, both inclusive.

[Schedule IV. refers to England and Schedule V. to Scotland.]

Sixth Schedule.

Acts relating to Ireland.

A description or citation of a portion of an Act is inclusive of the words, section, or other part first or last mentioned, or otherwise referred to as forming the beginning or as forming the end of the portion comprised in the description or citation.

Acts of the Parliament of Ireland.

Session and Chapter.	Title.	Extent of Repeal.
10 Hen. 7, c. 22, .	An Act confirming all the statutes made in England.	So much of the same as extends to Ireland the provisions of the Acts of the Parliament of England following; namely, 7 Hen. 4, chapter fifteen, 8 Hen. 6, chapter seven, from "and such as have the "greatest number" to "shall lose their wages," and from "and that in "every writ that shall "hereafter go forth" to the end of the chapter, 23 Hen. 6, chapter fourteen.
35 Geo. 3, c. 29, .	An Act for regulating the election of members to serve in Parliament, and for repealing the several Acts therein mentioned.	Section three, sections five to thirteen, sections fifteen to eighteen, section twenty.

Acts of the Parliament of the United Kingdom.

1 Geo. 4, c. 11, .	An Act for the better regulation of polls, and for making further provision touching the election of members to serve in Parliament for Ireland.	Sections two and three, section five from the words "and that such sheriff" to the end of that section, sections six to twenty-one, section twenty-three, sections forty-one and forty-two.

*

Sixth Schedule—*continued.*

Session and Chapter.	Title.	Extent of Repeal.
9 Geo. 4, c. 82.	An Act to make provision for the lighting, cleansing, and watching of cities, towns, corporations, and market towns in Ireland in certain cases.	So much of sections twelve and sixteen as prescribes the mode of election of commissioners.
4 Geo. 4, c. 55.	An Act to consolidate and amend the several Acts now in force, so far as the same relate to the election and return of members to serve in Parliament for counties of cities and counties of towns in Ireland.	Section thirty-three from the words "and that such sheriffs" to the end of that section, sections thirty-four to forty-seven, sections forty-nine to fifty-nine, sections sixty to sixty-two, sections sixty-four and sixty-five, sections sixty-eight to seventy, seventy-two, seventy-six, and seventy-seven.
2 & 3 Will. 4, c. 88.	An Act to amend the representation of the people of Ireland.	Section thirty, section forty-eight, and sections forty-nine to fifty-four.
3 & 4 Vict., c. 108.	An Act for the regulation of municipal corporations in Ireland.	Section sixty-four from the words "by delivering to "the mayor or barrister" to the end of that section, and so much of that section as relates to assessors; section sixty-five from "and shall be so divided" to "poll at each compart-"ment," and from "in "case the booths" to "at "each place;" the words "are you the person whose "name is signed as A. B "to the voting paper now "delivered in by you," in section sixty-six; section sixty-eight from "and the "mayor shall cause the "voting papers" to the end of that section, and so much of the rest of that section as relates to assessors; and so much of section seventy as relates to ward assessors.

35 *and* 36 *Vict., c.* 33.

Sixth Schedule—*continued*.

Session and Chapter.	Title.	Extent of Repeal.
6 & 7 Vict., c. 93,	An Act to amend an Act of the third and fourth years of Her present Majesty for the regulation of municipal corporations in Ireland.	Section twenty-three.
9 & 10 Vict., c. 19,	An Act to amend an Act of the second and third years of His late Majesty by providing additional booths or polling places at elections in Ireland where the number of electors whose names shall begin with the same letter of the alphabet shall exceed a certain number.	The whole Act.
13 & 14 Vict., c. 68,	An Act to shorten the duration of elections in Ireland, and for establishing additional places for taking the poll thereat.	Section one, section three, section four, sections ten to fourteen, so much of section fifteen as prescribes the interval between the election and the polling, section sixteen, section nineteen from "and that "all the deputies" to "at "the expense of the candi-"dates," section twenty, section twenty-two.
13 & 14 Vict., c. 69,	An Act to amend the laws which regulate the qualification and registration of parliamentary voters in Ireland, and to alter the law for rating immediate lessors of premises to the poor rate in certain boroughs.	Sections eighty-six, ninety-eight, ninety-nine; section one hundred; sections one hundred and one and one hundred and two, sections one hundred and four and one hundred and five.
17 & 18 Vict., c. 102,	The Corrupt Practices Prevention Act, 1854.	Section eleven, and Schedule B.

Sixth Schedule—*continued.*

Session and Chapter.	Title.	Extent of Repeal.
17 & 18 Vict., c. 103,	The Towns Improvement (Ireland) Act, 1854.	So much of section twenty-four as incorporates the sections of 10 & 11 Vict. c. 16, following; that is to say,—sections twenty-three, twenty-six, and twenty-seven; section twenty-eight from the words " and shall be conducted in manner following " to " carefully preserved by the presiding officer, and," the question numbered I., section thirty from " the returning officer " to " each person and," and section thirty-one, and so much of any Act as incorporates the part of the said section twenty-four hereby repealed.
25 & 26 Vict., c. 62,	An Act to amend the law relating to the duration of contested elections for counties in Ireland, and for establishing additional places for taking the poll thereat.	Part of section four, namely, so much as prescribes the interval between the day fixed for the election and the polling; section five, sections eight to ten.
25 & 26 Vict., c. 92,	An Act to limit the time for proceeding to elections in counties and boroughs in Ireland.	Section one, and section two from the words " and in every city or town " to the end of that section.
31 & 32 Vict., c. 49,	An Act to amend the representation of the people in Ireland.	Section twelve from the words " several boroughs " to the word " Cork " and the words " and county of the city of Limerick."
31 & 32 Vict., c. 112,	An Act to amend the law of registration in Ireland.	Sections four to thirty; section thirty-eight.

CORRUPT PRACTICES (MUNICIPAL ELECTIONS) ACT, 1872.

(35 & 36 Vict., c. 60).

An Act for the better prevention of Corrupt Practices at Municipal Elections, and for establishing a tribunal for the trial of the validity of such Elections. [6th August, 1872.]

Whereas it is expedient to make provision for the better prevention of corrupt practices at municipal elections, and for establishing a tribunal for the trial of the validity of such elections:

*　　*　　*　　*　　*　　*　　*

Preliminary.

1. This Act may be cited for all purposes as the "Corrupt Practices (Municipal Elections) Act, 1872."

2. In this Act, except where the context otherwise requires, the following words and expressions shall respectively be construed as follows, viz.:

(1.) " Borough " means a place for the time being subject to the provisions of the Act of the fifth and sixth of William the Fourth, chapter seventy-six, intituled " An Act to provide " for the regulation of municipal corporations in England and " Wales," as amended by the Acts amending the said Act:

"Office" means the office of mayor, alderman, councillor, auditor, or assessor, of a borough or ward of a borough:

" Election " means an election to an office:

" Candidate " means a person elected, or who has been nominated or has declared himself a candidate for election to an office:

" Canvasser " means any person who solicits or persuades, or attempts to persuade, any person to vote or to abstain from voting at an election, or to vote or to abstain from voting for any candidate at an election:

" Register " includes a burgess roll or ward list:

" Voter " means a person included in a register or who voted or claimed to vote at an election:

" Returning officer " means a person under whatever designation presiding at an election:

" Election court " means an election court constituted and acting under the provisions of this Act for the trial of a petition respecting an election:

" Superior court " means the Court of Common Pleas at Westminster:

" Prescribed " means prescribed by general rules to be made under the provisions of this Act.

(2.) This Act shall so far as is consistent with the tenor thereof be construed as one with the Acts for the time being in force relating to boroughs and to elections in boroughs.

Part I.

Corrupt Practices at Municipal Elections.

3. The offences of bribery, treating, undue influence, and personation, shall be deemed to be corrupt practices at an election for the purposes of this Act.

The terms "bribery," "treating," "undue influence," and "personation," shall respectively include anything committed or done before, at, after, or with respect to an election, which if done before, at, after, or with respect to an election of members to serve in Parliament would render the person committing or doing the same liable to any penalties, punishments, or disqualifications, for bribery, treating, undue influence, or personation, as the case may be, under any Act for the time being in force with respect to elections of members to serve in Parliament.

Any person who is guilty of a corrupt practice at an election shall be liable to the like actions, prosecutions, penalties, forfeitures, and punishments, as if the corrupt practice had been committed at an election of members to serve in Parliament.

4. Where it is found by the report of an election court acting under the provisions of this Act that any corrupt practice has been committed by or with the knowledge and consent of any candidate at an election, such candidate shall be deemed to have been personally guilty of corrupt practices at the election, and his election, if he has been elected, shall be void, and he shall (whether he was elected or not) during seven years from the date of the report be subject to the following disqualifications; viz.,

(1). He shall be incapable of holding or exercising any municipal office or franchise, and of having his name placed on the register, or voting at any municipal election:
(2). He shall be incapable of acting as a justice of the peace and of holding any judicial office:
(3). He shall be incapable of being elected to and of sitting or voting in Parliament:
(4). He shall be incapable of being registered or voting as a parliamentary voter:
(5.) He shall be incapable of being employed by any candidate in any parliamentary or municipal election:
(6.) He shall be incapable of acting as overseer or as guardian of the poor.

If any person is upon an indictment or information found guilty of any corrupt practice at an election, or is in any action or proceeding adjudged to pay a penalty or forfeiture for any corrupt practice at an election, he shall, whether he was a candidate at the election or not, be subject during seven years from the date of the conviction or judgment to all the disqualifications mentioned in this section.

If at any time after any person has become disqualified by virtue of this Act, the witnesses, or any of them, on whose testimony such person has so become disqualified, are upon the prosecution of such person convicted of perjury in respect of such testimony, it shall be lawful for such person to move the superior court to order, and the superior court shall, upon being satisfied that such disqualification was procured by reason of perjury, order that such disqualification shall thenceforth cease and determine, and the same shall cease and determine accordingly.

5. If it is found by an election court acting under the provisions of this Act, that a candidate has by an agent been guilty of any corrupt practice at an election, or that any act hereinafter in this Act declared to be an offence against this Act has been committed at an election by a candidate or by an agent for a candidate with the candidate's knowledge and consent, the candidate shall during the period for which he was elected to serve, or for which, if elected, he might have served, be disqualified for being elected to and for holding any municipal office in the borough for which the election was held, and if he was elected his election shall be void.

6. An election for a borough or a ward thereof shall be wholly avoided by such general corruption, bribery, treating, or intimidation at the election for such borough or ward as would by the common law of Parliament avoid an election of members to serve in Parliament for a parliamentary borough.

7. No person who is included in a register for a borough or ward thereof as a burgess or citizen shall be retained or employed for payment or reward by or on behalf of a candidate at an election for such borough or any ward thereof as a canvasser for the purposes of the election.

If any person is retained or employed by or on behalf of a candidate at an election in contravention of this prohibition, such person and also the candidate or other person by whom he is retained or employed shall be deemed to be guilty of an offence against this Act, and shall be liable on summary conviction before two justices of the peace to a penalty not exceeding ten pounds.

An agent or canvasser who is retained or employed for payment or reward for any of the purposes of an election shall not vote at the election, and if he votes he shall be guilty of an offence against this Act, and shall be liable on summary conviction before two justices of the peace to a penalty not exceeding ten pounds.

8. If a candidate or an agent for a candidate pays or agrees to pay any money on account of the conveyance of a voter to or from

the poll, such candidate or agent shall be deemed to be guilty of an offence against this Act, and shall be liable on summary conviction before two justices of the peace to a penalty not exceeding five pounds.

9. The costs and expenses of a prosecutor and his witnesses in the prosecution of any person for either of the corrupt practices of bribery, undue influence, or personation at an election, together with compensation for trouble and loss of time, shall, unless the court before which such person is prosecuted otherwise directs, be allowed, paid, and borne in the same manner in which they may be allowed, paid, and borne in cases of felony.

The clerk of the peace of the county in which a borough is situate, or in the case of a borough which is a county of a city or a county of a town or in which there is a clerk of the peace, the clerk of the peace of such county of a city or county of a town or borough, shall, if he is directed by an election court acting under the provisions of this Act to prosecute any person for either of the corrupt practices of bribery, undue influence, or personation at the election in respect of which the court acts, or to sue or proceed against any person for penalties for bribery, treating, undue influence, or any offence against this Act at such election, prosecute, sue, or proceed against such person accordingly.

10. The votes of persons in respect of whom any corrupt practice is proved to have been committed shall be struck off on a scrutiny.

Subject to the provisions of this section a register shall for all purposes be conclusive as to the right of the persons included therein to vote at an election for the purposes whereof such register is in force; but nothing in this section shall entitle any person to vote who is by any Act or law prohibited from voting at an election on the ground of any disqualification by office or disability, nor shall relieve any such person from any penalty, liability, or punishment to which he may by law be subject by reason of his voting at an election.

11. The provisions of the Acts for the time being in force for the detection of personation and for the apprehension of persons charged with personation at a parliamentary election shall apply in the case of a municipal election.

Part II.

Election Petitions.

12. The election of any person at an election for a borough or ward may be questioned by petition before an election court constituted as hereinafter in this Act provided, and hereinafter in this Act referred to as the "court," on the ground that the election was as to the borough or ward wholly avoided by general bribery,

treating, undue influence, or personation, or on the ground that the election of such person was avoided by corrupt practices or offences against this Act committed at the election, or on the ground that he was at the time of the election disqualified for election to the office for which the election was held, or on the ground that he was not duly elected by a majority of lawful votes.

An election shall not, except in the manner provided by this Act, be questioned upon an information in the nature of a quo warranto or by or in any process or manner whatsoever for a matter for which it might be questioned under the provisions of this Act.

[Sections 13, 14, and Sub-Sections (1), (2), and (3) of Section 15 do not apply to Ireland].

*   *   *   *   *   *

15. The following provisions shall have effect with respect to the trial of a petition :

(4.) At the conclusion of the trial the court shall determine whether the person whose election is complained of, or any and what other person, was duly elected, or whether the election was void, and shall forthwith certify in writing the determination to the superior court, and upon the certificate being given the determination shall be final to all intents and purposes as to the matters at issue on the petition :

(5.) Where any charge is made in a petition of any corrupt practice or offence against this Act having been committed at the election to which the petition refers, the court shall, in addition to the certificate, and at the same time, report in writing to the superior court as follows :

(a.) Whether any corrupt practice or offence against this Act has or has not been proved to have been committed by or with the knowledge and consent of any candidate at the election, and the nature of such corrupt practice or offence against this Act ;

(b.) The names of all persons (if any) who have been proved at the trial to have been guilty of any corrupt practice or offence against this Act ;

(c.) Whether any corrupt practices have, or whether there is reason to believe that any corrupt practices have extensively prevailed at the election to which the petition relates, in the borough or in any ward thereof ;

The court may at the same time make a special report to the superior court as to any matters arising in the course of the trial, an account of which, in the judgment of the court, ought to be submitted to the superior court :

(6.) Where, upon the application of any party to a petition made in the prescribed manner to the superior court, it appears to that court that the case raised by the petition can be conveniently stated as a special case, that court may direct the same to be stated accordingly, and any such special case shall be heard before the superior court, and the decision of the superior court shall be final:

(7.) If it appear to the court on the trial of a petition that any question of law as to the admissibility of evidence, or otherwise, requires further consideration by the superior court, the court may postpone the granting of a certificate until such question has been determined by the superior court, and for this purpose may reserve any such question, in like manner in which questions may be reserved by a judge on a trial at nisi prius:

(8.) On a trial of a petition, unless the court otherwise directs, any charge of a corrupt practice or offence against this Act may be gone into, and evidence in relation thereto received before any proof has been given of agency on behalf of any candidate in respect of such corrupt practice or offence:

(9.) On the trial of a petition complaining of an undue election and claiming the office for some person, the respondent may give evidence to prove that such person was not duly elected, in the same manner as if he had presented a petition against the election of such person:

(10.) The trial of a petition shall be proceeded with notwithstanding that the respondent has ceased to hold the office his election to which is questioned by the petition:

(11.) A copy of any certificate or report made to the superior court upon the trial of a petition or a statement of any decision made by the superior court shall by the superior court be transmitted to one of Her Majesty's Principal Secretaries of State:

(12.) A copy of any certificate made by the court to the superior court, or in case of a decision by the superior court upon a special case a statement of such decision shall be certified by the superior court, under the hands of two or more judges of the superior court, to the town clerk of the borough to which the petition relates.

16. The following provisions shall have effect with respect to witnesses at the trial of a petition:

(1.) Witnesses shall be summoned and sworn in the same manner as nearly as circumstances admit, as witnesses at a trial at nisi prius, and shall be liable to the same penalties for perjury:

(2.) On the trial of a petition the court may, by order in writing compel the attendance of any person as a witness who appears to the court to have been concerned in the election to which the petition refers, and any person refusing to obey such order shall be guilty of contempt of court. The election court may examine any witness so compelled to attend, or any person in court although such witness is not called and examined by any party to the petition. After the examination of a witness by the election court such witness may be cross-examined by or on behalf of the petitioner and respondent or either of them :

(3.) The provisions of the seventh section of the Act of the twenty-sixth and twenty-seventh of Her Majesty, chapter twenty-nine, relating to the examination and indemnity of witnesses, shall apply to any witness appearing before the court on the trial of a petition under this Act, and the certificate shall be given by the court ; provided always, that the giving or refusal to give such certificate by the court shall be final and conclusive, and shall not be questioned by any proceeding or in any court whatsoever :

(4.) The reasonable expenses incurred by any person in appearing to give evidence at the trial of a petition according to the scale allowed to witnesses on the trial of civil actions at the assizes, may be allowed to such person by a certificate of the court or of the prescribed officer, and such expenses, if the witness was called and examined by the court, shall be deemed part of the expenses of providing a court, and in other cases shall be deemed to be costs of the petition.

17. The following provisions shall have effect with respect to the withdrawal and abatement of petitions :

(1.) A petition shall not be withdrawn without the leave of the court or superior court upon special application, to be made in and at the prescribed manner, time, and place ;

No such application shall be made for the withdrawal of a petition until the prescribed notice has been given in the borough to which the petition relates, of the intention of the petitioner to make an application for the withdrawal of his petition :

(2.) On the hearing of the application for withdrawal any person who might have been a petitioner in respect of the election to which the petition relates, may apply to the court or superior court to be substituted as a petitioner for the petitioner so desirous of withdrawing the petition ;

The court or superior court may, if it think fit, substitute as a petitioner any such applicant as aforesaid ; and may further, if the proposed withdrawal is in the opinion of the court or superior court induced by any corrupt bargain or consideration, by order direct that the security given on behalf of the original petitioner shall remain as security for any costs that may be incurred by the substituted petitioner, and that to the extent of the sum named in such security, the original petitioner and his sureties shall be liable to pay the costs of the substituted petitioner :

(3.) If no such order is made with respect to the security given on behalf of the original petitioner, security to the same amount as would be required in the case of a new petition, and subject to the like conditions, shall be given on behalf of the substituted petitioner before he proceeds with his petition, and within the prescribed time after the order of substitution :

(4.) Subject as aforesaid a substituted petitioner shall stand in the same position as nearly as may be, and be subject to the same liabilities, as the original petitioner ;

If a petition is withdrawn, the petitioner shall be liable to pay the costs of the respondent ;

Where there are more petitioners than one, no application to withdraw a petition shall be made except with the consent of all the petitioners :

(5.) A petition shall be abated by the death of a sole petitioner or of the survivor of several petitioners :

The abatement of a petition shall not affect the liability of the petitioner or of any other person to the payment of costs previously incurred ;

On the abatement of a petition the prescribed notice of such abatement having taken place shall be given in the borough to which the petition relates, and within the prescribed time after the notice is given, any person who might have been a petitioner in respect of the election to which the petition relates, may apply to the court or superior court in and at the prescribed manner, time, and place, to be substituted as a petitioner ;

The court or superior court may, if it think fit, substitute as a petitioner any such applicant who is desirous of being substituted and on whose behalf security to the same amount is given as is required in the case of a new petition.

18. The following provisions shall have effect with respect to the withdrawal and substitution of respondents upon a petition :

(1.) If before the trial of a petition either of the following events happens in the case of a respondent other than a returning officer ; viz.,

(*a*.) If he dies, resigns, or otherwise ceases to hold the office to which the petition relates ; or

(*b*.) If he gives the prescribed notice that he does not intend to oppose the petition ;

Notice of such event having taken place shall be given in the borough to which the petition relates, and within the prescribed time after the notice is given any person who might have been a petitioner in respect of the election to which the petition relates, may apply to the court or superior court to be admitted as a respondent to oppose the petition, and such person shall be admitted accordingly, and any number of persons not exceeding three may be so admitted:

(2.) A respondent who has given the prescribed notice that he does not intend to oppose the petition, shall not be allowed to appear or act as a party against such petition in any proceedings thereon.

19. The following provisions shall have effect with respect to costs on the trial of a petition:

(1.) All costs, charges, and expenses of and incidental to the presentation of a petition, and to the proceedings consequent thereon, with the exception of such costs, charges, and expenses as are by this Act otherwise provided for, shall be defrayed by the parties to the petition in such manner and in such proportions as the court by which the petition is tried may determine; and in particular any costs, charges, or expenses which in the opinion of the court by which the petition is tried have been caused by vexatious conduct, unfounded allegations, or unfounded objections on the part either of the petitioner or the respondent, and any needless expense incurred or caused on the part of petitioner or respondent, may be ordered to be defrayed by the parties by whom it has been incurred or caused, whether such parties are or not on the whole successful:

(2.) The costs may be taxed in the prescribed manner, but according to the same principles as costs between attorney and client in a suit in the High Court of Chancery, and such costs may be recovered in the same manner as the costs of an action at law, or in such other manner as may be prescribed.

(3.) If any petitioner neglect or refuse for the space of three months after demand to pay to any person summoned as a witness on his behalf, or to the respondent, any sum certified to be due to him for his costs, charges, and expenses, and if such neglect or refusal be, within one year after such demand, proved to the satisfaction of the superior court, every person who has entered into a recognizance relating to such petition under the provisions of this Act shall be held to have made default in his said recognizance, and the prescribed officer shall thereupon certify such recognizance to be forfeited, and the same shall be dealt with in the same manner as a forfeited recognizance under the provisions of the Parliamentary Elections Act, 1868.

20. The following provisions shall have effect with reference to the reception of the court upon the trial of a petition: * * *

(Sub-sections (1) & (2) do not apply to Ireland.)

(3.) The court may employ such officers and clerks as may be allowed by general rules to be made under the provisions of this Act :

(4.) A shorthand writer shall attend at the trial of a petition, and shall be sworn by the court faithfully and truly to take down the evidence given at the trial, and shall take down the evidence at length, and a copy of the evidence so taken shall accompany the certificate of the said court, and the expenses of the shorthand writer, according to a scale to be prescribed, shall be deemed to be part of the expenses incurred in receiving the court.

21. The following provisions shall have effect with respect to jurisdiction, and to general rules :

(1.) The judges for the time being on the rota for the trial of election petitions under the provisions of the Parliamentary Elections Act, 1868, may from time to time make, revoke, and alter general rules for the effectual execution of this Act, and of the intention and object thereof, and the regulation of the practice, procedure and costs of petitions, and the trial thereof, and the certifying and reporting thereon :

Any general rules made as aforesaid shall, in so far as they are not inconsistent with any of the provisions of this Act, be deemed to be within the powers conferred by this Act, and shall be of the same force as if they were enacted in the body of this Act ;

Any general rules made in pursuance of this section shall be laid before Parliament within three weeks after they are made, if Parliament be then sitting, and if Parliament be not then sitting, within three weeks after the beginning of the then next session of Parliament :

(2.) Until general rules have been made in pursuance of this Act, and so far as such rules (when made), and the provisions of this Act, do not extend, the principles, practice, and rules which are for the time being observed in the case of election petitions under the provisions of the Parliamentary Elections Act, 1868, shall be observed so far as may be by the court and superior court in the case of petitions under this Act :

(3.) The duties to be performed by the prescribed officer under this Act shall be performed by the prescribed officer of the superior court :

(4.) The rules and principles with regard to agency and evidence, and with regard to a scrutiny, and with regard to the declaring any person to be elected in the room of any other person who is declared to have been not duly elected, which are applicable in the case of parliamentary election petitions shall be applied so far as they are applicable in the case of a petition under this Act :

(5.) The superior court shall, subject to the provisions of this Act, have the same powers, jurisdiction, and authority with reference to an election petition and the proceedings thereon as it would have if the petition were an ordinary cause within its jurisdiction.

Miscellaneous Provisions.

22. The remuneration and allowances to be paid to a barrister for his services in respect of the trial of a petition, and to any officers, clerks, or shorthand writers employed under the provisions of this Act shall be fixed by a scale which shall be made and may be varied from time to time by the election judges on the rota for the trial of election petitions under the provisions of the Parliamentary Elections Act, 1868, with the approval of the Commissioners of Her Majesty's Treasury, or any two or more of them, and the amount of any such remuneration and allowances shall be paid by the said Commissioners, and shall be repaid to the said Commissioners on their certificate, by the treasurer of the borough to which the petition relates, out of the borough fund or rate:

Provided that the court at its discretion may order that the whole or any part of such remuneration and allowances, or the whole or any part of the expenses incurred by a town clerk for receiving the court under the provisions of this Act, shall be repaid to the said commissioners or to the town clerk, as the case may be, in the cases, by the persons, in the manner following; viz.,

(a.) When in the opinion of the court a petition is frivolous and vexatious, then by the petitioner;

(b.) When in the opinion of the court a respondent has been personally guilty of corrupt practices at the election, then by such respondent:

And any order so made for the repayment of any sum by a petitioner or respondent may be enforced in the same way as an order for payment of costs; but any other costs or expenses payable by such petitioner or respondent to any party to the petition shall be satisfied out of any deposit or security made or given under the provisions of this Act before such deposit or security is applied for the repayment of any sum under an order made in pursuance of this section.

23. Where a candidate who has been elected to an office at an election is by a certificate of the court, or by a decision of the superior court, declared not to have been duly elected, acts done by him in execution of such office before the time when the certificate or decision is certified to the town clerk, shall not be invali-

dated by reason of his being so declared not to have been duly elected.

24. Where upon a petition the election of any person to an office has been declared void, and no other person has been declared elected in his room, a new election shall forthwith be held to supply the vacancy in the same manner as in the case of an extraordinary vacancy in the office; and for the purposes of any such new election any duties to be performed by a mayor, alderman, or any officer, shall, if such mayor, alderman, or officer has been declared not elected, be performed by a deputy, or other person who might have acted for him if he had been incapacitated by illness.

25. In reckoning time for the purposes of this Act, Sunday, Christmas Day, Good Friday, and any day set apart for a public fast or public thanksgiving shall be excluded.

26. No person who has voted at an election by ballot shall in any proceeding to question the election be required to state for whom he has voted.

27. This Act shall not apply to Scotland.

28. This Act shall apply to Ireland; provided as follows:

(1.) "The superior court" means the Court of Common Pleas at Dublin:

(2.) "Borough" means a place for the time being subject to the provisions of the Act of the third and fourth of Her Majesty, chapter one hundred and eight, intituled "An Act for the regulation of Municipal Corporations in Ireland," the Act of the ninth of George the Fourth, chapter eighty-two, the Towns Improvement (Ireland) Act, 1854, or of any local and personal Act providing for the election of commissioners in any towns or places for purposes similar to the purposes of the said Acts:

(3.) "Office" means either of the offices of mayor, alderman, councillor, commissioner, municipal commissioner, town commissioner, township commissioner, or assessor, of any borough:

(4.) "Town clerk" includes a clerk to commissioners:

(5.) "Borough rate or fund" includes any rate, fund, or assessment out of which the expenses of any election to an office in a borough may be defrayed:

(6.) "County court" means a civil bill court:

(7.) "Register" has the same meaning as the term "Register of Voters" in Part II. of the First Schedule to the Ballot Act, 1872, as applied to Ireland:

(8.) "One of Her Majesty's Principal Secretaries of State" shall be construed to mean the Chief Secretary to the Lord Lieutenant of Ireland for the time being:

(9.) Petitions questioning the election of any person to any office at an election for a borough or ward on the grounds set forth in section 12 of this Act may be presented to the court as defined by the Local Government (Ireland) Act, 1871, and the same shall be presented and tried in the manner and subject to the provisions of the said Act relating to controverted elections as the same are modified by this Act; and the terms "election court" or "court" and "prescribed" in this Act shall be construed to have the same meanings respectively as the terms "court" and "prescribed" in the said Act:

(10.) Where under the provisions of this Act any general rules may be made, the same shall be made by the court in the manner and subject to the provisions of section 21 of the Local Government (Ireland) Act, 1871:

(11.) Sections 13 and 14, sub-sections (1.), (2.), and (3.) of section 15, and sub-sections (1.) and (2.) of section 20, shall not extend or apply to Ireland.

29. The Acts mentioned in the Schedule to this Act are repealed to the extent therein mentioned; but such repeal shall not affect the validity or invalidity of anything already done or suffered, or any offence already committed, or any remedy or proceeding in respect thereof, or the proof of any past act or thing.

SCHEDULE.

Acts Repealed.

5 & 6 Will. 4. c. 76, ss. 54 to 56, both inclusive.
22 Vict. c. 35. ss. 9 to 14, both inclusive.
3 & 4 Vict. c. 108, ss. 90, 91.

MUNICIPAL ELECTIONS ACT, 1875.

(38 and 39 Vict., c. 40.)

An Act to amend the Law regulating Municipal Elections.

[19th July, 1875].

Be it enacted, etc.—

1. The following provisions shall be enacted and apply to nominations at all municipal elections of councillors, auditors, and assessors after the passing of this Act:

1. Nine days at least before any such election the town clerk shall prepare, sign, and publish a notice in the form No. 1. set forth in the First Schedule to this Act, or to the like effect, by causing the same to be placed on the door of the Town Hall, and in some conspicuous parts of the borough or ward for which any such election is to be held.

2. At any such election every candidate shall be nominated in writing; the writing shall be subscribed by two enrolled burgesses of such borough or ward as proposer and seconder, and by eight other enrolled burgesses of such borough or ward as assenting to the nomination. Each candidate shall be nominated by a separate nomination paper, but the same burgesses, or any of them, may subscribe as many nomination papers as there are vacancies to be filled, but no more. Every person nominated shall be enrolled on the burgess roll of the borough, or a person whose name is inserted in the separate list at the end of the burgess roll, as provided by section three of the Act thirty-two and thirty-three Victoria, chapter fifty-five, and shall be otherwise qualified to be elected. The nomination paper shall state the surname and other names of the person nominated, with his place of abode and description, and shall be in the form No. 2. set forth in the First Schedule to this Act, or to the like effect. And the town clerk shall provide nomination papers, and shall supply any enrolled burgess with as many nomination papers as may be required, and shall, at the request of any such person, fill up a nomination paper in manner prescribed by this Act.

3. Every nomination paper subscribed as aforesaid shall be delivered by the candidate himself, or his proposer or seconder, to the town clerk, seven days at least before the day of election, and before five o'clock in the afternoon of the last day on which any such nomination paper may by law be delivered; the town clerk shall forthwith send notice of such nomination to each person nominated. The mayor shall attend at the Town Hall on the day next after the last day for the delivery of nominations to the town clerk between the hours of two and four in the afternoon, and shall decide on the validity of every objection made to a nomination paper, such objection to be made in writing. The candidate nominated by each nomination paper, and one other person, appointed by or on behalf of the candidate as hereinafter mentioned, and no person other than aforesaid, shall, except for the purpose of assisting the mayor, be entitled to attend such proceedings, and each candidate and the person appointed by him shall, during the time appointed for the attendance of the mayor for the purposes for this section, have respectively power to object to the nomination paper of every person nominated at the same election. The decision of the mayor, which shall be given in writing, shall, if disallowing any objection to a nomination paper, be final, but if allowing the same shall be subject to reversal on petition questioning the election or return. The appointment by or on behalf of candidates of persons as aforesaid

38 *and* 39 *Vict.*, c. 40.

shall be made in writing under the hand of the candidate, or, in case he is absent from the United Kingdom, then under the hand of his proposer or seconder, and shall be delivered to the town clerk before five o'clock in the afternoon of the last day on which nomination papers may by law be delivered.

The town clerk shall at least four days before the day of election cause the surnames and other names of all persons duly nominated, with their respective places of abode and descriptions, and the names of the persons subscribing their respective nomination papers as proposers and seconders, to be printed and placed on the door of the Town Hall, and in some conspicuous parts of the borough or ward for which such election is to be held.

4. Section eight of the Act of twenty-second Victoria, chapter thirty-five, so far as the same is now in force, shall apply to nominations of councillors, auditors, and assessors, duly made and allowed under this Act.

Section three of the Ballot Act, 1872, shall apply to nomination papers under this Act, and so applied, the word "returning officer" shall be taken to include town clerk in reference to the delivery of such nomination papers.

2. The nomination of a person who is absent from the United Kingdom shall be void, unless his written consent given within one month of the day of his nomination before two witnesses be produced at the time of his nomination.

3. At any municipal election of councillors, auditors, or assessors, the power and duty of the mayor, under section twenty of the Ballot Act of 1872, to provide everything which in the case of a parliamentary election is required to be provided by the returning officer for the purpose of a poll, shall (save as to the appointment of the alderman as returning officer for any ward) extend to the appointment of officers for taking the poll and counting the votes recorded at such election.

4. The provisions contained in rules 16 and 19 of the first schedule to the Ballot Act, 1872, shall not apply to any such election, but the mayor shall furnish every polling station with such number of compartments in which the voters can mark their votes screened from observation, and furnish each presiding officer with such number of ballot papers, as in the judgment of the mayor shall be necessary for effectually taking the poll at such election in other respects in the manner provided by the Ballot Act, 1872. Where more candidates are nominated than there are vacancies to be supplied, the mayor shall at least four days before the day of election, give such public notice as may be required by law of the situation, division, and allotment of polling places for taking the poll at any municipal election, and of the description

of persons entitled to vote thereat and at the several polling stations.

5. At any municipal election a person shall not be entitled to sign or subscribe any nomination paper, or to vote, unless his name is on the burgess roll for the time being in force in the borough, or on the ward list for the time being in force for the ward, for which such election shall be held; and every person whose name is on such burgess roll or ward list, as the case may be, shall be entitled to sign or subscribe any nomination paper, and to demand and receive a ballot paper, and to vote; provided that nothing in this section shall entitle any person to do any of the acts aforesaid who is prohibited from doing such acts or any of them by law, or relieve such person from any penalties to which he may be liable for doing any such act.

6. At the poll at any election of auditors and assessors one ballot paper only shall be used by any person voting. In such ballot paper the names of the candidates for the respective offices shall be separate, and distinguished so as to show the office for which they are respectively candidates, and the ballot paper shall be in the Form No. 3. set forth in the First Schedule to this Act or to the like effect, and the provisions of the Ballot Act, 1872, shall at any such election be altered and varied accordingly; provided always, that in counting the votes every such ballot paper shall be deemed to be a separate ballot paper in respect of each office, and any objections thereto shall be considered and dealt with accordingly.

7. Where more candidates are nominated at any municipal election than there are vacancies to be filled at such election, any of such candidates may withdraw from his candidature by notice signed by him and delivered to the town clerk not later than two o'clock in the afternoon of the day next after the last day for the delivery of nomination papers to the town clerk; provided that such notices shall take effect in the order in which they are delivered to the town clerk, and that no such notice shall have effect so as to reduce the number of candidates ultimately standing nominated below the number of the vacancies to be filled.

8. Any notice required by law to be given or published by the mayor or other returning officer or town clerk in connexion with any municipal election may, as to auditors and assessors, be comprised in one notice, and with respect to the election of councillors in any borough divided into wards, may comprise the matter necessary to such notice for the several wards in the borough, and it shall not be necessary to issue a separate notice for each ward.

9. Section eleven of the Act sixteenth and seventeenth Victoria, chapter seventy-nine, shall be read as if fourteen days were therein inserted instead of ten days, and the day for holding the election in the case of any extraordinary vacancy in the office of councillor,

auditor, or assessor in any borough (whether such borough shall be divided into wards or not) shall be fixed by the mayor.

10. The town council of any borough may by order divide any such borough or any ward or wards of such borough into polling districts in such manner as they may think most convenient for taking the votes of the burgesses at a poll, and the overseer shall, so far as practicable, make out the list of burgesses in such manner as to divide the names in conformity with such polling districts.

11. In reckoning time for the purpose of this Act, Sunday, Christmas Day, Good Friday, and any day set apart for a public holiday, fast, or public thanksgiving, shall be excluded.

12. The several Acts of Parliament mentioned in the Second Schedule to this Act shall be repealed to the extent specified in the third column of such schedule, but such repeal shall not affect the validity or invalidity of anything already done or suffered, or any remedy or proceeding in respect thereof, or the proof of any past act or thing.

13. This Act shall, as far as consistent with the tenor thereof, be construed as one with the Act fifth and sixth William the Fourth, chapter seventy-six, and the Acts amending the same, and the Acts for the time being in force relating to elections of councillors, auditors, and assessors in boroughs.

14. This Act may for all purposes be cited as "The Municipal Elections Act, 1875."

15. This Act shall continue in force for so long only as the Ballot Act, 1872, continues in force.

FIRST SCHEDULE.

Form No. 1.

NOTICE.

Borough of   .   Election of [Councillors, *or* Auditors, *or* Assessors, *as the case may be*] for the [Ward or several Wards of the] Borough.

Take Notice.

1. That an election of [*here insert the number of Councillors, Auditors, or Assessors, as the case may be*] for the [Ward or several Wards of the] said Borough will be held on the   day of

2. Candidates must be nominated by writing, subscribed by two enrolled burgesses as proposer or seconder, and by eight other enrolled burgesses as assenting to the nomination.

3. Candidates must be duly qualified for the office to which they are nominated, and the nomination paper must state the surname and other names of the person nominated, with his place of abode and description, and may be in the following form, or to the like effect:

(Set out Form No. 2.)

4. Each candidate must be nominated by a separate nomination paper, but the same burgesses or any of them may subscribe as many nomination papers as there are vacancies to be filled for the borough [or ward], but no more.

5. Every person who forges a nomination paper, or delivers any nomination paper knowing the same to be forged, will be guilty of misdemeanor, and be liable to imprisonment for any term not exceeding six months, with or without hard labour.

6. Nomination papers must be delivered by the candidate himself, or his proposer or seconder, to the town clerk at his office before five o'clock in the afternoon of   day the   day of   next.

7. The mayor will attend at the Town Hall, on   day the   day of   , from two to four o'clock in the afternoon, to hear and decide objections to nomination papers.

8. Forms of nomination papers may be obtained at the town clerk's office; and the town clerk will, at the request of any enrolled burgess, fill up a nomination paper.

Dated this   day of   18   .

A.B., Town Clerk.

Form No. 2.

NOMINATION PAPER.

Borough of   . Election of Councillors, Auditors, or Assessors for   Ward in the said Borough [or the said Borough], to be held on the   day of   18   .

We, the undersigned, being respectively enrolled burgesses, hereby nominate the following person as a candidate at the said election.

Surname.	Other Names.	Abode.	Description.

(Signed) A.B. of*
C.D. of*

* The number on the Burgess Roll of the Burgess subscribing, with the situation of the property in respect of which he is enrolled on the Burgess Roll.

We, the undersigned, being respectively enrolled burgesses, do hereby assent to the nomination of the above person as a candidate at the said election.

Dated this   day of   18   .

(Signed)   E.F. of*
           G.H. of*
           I.J. of*
           K.L. of*
           M.N. of*
           O.P. of*
           Q.R. of*
           S.T. of*

* The number on the Burgess Roll of the Burgess subscribing, with the situation of the property in respect of which he is enrolled on the Burgess Roll.

Form No. 3.

Ballot Paper.

Form of Front of Ballot Paper.

For Auditors.

Counterfoil. No.		
Note.—The Counterfoil is to have a Number to correspond with that on the back of the Ballot Paper.	1	Cade. (John Cade, of 22, Wellclose Place, Accountant.)
	2	Johnson. (Charles Johnson, of 7, Albion Street, Gentleman.)
	3	Thompson. (William Thompson, of 14, Queen Street, Silversmith.)

For Revising Assessor.

1	Bacon. (Charles Bacon, of 29, New Street, Solicitor.)
2	Byron. (James Byron, of 45, George Street, Commission Agent.)
3	Wilson. (George Wilson, of 22, Hanover Square, Gentleman.)

Form of Back of Ballot Paper.

No.   Election of Auditors [or Assessors] for the Borough of
      to be held on the   day of   18 .

The Number on the back of the Ballot Paper is to correspond with that on the Counterfoil.

SECOND SCHEDULE.

Session and Chapter.	Title of Act.	Extent of Repeal.
5 & 6 Will. 4, c. 76.	An Act to provide for the regulation of Municipal Corporations in England and Wales.	So much of section 47 as relates to the fixing of the day of election by the alderman.
22 Vict., c. 35.	The Municipal Corporation Act, 1859.	Sections 5, 6, 7, and Schedules
32 & 33 Vict., c. 55.	An Act to shorten the term of residence required as a qualification for the Municipal Franchise, and to make provision for other purposes.	Sections 6 and 7.
35 & 36 Vict., c. 33.	The Ballot Act, 1872.	Directions in the Schedule to the Act as to the form of nomination papers at Municipal Elections.

MUNICIPAL ELECTIONS ACT (IRELAND), 1879.

42 & 43 Vict., c. 53.

An Act to amend the Law regulating Municipal Elections in Ireland.   [15th August, 1879.]

Be it enacted, etc.

1. This Act may be cited as the Municipal Elections (Ireland) Act, 1879.

2. From and after the passing of this Act, the Municipal Elections Act, 1875, shall extend and apply to all municipal boroughs in Ireland in which the Act passed in the session of Parliament held in the third and fourth years of the reign of Her present Majesty, chapter one hundred and eight, intituled "An Act for "the Regulation of Municipal Corporations in Ireland" is in force, subject to the following provisions:

(1.) The thirteenth section of the said Municipal Elections Act shall be read as if the Act passed in the session of Parliament held in the third and fourth years of the reign of Her present Majesty, chapter one hundred and eight and the Acts amending the same, were mentioned in the said thirteenth section instead of the Act of the fifth and sixth years of King William the Fourth, chapter seventy-six, and the Acts amending the same:

(2.) The term "councillor" in the said Municipal Elections Act shall extend to and include an alderman:

(3.) If any extraordinary vacancy happens in the office of any alderman, councillor, auditor, or assessor, the election to supply such vacancy shall take place not later than fourteen days after notice shall have been given to the mayor or town clerk by any two burgesses, anything to the contrary notwithstanding; and the day for holding any such election in any borough (whether the borough shall be divided into wards or not) shall be fixed by the mayor:

(4.) The duty imposed upon the overseers by the tenth section of the said Act with respect to the making of lists shall be discharged by the town clerk:

(5.) The forms in the schedule to the said Act shall be amended by adding the word "alderman" wherever it may be necessary.

3. So much of the eighty-first and eighty-second sections of the said Act of the Session of Parliament of the third and fourth years of Her present Majesty, chapter one hundred and eight, as relates to the fixing of the day of election by the alderman shall be and is hereby repealed.

TOWN COUNCILS AND LOCAL BOARDS ACT, 1880.

43 Vict., c. 17.

An Act to abolish the property qualification for members of Municipal Corporations and Local Governing Bodies.

[24th March, 1880.]

Be it enacted, etc.

1.—(1.) Subject as in this section mentioned, every person shall be qualified to be elected and to be a member of a local authority who is at the time of election qualified to elect to any membership of that authority.

(2.) For the purposes of this section the term "local authority" means,—

(a.) The council of a borough under the Municipal Corporations Act, 1835, or any Act amending the same:

(b.) In Ireland, the town council of any town corporate, commissioners appointed by virtue of an Act made in the ninth year of King George the Fourth, intituled "An Act to "make provision for the lighting, cleansing, and watching of "cities and towns corporate, and market towns in Ireland in "certain cases," and any municipal town or township commissioners appointed under any general or local Act.

(3.) The qualifications mentioned in this section shall be alternatives for and shall not repeal or take away any other qualification.

(4.) Nothing in this section shall qualify any person for any office who is disqualified for the office by the existing law by reason of office, contract, bankruptcy, or any other matter of disqualification or disability.

(5.) If a person qualified under this section ceases for six months to reside within the borough or district in which he has been elected to an office, he shall cease to be qualified under this section and his office shall become vacant, unless he was at the time of his election and continues to be qualified in some other manner.

2. This Act may be cited as the Town Councils and Local Boards Act, 1880.

3. This Act shall extend to Ireland but not to Scotland.

ELECTIONS (HOURS OF POLL) ACT, 1885.

(48 VICT., c. 10.)

An Act to extend the Hours of Polling at Parliamentary and Municipal Elections. [28th April, 1885.]

Be it enacted, etc.

1. At every parliamentary and every municipal election within the meaning of this Act, the poll (if any) shall commence at eight o'clock in the forenoon, and be kept open till eight o'clock in the afternoon of the same day and no longer.

2. In this Act—

* * * * * *

The expression "municipal election" means an election of a councillor, commissioner of police, or auditor, or (in Ireland) an alderman or any commissioner, in any municipal borough or in any ward thereof:

The expression "municipal borough" means,—

* * * * * * *

As regards Ireland, a borough subject to the Act of the session of the third and fourth years of the reign of Her present Majesty, chapter one hundred and eight, intituled "An Act for the Regulation of Municipal Corporations in Ireland," and the Acts amending the same, and includes a place subject to the Act of the ninth year of the reign of King George the Fourth, chapter eighty-two, or to the Towns Improvement (Ireland), Act, 1854, or to any local Act providing for the election of commissioners in any town or place for purposes similar to the purposes of the above-mentioned Acts.

3. Upon this Act coming into operation the Parliamentary Elections (Metropolis) Act, 1878, and the Elections (Hours of Poll) Act, 1884, shall be repealed, without prejudice to anything previously done in pursuance thereof.

4. This Act may be cited as the Elections (Hours of Poll) Act, 1885.

5. This Act shall come into operation at the end of this present Parliament.

MUNICIPAL VOTERS RELIEF ACT, 1885.
(48 VICT., c. 9.)

An Act to relieve Municipal Voters from being disqualified in consequence of letting their dwelling-houses for short periods. [28th April, 1885.]

Whereas by the House Occupiers Disqualification Removal Act, 1878, provision was made that a man should be entitled to be registered as an inhabitant occupier of a dwelling-house under the third section of the Representation of the People Act, 1867, notwithstanding that during a part of the qualifying period not exceeding four months in the whole, he should by letting, or otherwise, have permitted the qualifying premises to be occupied as a furnished house by some other person:

And whereas similar provision was made as regards Scotland by the House Occupiers Disqualification Removal (Scotland) Act, 1878:

And whereas it is expedient to extend the said Acts to voters at municipal elections:

Be it therefore enacted, etc.

1. This Act may be cited as the Municipal Voters Relief Act, 1885.

2. From and after the passing of this Act a man shall not be disqualified from being enrolled or voting as a burgess at any municipal election in a borough, in respect of the occupation of any house, by reason only that during a part of the qualifying period, not exceeding four months in the whole, he has, by letting or otherwise, permitted such house to be occupied as a furnished dwelling-house by some other person, and during such occupation by another person has not resided in or within seven miles of the borough.

3. In this Act—

The expression "burgess" has, in England, the same meaning as in the Municipal Corporations Act, 1882, and in Scotland and Ireland means a person entitled to vote at a municipal election in Scotland and Ireland respectively.

The expression "municipal election" has, in England, the same meaning as in the Municipal Corporations Act, 1882, and in Scotland and Ireland has the same meaning as that expression is defined to have with reference to Scotland and Ireland respectively by the Ballot Act, 1872.

4. Whereas in the municipal borough of Dublin the qualifying period of occupation is a period of two years and eight months, ending the last day of August, and it is expedient that such

qualifying period should be reduced: Be it enacted, that from and after the passing of this Act the qualifying period of occupation in the said municipal borough shall be a period of twelve months preceding the first day of September, instead of such period of two years and eight months.

MEDICAL RELIEF DISQUALIFICATION REMOVAL ACT, 1885.

48 & 49 VICT., c. 46.

An Act to prevent Medical Relief disqualifying a person from voting. [6th August, 1885.]

Be it enacted, etc.

1. This Act may be cited as the Medical Relief Disqualification Removal Act, 1885.

Medical Relief not to disqualify.

2.—(1.) Where a person has in any part of the United Kingdom received for himself, or for any member of his family, any medical or surgical assistance, or any medicine at the expense of any poor rate, such person shall not by reason thereof be deprived of any right to be registered or to vote either— * * * *

(b) as a voter at any municipal election; or

(c) as a burgess; or

(d) as a voter at any election to an office under the provisions of any statute; * * * *

Definition of Medical and Surgical Assistance.

4. The term "medical or surgical assistance" in this Act shall include all medical and surgical attendance, and all matters and things supplied by or on the recommendation of the medical officer having authority to give such attendance and recommendation at the expense of any poor rate.

PUBLIC BODIES CORRUPT PRACTICES ACT, 1889.

52 & 53 VICT., c. 69.

An Act for the more effectual Prevention and Punishment of Bribery and Corruption of and by Members, Officers, or Servants of Corporations, Councils, Boards, Commissions, or other Public Bodies. [30th August, 1889.]

Corruption in Office a Misdemeanor.

1.—(1.) * * * * *

(2.) Every person who shall by himself or by and in conjunction with any other person corruptly give, promise or offer any gift, loan, fee, reward, or advantage whatsoever to any person, whether for the benefit of that person or of another person, as an inducement to or reward for or otherwise on account of any member, officer, or servant of any public body as in this Act defined, doing or forbearing to do anything in respect of any matter or transaction whatsoever, actual or proposed, in which such public body as aforesaid is concerned, shall be guilty of a misdemeanor.

Penalty for Offences.

2. Any person on conviction for offending as aforesaid shall, at the discretion of the court before which he is convicted,—

   (*a*) be liable to be imprisoned for any period not exceeding two years, with or without hard labour, or to pay a fine not exceeding five hundred pounds, or to both such imprisonment and such fine; and

   (*b*) in addition be liable to be ordered to pay to such body, and in such manner as the court directs, the amount or value of any gift, loan, fee, or reward received by him or any part thereof; and

   (*c*) be liable to be adjudged incapable of being elected or appointed to any public office for seven years from the date of his conviction, and to forfeit any such office held by him at the time of his conviction; and

   (*d*) in the event of a second conviction for a like offence he shall, in addition to the foregoing penalties, be liable to be adjudged to be for ever incapable of holding any public office, and to be incapable for seven years of being registered as an elector, or voting at an election either of members to serve in Parliament or of members of any public body, and the enactments for preventing the voting and registration of persons declared by reason of corrupt practices to be incapable of voting shall apply to a person adjudged in pursuance of this section to be incapable of voting;   *   *   *   *

Savings.

3.—(1.) Where an offence under this Act is also punishable under any other enactment, or at common law, such offence may be prosecuted and punished either under this Act, or under the other enactment, or at common law, but so that no person shall be punished twice for the same offence.

(2.) A person shall not be exempt from punishment under this Act by reason of the invalidity of the appointment or election of a person to a public office.

Restriction on Prosecution.

4.—(1.) A prosecution for an offence under this Act shall not be instituted except by or with the consent of the Attorney General.

(2.) In this section the expression "Attorney General" * * * * * as respects Ireland means the Attorney or Solicitor General for Ireland.

Expenses of Prosecution.

5. The expenses of the prosecution of an offence against this Act shall be defrayed in like manner as in the case of a felony.

Interpretation.

7. In this Act—

The expression " public body " means any council of a county or county of a city or town, any council of a municipal borough, also any board, commissioners, select vestry, or other body which has power to act under and for the purposes of any Act relating to local government, or the public health, or to poor law or otherwise to administer money raised by rates in pursuance of any public general Act, but does not include any public body as above defined existing elsewhere than in the United Kingdom :

The expression " public office " means any office or employment of a person as a member, officer, or servant of such public body :

The expression " person " includes a body of persons, corporate or unincorporate :

The expression " advantage " includes any office or dignity, and any forbearance to demand any money or money's worth or valuable thing, and includes any aid, vote, consent, or influence, or pretended aid, vote, consent, or influence, and also includes any promise or procurement of or agreement or endeavour to procure, or the holding out of any expectation of any gift, loan, fee, reward, or advantage, as before defined.

9. The provisions of the Criminal Law and Procedure (Ireland) Act, 1887, shall not apply to any trial under the provisions of this Act.

10. This Act may be cited as the Public Bodies Corrupt Practices Act, 1889.

INDEX.

A

ACTS OF PARLIAMENT BEARING ON MUNICIPAL ELECTIONS IN IRELAND, 210-213.

ADVERTISEMENTS (see *Publication*).

AGE:
What constitutes full, 56.

AGENTS:
Three classes of, 81.
"Expense" unnecessary, 81.
Appointment of authorized, 81.
Appointment of at municipal elections upheld by legal decisions, 82.
What constitutes, 83.
Relation between Candidate and, 83.
Liability of Candidate for act of, 83.
If treacherous, 83.
Must make declaration of secrecy, 83.
Returning Officer, his partner or clerk may not act as, 84.
Scheduled briber not to be appointed as, 84.
A reasonable number of—only to be appointed, 84.
Candidate may undertake the duties of, 84.
Notice of names and addresses of—to be sent to Returning Officer, 84.
No one whose name is on Register to be employed as paid canvasser, 84.
Penalty on person so acting, 84.
Penalty on paid—who vote, 84.
Vote of paid—bad, even if given for another candidate, 84.
Retainer to act as—to incapacitate from voting for other candidate, 84.
Refreshments to—if paid, 85.
—— if voluntary, 85.
Ballot box to be shown empty to, 85.
Duties of—in regard to personation, 85.

AGENTS—*continued.*
Votes of certain electors to be taken in presence of, 85.
Bribery by wife of, 85.
May be removed from polling station, 85.
May affix seals to ballot boxes, &c., 85.
Notice of time and place of counting of votes to be sent to, 85.
Persons proved guilty of corrupt practices may not be employed as, 85.
Counting of votes—may attend at, 85.
Ballot boxes to be opened in the presence of, 86.
To be present at counting of votes, 86.
Unless with consent of—votes may not be counted between 7 P.M. and 9 A.M, 86.
May copy Returning Officer's report, 86.
Prohibited from paying for conveyance for voters under penalty, 86.
Authorized in certain boroughs to attend at nomination of Candidates, 86.
Absence of—will not invalidate anything done, 86.
Vacancy in office of—may be filled up, 86.
Notice of appointment of successor, 86.
Not authorized to interfere with ballot papers, 163.
May inspect bad or doubtful ballot papers, 163.
Vote of paid—who retired before poll commenced—bad, 196.
Single corrupt act by—avoids election, 135.

ALDERMEN:
Form of declaration to be made by, 187.
Fine for resignation of office of, 188.
Disqualifications for office of, 188.

G

ALDERMEN—continued.
  Penalties on—for acting if disqualified, 188.
  Qualifications for office of, 188.
  How elected, 188.
  Term of office of, 188.
  If incapable of acting, 188.

ALIENS:
  Disqualified, 48–55, 67.
  Definition of, 68.
  Children of, 68.
  Notice by Town Clerk to, 69.
  If naturalized, may vote, 69.

ARREST:
  For disturbing proceedings at nominations, 103.
  For personation, 144.
  For misconduct at polling station, 146.

ASSESSORS:
  Declaration to be made by, 187.
  Appointment of, 188.

AUDITORS:
  Election of abolished—except in certain towns, 96.
  How elected, 188.
  Who are disqualified for, 188.
  Where still elected, 189.

B

BALLOT ACT:
  Acts (Irish) repealed or amended by, Ap. lv.
  Schedules to have effect as part of, 164.
  Rules to point out manner of doing what sections enact shall be done, 164.

BALLOT BOXES:
  To be supplied by Returning Officer, 117.
  Construction of, 129.
  To be shown empty before commencement of poll, 132.
  Should be kept in view of presiding officer, 132.
  To be locked and sealed during poll, 132.
  Undue interference with, 134.
  To be sealed up at close of poll, 148.
  To be delivered to Returning Officer at close of poll, 148.

BALLOT PAPERS:
  To be provided by Returning Officer, 117.
  Voters not to be interfered with when marking, 125.
  Voter not to be induced to display—after marking, 125.
  To contain list of candidates, 126.
  Printed number on back of, 126.
  To have counterfoil attached, 126.
  Prescribed form of, 127.
  To be made up in form of cheque books, 128.
  To be numbered consecutively, 128.
  If insufficient supply of—election avoided, 128.
  Official stamp for marking—to be kept secret, 129.
  Voter to state his name and address when applying for, 132.
  Not be given out after 8 o'clock, P.M., 132.
  To be marked on both sides with official mark, 133.
  Counterfoil to have register number of elector entered on, 133.
  How to be marked, 133.
  To be marked secretly—mandatory, 133.
  Penalties for offences in regard to, 134.
  Who are entitled to receive, 134.
  Names of persons twice nominated not to be printed on, 134.
  Questions which may be asked voter on applying for, 135.
  In certain cases may be marked by presiding officer, 141.
  Tendered, 142.
  ——— to be of a different colour, 142.
  ——— not to be counted, 142.
  ——— may be counted on scrutiny, 142.
  ——— if put by mistake into ballot box, 142.
  ——— omission to endorse applicant's name on, 143.
  To apply for—is to tender to vote, 143.
  If spoilt, how to be dealt with, 147.
  Unused and spoilt—to be placed together, 148.
  To be made into packets after closing of the poll, 148.
  Account of—by presiding officer, 149.
  During intervals in counting—to be properly secured, 160.
  To be mixed and counted before votes are counted, 161.

BALLOT PAPERS—*continued.*
  Faces of—to be kept upward in counting, 163.
  Agents not to interfere with, 163.
  Returning Officer must himself decide as to validity of, 163.
  —— his decision final in regard thereto, 163.
  On what grounds to be rejected, 163.
  Principles for determining validity of, 164.
  Not to be marked so as to lead to identification, 165.
  Peculiarly marked—illustrations of, 166.
  If torn across, 171.
  If vote uncertain as to any candidate, not to be counted, 177.
  Decisions in regard to, 166–179.
  Marked on back, 178.
  —— with peculiar ink, 178.
  —— without discolouring the paper, 179.
  —— with register number of voter, 179.
  When wrapped up in declaration of inability to read, 179.
  Liability of presiding officer for want of official mark on, 180.
  If not marked on back with official stamp, 181.
  —— on face, 181.
  Omission by presiding officer to enter voter's number on counterfoil, 181.
  If name of candidate entered twice on, 182.
  Endorsement on, rejected, 183.
  To be sealed up in packets after counting of votes, 183.
  Returning Officer to verify account of, 183.
  Who to have custody of, 185.
  When may be destroyed, 185.
  Inspection of counterfoils and counted ballot papers; how to be obtained, 207.

BALLOT PAPER ACCOUNT:
  To be furnished by presiding officer, 148.
  Form of, 149.
  To be verified by Returning Officer, 183.

BANKRUPT (see *Disqualifications*).
  If uncertified—disqualified, 78.
  Compounding with creditors not a disqualification under Towns Improvement (Ireland) Act, 1854, 78.

BANK HOLIDAYS:
  To be computed as ordinary days, 109.

BET (see *Wager*).

BLACKROCK TOWNSHIP:
  Two classes of voters in, 56.
  Immediate lessors, property qualification of, 57.
  —— payment of rates by, 57.
  —— names of, to be on Township Ratebook, 57.
  —— Notice to, 58.
  Rated occupiers, qualifications of, 59.
  Women, disqualified to vote, 59.
  Claim to be rated for relief of the poor—when it may be made, 59.
  Form of application, 60.
  Occupation, does not imply residence, 60.
  Weekly or monthly tenants not qualified, 61.
  Receipt of parochial relief does not disqualify, 61.
  Bankruptcy not a disqualification for voting, 61.
  Voter, if qualified for two wards, 61.
  Payment of poor rates by voter in, 62.
  —— Township rates, 62.
  —— When to be paid, 63.
  —— Notice in regard to payment of, 67.
  Aliens disqualified, 67.
  Felons disqualified, 70.
  Joint occupiers not entitled to vote 71.
  Police not disqualified, 71.

BLINDNESS (see *Voters*).

BOOTHS (see *Polling Stations*).

BOROUGH:
  Municipal, defined, 23.
  Division of, into four classes, 24.
  Division of, into polling districts, 118 (See *Polling Stations*).

BRIBERY:
  Appointment of scheduled briber as agent—prohibited, 84.
  Retainer to voter to act as agent—thereby to prevent him from voting, not, 84.
  Defined, 192.
  Penalty for, 193.
  Person receiving bribe, deemed guilty of, 193.
  Corrupt payment of rates is, 193.

G 2

BRIBERY—*continued.*
　When candidate liable for—by his agent, 194.
　A single act of — clearly proved, avoids election, 195.
　Conveyance of voters to and from poll, when, 196.
　—— When not, 196.
　Wager may be, 197.
　Payment of voter's travelling expenses, when, 196.
　—— For colourable services is, 197.
　Payment to elector's children for services, may be, 197.
　Payment to induce a person to personate his father and vote, is, 197.
　Paying excessive prices for services is, 197.
　Offer of bribe to disqualified person is, 197.
　Payment to workmen for wages lost through coming to vote is, 197.
　Promising advantage to elector without condition is, 197.
　General—though not traced to candidate, avoids election, 198.
　At common law, 198.
　Time of giving bribe unimportant, 198.

BURGESS ROLL:
　How to be prepared, 24.
　Form of book to be prepared by Town Clerk for, 25.
　Names of what persons to be entered therein, 24.
　Separate books for each ward, 26.
　Rate Collector to be summoned to make entries of payment of rates in the books, 26.
　Treasurer of borough to attend, 26.
　If no Treasurer, Mayor to attend, 26.
　Entries in book to be signed, 26.
　Notice to be given by Town Clerk on completion of entries, 26.
　Book may be perused without fee, 26.
　—— Town Clerk to supply copy or extract, if required, on payment of fee, 27.
　—— Penalty on Mayor, Treasurer, or Collector for neglect of duties in regard to, 27.
　Town Clerk to make alphabetical list of persons entitled to be enrolled on—on or before 20th Sept., 27.
　—— To deliver copy to Mayor, 27.
　Original list may be perused without fee between 20th and 30th Sept., 27.

BURGESS ROLL—*continued.*
　List to be published for eight days next preceding 1st October, 27.
　Notice may be given by persons whose names are omitted from list, 27.
　Notice—as to persons whose names are objected to, 27.
　Publication of names of claimants, 28.
　—— of persons objected to, 28.
　Revision of lists by Court (see Revision Court).
　Lists when revised by Court to be delivered to Town Clerk, 29.
　Names to be entered in book, 29.
　To be completed before 20th Nov., 29.
　If not made out, old one to remain in force, 29.
　Mayor to provide copies of, for each polling station, 29.
　Burgesses omitted from—remedy of, 30.
　Right of anyone to be on—may be questioned, 30.
　Freemen's—(see *Freemen's Roll*).
　Conclusiveness of, 137.

C

CANDIDATES defined, Ap. lix.
　If disqualified—votes given for, after notice, thrown away, 78.
　Form of notice of disqualification to be given, 79.
　Not liable for acts of treacherous agent, 83.
　Nomination of (see *Nomination*).
　May undertake duties of agent, 84.
　Penalty on—for employment of voter as paid canvasser, 84.
　May be present at nominations, 104.
　Withdrawal of, 108.
　Right of—to be present at poll, 126.
　—— to be present at counting of votes, 126.
　Penalty for corrupt practices (see *Corrupt Practices*).

CANVASSERS defined, Ap. lix.

CIRCULARS:
　Fraudulent (see *Fraudulent Devices*).

CLERGY:
　Disqualified for election, 75-77.
　Not disqualified for election under 9 Geo. IV., c. 82, 75.
　Dissenting minister—meaning of, 75.
　Undue influence of, 200.

COMMISSIONERS (see *Town Councillors*).

COMPARTMENTS:
Polling—how many at each station, 119.
How to be constructed, 120.

CONSTABLES (see *Police*).

CONTRACTS (see *Disqualifications*).
Meaning of, 75.
With Council—when a disqualification, 75-77.

CONVEYANCE OF VOTERS to and from poll, 196.

CONVICTS (see *Felons*).

CORRUPT PRACTICES:
Appointment of agent to detect, 82.
Defined, 191.
Bribery (see *Bribing*).
Treating (see *Treating*).
Undue influence (see *Undue Influence*).
Personation (see *Personation*).
Disqualifications incurred by candidate through, 202.
—— by any person guilty of, 202.

COUNTERFOILS (see *Ballot Papers*).

COUNTING VOTES (see *Votes*).

D

DAYS:
Meaning of "Days at least," 31.
Clear—how to be reckoned, 31.
Sunday—if election falls on, 31.

DEAF AND DUMB (see *Voters*).

DEATH:
Of agent, 86.
Returning Officer, 87-187.
Presiding Officer, 92.

DECLARATIONS:
Of secrecy, by whom to be made, 123.
—— form of, 124.
—— when to be made, 124.
—— notice as to, 124.
—— penalties for violation of, 125.
—— omission by Returning Officer, &c., to take, 125.
—— Candidate need not make, 126.
Of inability to read—form of, 142.
—— To be made in presence of agents, 141.
—— Returning Officer to provide sufficient supply of forms of, 142.

DECLARATIONS—*continued*.
To be made into packets after close of poll, 157.
—— by persons elected, 74, 77, 187.
(See *Secrecy*.)

DENIZEN, definition of, 68.

DISQUALIFICATIONS:
Of Commissioners and Town Councillors (see *Town Councillors*).
Voters (see *Voters*).

DISSENTING MINISTERS (see *Clergy*).

DOCUMENTS.—ELECTION:
Town Clerk to have charge of, 185.

DRUNKEN PERSONS (see *Voters*).

E

ELECTION, MUNICIPAL—defined, Ap. xli.
Notice of, 96, 110.
Declaration of poll, if uncontested, 116.
Polling Station for (see *Polling Station*).
Expenses of, 117.
What must be provided for if contested, 117.
Day of, 130.
If held on wrong day, 130.
Result of contested—when and by whom to be declared, 186.
Controverted (see *Petitions*).
If avoided, how vacancies to be filled in towns, 205.
—— in boroughs, 206.
When avoided (see *Corrupt Practices*).

ELECTORS (see *Voters*).

EQUALITY of votes, 182, 186.

EXPENSES:
Of Candidates at Municipal Elections, 81.
Of Elections (see *Elections*).
Travelling—of voters, 196.

F

FELONS:
Disqualified to vote, 48, 55, 70.
—— for election, 78.

FRAUDULENT devices, 201.

FREEMEN:
  Existing rights of voting preserved, 41, 46.

FREEMEN'S ROLL:
  Who is to prepare, 30.
  Revision in boroughs under—3 & 4 Vic., c. 108, 30; 9 Geo. IV., c. 82, 30.
  Free perusal of—to be allowed, 30.
  Admission or rejection of claimant by Mayor subject to appeal, 30.

FURNISHED HOUSE:
  Person who lets—for more than a year ceases to be an occupier, 61.
  Person in occupation of—for more than a year becomes the occupier, 61.

G

GRAND JURY RATES (see *Rates*).

H

HOUSEHOLDER (see *Voters Lists*).
  What constitutes, 47.

I

IDIOTS (see *Voters*).

IMMEDIATE LESSORS:
  Property qualification of, to vote, under Towns Improvement (Ireland) Act, 1854, 49.
  Qualified to vote under Towns Improvement (Ireland) Act, 1854, if in occupation of premises valued at over £4, 49.
  Joint, not qualified to vote, 54.
  Meaning of term, 56.
  Not liable for rates, with certain exceptions, 57.
  Name to be on township rate book, 57.
  Property qualification of, in Blackrock Township, 57.
  Notice to, 58.

INHABITANT:
  Continued residence not requisite to constitute a, 43.

INTIMIDATION (see undue *Influence*).

J

JEW:
  When poll is taken on Saturday, vote may be marked for, 141.

JOINT OCCUPIERS (see *Occupier*).

JOINT IMMEDIATE LESSORS (see *Immediate Lessors*).

L

LOCAL AUTHORITY:
  Meaning of, 72.

LODGERS:
  Not qualified, 53.

LUNATICS (see *Voters*).

M

MAYOR (see *Returning Officer* and *Burgess Roll*).
  To be Returning Officer, 87.
  Time of election of, 186.
  Duration of office of, 186.
  In case of equality of votes for, 186.
  Vacancy in office of, 187.
  Form of declaration to be made by, 187.
  Fine for non-acceptance of office of, 187.
  Fines for resignation of office of, 188.
  Qualifications of, 188.
  Disqualifications for office of, 188.

MINORS:
  What constitutes full age, 56.

MISDEMEANOUR (see *Offences*).

MONTHLY TENANTS:
  Not qualified under Towns Improvement (Ireland) Act, 1854, 53.

MUNICIPAL COMMISSIONERS:
  Only one borough under, 42.

N

NATURALIZED person may vote, 69.

NEWSPAPER:
  Interest in, not a disqualification, 77.

NOMINATIONS:
  Cause of confusion in regard to, 94.
  Uniformity of, destroyed by M. E. (I.) A., 1879, 95.
  Two different modes of carrying out, 95.

NOMINATIONS—continued.

How to be conducted in Township of Rathmines and Rathgar, 95.
How to be conducted in Boroughs under 3 & 4 Vic., c. 108, 96.
Form of notice of election to be published, 96.
Form of nomination paper in boroughs under 3 & 4 Vic., c. 108, 97.
When a defective notice in regard to, may render election void, 98.
Need not be on forms supplied by Town Clerk, 98.
Time for delivery of, in boroughs under 3 & 4 Vic., c. 108, 98.
Persons nominated to be notified by Town Clerk, 98.
Same elector cannot subscribe more nomination papers than there are vacancies, 99.
Papers—by whom to be delivered, 99.
Decision of Returning Officer in regard to objections to nomination papers, 100.
—— not always final if he disallows objection to, 100.
Returning Officer not entitled to decide objection in regard to qualifications of candidate, 101.
—— cannot refuse to put a notoriously disqualified candidate in nomination, 101.
—— decision of, to be given in writing, 100.
—— his decision, disallowing an objection in regard to form of nomination paper, is final, 101.
Difference of effect of disallowing an objection and refusing to entertain it, 101.
Signature of nominators must precede that of assentors, 102.
If different for same person, only one to be published, 103.
Duty of Returning Officer in regard to double, 103.
Endorsement of Town Clerk on nomination papers, 103.
Forms to be supplied for, 103.
Proceedings at, 103.
Persons disturbing proceedings at, 103.
Persons who may be present at, 104.
Appointment of agents to attend proceedings at, 104.

NOMINATIONS—continued.

Objections to be in writing, 104.
Returning Officer may give his decision in regard to, after 4 o'clock, 104.
Liability of Returning Officer in regard to his decision on objections to, 104.
Conclusiveness of burgess roll in regard to, 104.
Those subscribing must be on the ward list of the ward for which they nominate the candidate, 105.
Of candidate by disqualified persons, 105.
All the names of a candidate must be given, 105.
A recognised abbreviation of the Christian name of person nominated does not invalidate, 105.
Of persons with compound names or titles, 105.
Signatures of the nominating and assenting burgesses sufficient, 106.
Description of property of those subscribing nomination papers need not be identical with that given on burgess roll, 106.
Number on burgess roll to be accurately given, 107.
Separate nomination papers for each candidate, 107.
Of persons absent from United Kingdom, 107.
Withdrawal of candidate, 108.
Publication of names of persons nominated, 108.
Computation of time in regard to, 109.
Penalties for offences in regard to, 109.
Property of nomination papers, in whom vested for purpose of prosecution, 109.

Mode of—in boroughs in which 3 & 4 Vic., c. 108, is not in force, 110.
Notice to be published by Town Clerk, 110.
How to be published, 111.
To be sent to Town Clerk two clear days before day of election, 112.
Publication of names of persons nominated, 112.
Town Clerk to supply nomination papers, 113.
Hour on third day up to which nomination papers are to be received, 113.

NOMINATION—*continued.*
  Persons nominating candidates must be qualified voters in ward for which they nominate candidates, 113.
  Invalid nomination papers, how to be dealt with, 114.
  Of candidate—without his consent, 114.

NOTICE (see *Returning Officer*).
  Of payment of rates, 26, 30, 67.
  What constitutes publication of, 32.
  How to be given under Ballot Act, 31, 32.
  To immediate Lessors, 58.
  Of disqualification of candidate, 78.
  Of appointment of agent, 82.
  Form of—to be given for elections under 3 & 4 Vic., c. 108, 96.
  In boroughs not under, 110.
  If defective, 98.
  Of withdrawal of candidate, 108.
  Signature of, 111.
  Of persons nominated, 112.
  Of situation of polling stations, 119.
  Re declaration of secrecy, 124.

O

OATH:
  Abolition of, as regards Returning Officer, &c., 123.
  Who may administer, 135.
  When it may be administered, 135.

OCCUPATION:
  What constitutes—in boroughs under Municipal Reform Act, 1841, 47.
  Meaning of, in towns under Towns Improvement (Ireland) Act, 1854, 53.

OCCUPIERS:
  Joint, if qualified under 9 Geo. IV., c. 82, 43.
  —— qualified to vote under Municipal Reform Act, 1840, 48.
  —— under Towns Improvement (Ireland) Act, 1854, 54.
  Person in occupation of furnished house for more than a year is, 61.
  Person who lets his house for more than one year ceases to be a, 61.
  Joint—not qualified to vote in Blackrock Township, 71.

OFFENCES—(see *Corrupt Practices*).
  In regard to nomination papers, 109.
  As to infringement of secrecy, 125, 144.
  In regard to ballot papers, 134.

OFFENCES—*continued.*
  Undue interference with ballot box, 134.
  Misconduct at polling stations, 146.
  By officers at elections, 93.

OWNER (see *Immediate Lessors*).

OFFICIAL MARK:
  To be supplied by Returning Officer, 129.
  To be kept secret, 129.
  To be shown to presiding officer, on back of ballot paper, 133.
  Presiding officer to stamp both sides of ballot paper, 133.
  Counterfeiting, 134.
  Ballot papers not marked with, 181.
  May be made by a perforating instrument, 181.

P

PAIRING votes (see *Voters*).

PAROCHIAL relief (see *Disqualifications*).

PAUPERS:
  Disqualified under Municipal Reform Act, 1840, 48.

PAYMENT:
  Of Rates (see *Rates*).
  Returning Officer not paid, 92.
  Presiding Officer not paid, 92.
  Of election expenses, 117.
  —— poll clerks, 117.
  —— voter's travelling expenses, 196.

PENALTIES (see *Offences*).

PENCILS:
  To be provided for marking votes, 129.

PERSONATION:
  Appointment of agent to detect, 82.
  Right of person to vote, though guilty of, 142.
  Definition of, 143.
  Punishment for, 143.
  A felony, 143.
  Returning Officer to prosecute persons guilty of, 143.
  Costs and expenses of prosecution, 143.
  A corrupt practice, 143.
  Disqualification of candidate guilty of, Ap. lx.
  Compensation to persons unjustly charged with, 144.

PETITIONS:
   On the ground of votes being incorrectly counted, 186.
   Grounds generally upon which an election may be questioned, 203.
   Time within which—must be presented, 204.
   —— how to be computed for this purpose, 204.
   Who may present, 204.
   Persons on whom copies of—are to be served, 204.
   Security for payment of costs of, 204.
   —— Amount of, 204.
   Powers of Election Court in regard to, 204.
   Rules to be made by Court in regard to, 205.
   Examination and expenses of witnesses at trial of, 205.
   Abatement and withdrawal of, 205.
   Substitution of respondent on trial of, 205.
   Costs of, 205.
   Reception of Court for trial of, 205.
   Jurisdiction and general rules of Court on trial of, 206.
   Expenses of Court, 206.
   No person required to state for whom he has voted, in any proceedings in connection with, 206.
   Inspection of documents in regard to—how to be obtained, 207.
   Fees for inspection of same, 208.

POLICE:
   Qualified to vote, 54–71.
   Required, to attend at election, 123.
   —— to make declaration of secrecy, 124.

POLL (see *Polling Stations*).
   Day of, 120.
   When, may be adjourned, notice as to, 147.

POLL BOOKS:
   Meaning of expression under Ballot Act, 144.

POLL CLERKS:
   Penalties for neglect of duty by, 93.
   Appointed by Returning Officer, 117.
   Payment of, 117.
   To take declaration of secrecy, 124.
   Power to administer oath, 135.

POLLING STATIONS:
   How to be distributed, 118.
   Place of Public Worship cannot be used for, 118.
   Room cannot be taken compulsorily for, 118.
   May be in a public house, 118.
   Rooms may be hired for, 118.
   If excessive number of voters allotted to, 118.
   Irregularities in distribution of, 119.
   Notice of situation, division and allotment of, to be given to electors, 119.
   Compartments, several may be constructed in one room, 119.
   —— number of—to be provided at each station, 119.
   —— construction of, 120.
   Faulty arrangements at, 121.
   To be arranged so as not to admit of violation of secrecy, 121.
   Plan of, 122.
   Name of ward to be posted outside of, 122.
   Directions for guidance of voters to be posted outside, and in the compartments of, 122.
   Attendance of constables at, 123.
   Declarations of secrecy to be made before the opening of, 124.
   Tickets of admission to, 125.
   Candidate to be admitted to, 126.
   Articles to be provided at, 128.
   Irregularities in opening or closing of, 131.
   Presiding officer to keep order at, 146.
   Penalty for misconduct at, 146.
   Disturbance at, 146.

POOR LAW RELIEF:
   What premises may be rated for, 49.
   Claim to be rated for, 60.
   Rates (see *Rates*).

PRESIDING OFFICER:
   Returning officer may act as, 91.
   Appointed by Returning Officer, 92.
   Must be a Commissioner or Alderman, 92.
   Not paid, 92.
   More than one may be appointed to each ward, 92.
   May act by poll clerk, except for arrest or expulsion of any person, 93.
   Declaration of secrecy by, 93.

PRESIDING OFFICER—*continued.*
  Penalties for neglect of duties by, 93.
  Omission of, to take declaration of secrecy—how far material, 125.
  When to close poll, 132.
  To show ballot box empty, 132.
  To mark ballot papers with official mark, 133.
  Liable to prosecution if he refuses to take vote of person whose name is on list, 136.
  Votes to be marked by, 141.
  Declarations of inability to read to be attested by, 142.
  Endorsement by, on tendered ballot papers, 142.
  When he may ask prescribed questions, and administer oath, 144.
  May order arrest of personators, 144.
  To maintain order at polling station, 146.
  May adjourn poll in case of riot, 147.
  Is not to destroy spoilt ballot paper, 147.
  Duties of—after close of poll, 147.
  Forms for report of, 149.
  Instructions to, 151.
  How far liable for omission to stamp ballot paper with official mark, 180.
  Liable for breach of ministerial duties, 180.
  Not liable for acts of poll clerk, 180.

PREMISES, valuation of (see *Valuation.*)

PROPOSER, (see *Nomination.*)

PUBLICATION of voters lists, 32.
—— of notices, 32.

PUBLIC HOUSE, (see *Polling Station.*)

Q

QUALIFICATIONS of voters (see *Voters*).
  Of Town Councillors and Commissioners (see *Town Councillors*).

QUESTIONS:
  Which may be asked voter, 135.
  When and by whom they may be put, 135.
  To be asked in very words of Act, 136.
  Evasive answer to, 136.
  Meaning of questions, 141.

R.

RACKRENT:
  Meaning of, 56.

RATES:
  Notice to be given in regard to payment of—under 3 & 4 Vic., c. 108, 26.
  Office to be kept open for payment of, 26.
  —— If not open, how payment to be made, 26.
  Vestry—abolished, 43.
  Poor—payment of, abolished in towns under Towns Improvement (Ireland) Act, 1854, 50.
  Grand Jury—payment of, abolished in towns under Towns Improvement (Ireland) Act, 1854, 50.
  Township—payment of, under Towns Improvement (Ireland) Act, 1854, 50.
  Collector to give information as to persons not in occupation during qualifying period, 61.
  Payment of—in the Blackrock Township, 62-7.

REFRESHMENT (see *Treating*).

REGISTER OF VOTERS (see *Voters List*) defined, Ap. xlix.
  Meaning of—in Ballot Act, 28.

RETURNING OFFICER:
  Deputy (see *Presiding Officer*).
  Who is, 87.
  If dead or unable to act, 87.
  Want of title in, does not vitiate election, 88.
  If a candidate, 89.
  To prosecute personators, 90.
  Liability of, 90.
  May act as presiding officer, 91.
  To appoint presiding officers, 92.
  Not paid, 92.
  Declaration of secrecy by, 93.
  —— may be made before, 93.
  Penalties for neglect of duty by, 93.
  Not act as agent for candidate, 93.
  Decision of, in regard to nomination papers, 100.
  Not always final if he disallows objections, 100.
  Not entitled to decide objections in regard to qualifications of candidate, 101.
  Decision final—in regard to disallowing an objection to form of nomination paper, 101.

RETURNING OFFICER—*continued*.
- Difference of effect of disallowing an objection, and refusing to entertain it, 101.
- If different nomination papers are for same person, only one to be published, 103.
- Duty of—in regard to double nominations, 103.
- Powers of, when sitting to adjudicate on nominations, 103.
- Not liable for decision given *bona fide*, 104.
- May give decisions as to nominations after 4 o'clock, 104.
- Notice of withdrawal of candidate to be given to, 108.
- If no contest, to declare candidate elected, 115.
- Duties of—in a contested election, 117.
- To provide polling stations, 117.
- What he is to provide at polling station, 117.
- To appoint and pay poll clerks, 117.
- —— counting assistants, if necessary, 117, 159.
- Expenses of election incurred by, 117.
- To give notice of situation of polling stations, and of the persons entitled to vote thereat, 119.
- Distribution of polling stations by, 118.
- To have directions to voters, posted up, 123.
- To provide attendance of constables, 123.
- Not required to take oath, 123.
- Omission to take declaration of secrecy, how far material, 125.
- To keep official stamp secret, 129.
- Notice of appointment of agents to be sent to, 158.
- To give notice to agents of time and place of counting votes, 158.
- Votes to be counted by—as soon as possible after poll, 160.
- Counting of votes by—to be proceeded with continuously, 160.
- During the intervals in the counting—to keep ballot papers, &c., properly secured, 160.
- Must himself decide as to validity of ballot papers, 163.
- His decision final as to validity of ballot papers, 163.
- In case of equality of votes how to act, 182.
- Not prohibited from voting, 182.

RETURNING OFFICER—*continued*.
- Endorsement by—on rejected ballot papers, 183.
- To report number of rejected ballot papers, and reasons for rejection, 183.
- To verify accounts of ballot papers, &c., furnished by presiding officer. 183.
- To report to council as to election, 183.
- To forward election documents, with report, to town clerk, 183.
- Must declare duly nominated candidate elected, who obtains majority of votes, 186.
- To publish number of votes obtained by each candidate, 186.

REVISION:
- Annual, of voters' lists by barrister, 30.

REVISION COURT: (Under 3 & 4 Vic., c. 108):
- How constituted, 28.
- When to be held, 28.
- Notice to be given in regard to holding, 28.
- Lists to go before, 28.
- Proceedings of, 29.
- Lists, when revised and signed, to be delivered to town clerk, 29.

RIOT:
- In event of, presiding officer may adjourn poll, 146.
- What constitutes, 147.
- Evidence in regard to, 156

ROOMS:
- May be hired for polling stations, 118.
- When room is taken in an unoccupied house, 118.

RULES:
- In Ballot Act to have same force as the Act, 164.

S

SCHEDULES IN BALLOT ACT:
- Same effect as part of Act, 164.

SCHEDULED BRIBER:
- Not to be employed as an agent, 84.

SCRUTINY (see *Votes*).

SECONDER (see *Nominations*).

SECRECY (see *Declarations of*).
Violation of, by candidate, 84.
Persons engaged at polling stations to maintain, 125.
Voters not to be induced to display ballot paper, 125.
When arrangements of polling stations are defective for voting secretly, 121.
Giving information as to persons who had voted at polling stations, 144 to 146.
No person on petition required to state for whom he voted, 206.

SECRETARY OF COMMISSIONERS (see *Town Clerk*).

SIGNATURE—printed, sufficient on election notices, 111.

STAMP (see *Official Mark*).

T

TENDERED VOTES (see *Voters* and *Ballot Papers*).
Ballot paper for—to be of a different colour, 142.
List of, 143.

TIME (see *Days*).
Bank holidays to be computed as ordinary days, 109.
Hours of election fixed by Dublin mean time, 132.

TOWN CLERK:
Duties of, in regard to burgess roll, 24 to 29.
Duties of, in regard to freemen's roll, 30.
To prepare list of voters in certain towns, 31.
Machinery for preparation of lists by —unsatisfactory, 32.
Not liable for error in lists of voters, 33.
Suggestions for preparation of lists by, 34.
To publish notice of nominations, 96, 110.
Defective notice by, 98.
Nomination papers to be delivered to, 98, 111.
Notice to be given by—to persons nominated, 98, 112.
Hours for delivery of nomination papers to, 98, 113.

TOWN CLERK—*continued*.
Should not allow nomination papers delivered to him out of his possession, 102.
Not authorized to deal with invalid nomination papers, 114.
Duties of—in regard to election, 115.
To be given charge of documents at close of election, 185.
To retain documents for one year, 185.

TOWN COUNCIL:
Regulations by, as to inspection of election accounts, 208.

TOWN COUNCILLORS (Commissioners included under this head).
Qualifications of—if resident, and entitled to vote, 72.
—— if not resident under 3 & 4 Vic., c. 108, 73.
—— if not resident in towns under Towns Improvement (Ireland) Act, 1854, 73.
—— if not resident in towns under 9 Geo. IV., c. 82, 74.
—— if not resident in townships under Local Acts, 74.
Contracts, when a disqualification for, 75-76.
Disqualifications under 9 Geo. IV., c. 82, 74.
—— in towns under Towns Improvement (Ireland) Act, 1854, 76.
—— in towns under Local Acts, 77.
—— in towns under 3 & 4 Vic., c. 108, 75, 78.
Disqualified by being in holy orders, 75, 77.
—— by being an officer of the council, or holding a place of profit, 75-76.
—— if found guilty of corrupt practices, 77.
Candidate disqualified for election if returning officer, 77.
—— disqualified by compounding with creditors under 3 & 4 Vic., c. 108, 75.
Interest in a newspaper, not a disqualification, 77.
Felons disqualified for, 78.
Bankrupts—if uncertified, 78.
Notice to be given of disqualification, 78.
Compounding with creditors, not a disqualification under Towns Improvement (Ireland) Act, 1854, 78.

TOWN COUNCILLORS—*continued.*
    Notice of disqualification of—form of, 79.
    —— how to be given, 80.
    If disqualification is notorious, notice need not be given, 79.
    Fact of disqualification must be established at the time, 80.
    Notice should not be given unless disqualification is certain, 80.
    Counter notice may be given, 80.
    " Commissioners," " Township Commissioners," " Town Commissioners," and " Municipal Commissioners," defined, 87.
    Penalty for acting as commissioner, without being qualified, 114.
    Co-option of, 191.

TOWNSHIP RATES (see *Rates*).

TREATING, defined, 198.
    Penalty on candidate for, 198.
    Meat, drink, &c., must be corruptly given to constitute, 199.
    Refreshment given on days of nomination or polling, 199.
    Refreshment to women may be, 200.
    Promise of an entertainment after election may be, 200.

U

UNDUE INFLUENCE defined, 200.
    Penalty for, 200.
    Clerical, 200.
    Intimidation, 200.
    Threatening to give up pew may be, 201.
    Watching voters at polling station, may be, 201.

V

VACANCIES: occasional, how to be filled up, 190.
    Co-option of commissioner to be made at special meeting, 191.
    Resignation of commissioner may be accepted at ordinary meeting, 191.
    Must be filled by open voting, 191.

VALUE—annual meaning of, 49.

VALUATION—amount of, necessary to entitle any one to be rated for the relief of the poor, 52.

VESTRY rate abolished, 43.

VOTES (see *Voters*).
    —— casting (see *Equality of Votes*).
    —— petition for recounting of, 186.

VOTES, COUNTING OF:

    Agents may attend at, 158.
    Notice of appointment of agent to be sent to returning officer, 158.
    Returning officer to give notice to agent of time and place of, 158.
    Non-attendance of agent at, 158.
    If agent dies, candidate may appoint successor to attend at, 159.
    Who may be present at, 159.
    Candidate may attend at, 159.
    Returning officer may appoint additional assistants, 159.
    No one (except candidates) who has not made declaration of secrecy to be present at, 159.
    Votes to be counted as soon as possible after close of poll, 160.
    Cannot be counted without agent's consent between 7 o'clock P.M. and 9 A.M., 160.
    To be proceeded with continuously, 160.
    During intervals in—documents to be sealed by returning officer, 160.
    —— constable to be left in charge of documents, 161.
    Method of procedure to be adopted at, 161.
    Suggested form for, 162.
    Ballot papers to be kept face upwards during, 163.
    Agents not authorized to interfere with assistants engaged in, 163.
    —— are entitled to inspect face of bad and doubtful ballot papers at, 163.
    Returning officer's decision final as to validity of votes, 163.
    Ballot papers to be rejected at, 163.
    Votes may be struck out on scrutiny, 166.
    Peculiarly-marked ballot papers—when to be counted, 178.

VOTERS:

    Qualifications of, 42–71.
    Qualifications of—in boroughs under 9 Geo. IV., c. 82, 42.
    Householders jointly rated — not qualified, 43.
    —— Under 3 & 4 Vic., c. 108, qualified, 48.

VOTERS —continued.
  Qualifications under Municipal Reform Act, 1840, 44.
  ——— Towns Improvement (Ireland) Act, 1854, 49.
  ——— Townships formed under local acts, 55.
  Votes for disqualified Candidate thrown away, 78.
  Joint immediate Lessors (see *Immediate Lessors*.)
  Notice to be given to, as to what station to vote at, 119.
  Directions for guidance of, 123.
  To state name and address when applying for ballot papers, 132.
  To show official mark on back of ballot paper to Presiding Officer, 133.
  To mark vote secretly, 133.
  To vote at polling station allotted to him, 134, 180.
  Questions he may be required to answer, 135.
  Cannot vote unless his name is on register, 137.
  Idiots, drunken persons, and lunatics, 140.
  When deaf and dumb persons may vote, 140.
  Voting in two wards, 140.
  ——— his father's name, 140.
  Not disqualified if inaccurately described on Register, 46, 140.
  Illiterate, 141.
  Incapacity to vote through blindness, 141.
  Jewish, 141.
  Personation by, 143.
  To vote without delay, 147.
  If ballot paper spoilt, how to act, 147.
  Must be of full age, 56.
  Not illegal to pair, 198.
  Not to be employed as paid canvassers, 195.
  Penalty for employment of, 195.
  Conveyance of, to poll, 196.
  Travelling expenses of, to poll, 196.
  Not required to disclose vote on petition, 206.

VOTERS' LISTS:
  Sale of printed copies of, 30.
  Annual revision of—by revising barrister, 30.
  Where made out by town clerk, 31.

VOTERS' LISTS—*continued*.
  When to be made out, 31.
  How to be made out, 31.
  To be printed, 31.
  Price to be charged for copies of, 31.
  Publication of, 31.
  When to be published, 31.
  Machinery for preparation of—unsatisfactory, 32.
  Town Clerk not liable for error in regard to, 33.
  Preparation of—a judicial act, 33.
  Conclusiveness of—on an election tribunal, 34.
  Difficulties in regard to preparation of, 34.
  Suggestions in regard to, 34.
  Form of notice of claim suggested, 36.
  ——— of objection, 37.
  ——— in which list to be published, 39.
  How to be prepared in boroughs under 9 Geo. IV., c. 82, 40.
  Mis-named on—does not disqualify voters, 46, 140.
  Marked copies of—inspection of, 108, 208.
  Copies of to be supplied at polling station, 117.
  No person entitled to vote unless his name is on, 137.
  Conclusiveness of, how shown, 137.
  Packet of marked copies of—to be forwarded to town clerk, 185.

W.

WAGER:
  When bribery, 197.

WEEKLY TENANTS:
  Entitled to vote in municipal borough of Dublin, 48.
  Not qualified to vote under Towns Improvement (Ireland) Act, 1854, 53.

WITHDRAWAL OF CANDIDATE, 108.

WOMEN:
  Disqualified to vote, 50.
  May vote in Belfast, 44.
  Baron Deasy's judgment in regard to voting of—under Towns Improvement (Ireland) Act, 1854, 51.

www.ingramcontent.com/pod-product-compliance
Lightning Source LLC
Chambersburg PA
CBHW022105230426
43672CB00008B/1292